THE
COPYRIGHT GUIDE

FOURTH EDITION

T0105411

THE
COPYRIGHT GUIDE

FOURTH EDITION

*How You Can Protect
and Profit from Copyrights*

LEE WILSON

Attorney-at-Law

ALLWORTH PRESS
NEW YORK

Allworth Press books may be purchased in bulk at special discounts for sales promotion, corporate gifts, fund-raising, or educational purposes. Special editions can also be created to specifications. For details, contact the Special Sales Department, Allworth Press, 307 West 36th Street, 11th Floor, New York, NY 10018 or info@skyhorsepublishing.com.

23 22 21 20 19   5 4 3 2 1

Published by Allworth Press, an imprint of Skyhorse Publishing, Inc., 307 West 36th Street, 11th Floor, New York, NY 10018. Allworth Press® is a registered trademark of Skyhorse Publishing, Inc.®, a Delaware corporation.

www.allworth.com

Cover design by Mary Belibasakis

Library of Congress Cataloging-in-Publication Data

Names: Wilson, Lee, 1951- author.
Title: The copyright guide: how you can protect and profiting from copyrights / Lee Wilson.
Description: Fourth edition. | New York, New York: Allworth Press, [2018] | Includes index.
Identifiers: LCCN 2017051397 (print) | LCCN 2017052845 (ebook) | ISBN 9781621536215 (e-book) | ISBN 9781621536208 (hardcover: alk. paper)
Subjects: LCSH: Copyright—United States—Popular works. | Copyright licenses—United States—Popular works.
Classification: LCC KF2995 (ebook) | LCC KF2995 .W475 2018 (print) | DDC 346.73048/2—dc23
LC record available at https://lccn.loc.gov/2017051397

Hardcover ISBN: 978-1-62153-620-8
Paperback ISBN: 978-1-62153-699-4
eBook ISBN: 978-1-62153-621-5

Printed in the United States of America

> **Note:** It is important to remember that although this book contains reliable information, the law changes, and interpretations of the law vary. No book can offer sufficient advice to guide anyone in a specific situation. Use the information in this book to educate yourself so that you can recognize when you have a problem. Then, ask a lawyer well versed in intellectual property law to advise you about your particular concerns if you feel that your own understanding of the law or skills for handling your problem are inadequate.

Contents

Contents

Introduction

This book is written for everyone who creates, acquires, or exploits copyrights. Copyright owners constitute an increasingly large segment of our society. This group includes painters; illustrators; photographers; filmmakers; sculptors; graphic designers; industrial designers; jewelry designers; textile designers; journalists; novelists; poets; screenwriters; playwrights; technical writers; copywriters; students; scholars; editors; researchers; songwriters; composers; record producers; recording artists; choreographers; computer software designers; and television and movie directors and producers; as well as newspaper, book, and magazine publishers; educational institutions; radio and television broadcasters; toy manufacturers; music publishers; record companies; movie studios; museums and art collectors; software companies; advertising agencies; poster companies; photo archives and stock photo houses; theatrical producers; dance companies; pop music tour promoters; and manufacturers of all sorts of consumer products. In fact, in today's world, unless you engage solely in a profession or occupation that produces and sells only tangible products, you must know something about the most common sort of intangible property—copyrights.

For anyone whose livelihood or avocation is centered in one of the US information industries, copyrights and the exploitation of copyrights are basic facts of life. No one in America escapes the effect of copyrights. There may be no spot in your house or school or office where you are not surrounded by copyrights. The copy and illustrations on the box your breakfast cereal comes in are copyrighted. Every book in your school locker, except for those published before 1923, is copyrighted. The professional journals or trade publications at your office are copyrighted, as is every single memorandum, letter, report, proposal, or other document you produce on the job. Copyrights float through the air as radio and television broadcasts and arrive in the mail as magazines and newspapers and show up in shopping bags as DVDs and bestselling novels and video games.

Of course, this proliferation of expression may be a mixed blessing. We are inundated by our own communications. Toddlers who can't read know the names of cartoon characters. College students who can't remember the date of the Norman Conquest can recite dialogue from reruns of TV sitcoms. Their grandmothers can recall the convolutions of plot from television soap operas for the last twenty-five years. And aging baby boomers can sing every word of popular songs from their youth, almost on key.

This is mostly because the United States is unique in its cultural affection for and legal protection of free expression. We forget that we are the only nation that has the First Amendment. Many other nations impose more restrictions on what their citizens can say and write and publish than we do. In fact, throughout history, during numerous periods and in various places, you could be imprisoned or killed simply for saying or writing the wrong thing; unfortunately, this is still the case in some places.

But not in America. The rebels and mavericks who sailed across the oceans in wooden boats to settle in what became the United States knew the value of free thought and free speech. They came here seeking both. They gave us the right to think what we want and say what we think.

But even before the enactment of the First Amendment, the men who wrote our Constitution acted to ensure the production of the works of art and intellect necessary to create and promote culture and learning in our infant nation. In article I, section 8, clause 8 of the main body of the original, un-amended Constitution, they gave Congress the power "to Promote the Progress of Science and useful Arts, by securing for limited Times to Authors and Inventors the exclusive Right to their respective Writings and Discoveries." Congress carried out this mandate by passing the first US copyright statute in 1790 and also by enacting a succession of patent statutes. You may think from reading the language of the Constitution that only authors of books are protected by copyright law. That is not the case.

Historically, American copyright law has interpreted broadly the "writings" granted constitutional protection. At the time of the enactment of the first copyright statute, only "maps, charts, and books" were protected. During the two centuries since, US copyright statutes (there have been several) and court decisions have extended copyright protection to new subjects of copyright as previously nonexistent classes of works emerged, needing protection. This system of enumerating the classes of "writings" protected by copyright worked well enough until it became obvious that technology would create new methods of expression faster than the courts and lawmakers could amend the then-current copyright statute to include emerging technologies within the scope of copyright protection. The present US copyright statute abandons the effort to enumerate every class of work protected by copyright and simply states that "copyright protection subsists . . . in original works of authorship fixed in any tangible medium of expression, *now known or later developed* [emphasis added], from which they can be perceived, reproduced, or otherwise communicated, either directly or with the aid of a machine or device." This language allows copyright to expand automatically to extend protection to new forms of expression, including many that the men who passed the first copyright statute could never have imagined. This is fortunate, because the revolution in communications that characterized the last half of the twentieth century shows no signs of abating. Indeed, it may have reached warp speed.

By recognizing property rights in creative works and awarding ownership of those rights to the creators of the works, our copyright statute encourages expression in every art form and medium. It balances the interests of creators against those of the public. Creators reap the profits from their works for the duration of copyright protection by limiting access to creative works to those who pay for the privilege of using them. The public immediately enjoys controlled access to the works artists, writers, and composers create, and, eventually, those works become public property, available for use by anyone. This is precisely what the founding fathers had in mind; James Madison cited copyright as an instance in which the "public good fully coincides with the claims of individuals."

So, the United States gives its citizens the right to say or otherwise express almost anything at all and rewards that expression, whether meritorious or mundane, by bestowing upon it a copyright. But what, exactly, is a copyright? A copyright is a set of rights that the federal copyright statute grants to the creators of literary, musical, dramatic, choreographic, pictorial, graphic, sculptural, and audiovisual works and sound recordings. Copyright law rewards creators by granting them the exclusive right to exploit and control their creations. With a few narrow exceptions, only the person who created the copyrighted work or someone to whom he or she has sold the copyright in the work or given permission to use the work is legally permitted to reproduce the work, to prepare alternate or "derivative" versions of the work, to distribute and sell copies of the work, and to perform or display the work publicly. Any unauthorized exercise of any of these rights is called "copyright infringement" and is actionable in federal court.

But this is only the beginning of the story. The rest follows in what I hope is a logical progression. I have practiced intellectual property law for nearly half my life, but I still find the concept of copyright and the elaborate structures that our world community has erected around it fascinating. The law says that a copyright is a set of exclusive rights that belongs, in most instances, to the person who creates the copyrighted work. That's true, but what copyrights really are is magic. There's something wonderful in the fact that in a mass culture like ours, where individual voices are obscured by the noise of the rat race, you can create, all alone and out of thin air and your own brain, something that pays the rent.

I hope you find copyrights as interesting as I do. They are one of the last means by which an individual person, unaffiliated with any large organization or institution, can change people's minds, lift their spirits, and feed their souls. Where's your pencil?

—Lee Wilson
Nashville, Tennessee

CHAPTER 1

Copyright Protection

Before you can begin to understand copyright—that invisible but powerful and infinitely expandable concept that governs so many of our dealings with each other—you must first learn what it is *not*. Two of the things that copyright is not are trademarks and patents. These three forms of intellectual property are more like cousins than triplets, but lots of people, even lawyers and judges, confuse them.

COPYRIGHTS COMPARED TO TRADEMARKS AND PATENTS

Although all three protect products of the human imagination, copyrights, trademarks, and patents are distinct but complementary sorts of intellectual property. Each is governed by a different federal law. The US patent statute originates in the same provision of the Constitution that gives rise to our copyright statute. Our federal trademark statute originates in the "commerce clause" of the Constitution, which gives Congress the power to regulate interstate commerce. Only our federal government regulates copyrights; copyright registrations are granted by the Copyright Office, which is a department of the Library of Congress. Similarly, only the federal government can grant a patent. However, although the federal government grants trademark registrations, so do all the fifty states.

COPYRIGHTS

Since January 1, 1978, in the United States, a copyright is created whenever a creator "fixes" in tangible form a work for which copyright protection is available. Under most circumstance, a copyright will endure until seventy years after the death of the creator of the copyrighted work; after copyright protection expires a work is said to have fallen into the "public domain" and anyone is free to use it. Registration of a copyright enhances the rights that a creator automatically gains by the act of creation, but it is not necessary for copyright protection. The chief limitation on the rights of copyright owners is that copyright protects only particular *expressions* of ideas rather than the ideas themselves. This means that several people can create copyrightable works based on the same idea; in fact, there is no infringement no matter how similar one work is to another unless one creator copied another's work.

TRADEMARKS

Trademarks are words or symbols that identify products or services to consumers. Unlike a copyright, in which the creator has protectable rights from the inception of the copyrighted work, rights in a trademark accrue only by use of the trademark in commerce and then belong to the company that applies the mark to its products rather than to the person who came up with the name or designed the logo that becomes the trademark. Roughly speaking, a company gains rights in a trademark in direct proportion to the duration and the geographic scope of its use of the mark; ordinarily, the company that first uses a mark gains rights in that mark superior to any other company that later uses it for the same product or services. Unauthorized use of a trademark is "trademark infringement."

As is the case with copyrights, registration enhances rights in trademarks but does not create them. It is generally easy to register a mark within a state, but federal trademark registration, which confers much greater benefits, is more difficult to obtain. Trademark rights last indefinitely; as long as a mark is used in commerce, its owners have protectable rights in it. (For more information about trademarks, see *The Trademark Guide*, by Lee Wilson, published by Allworth Press.)

PATENTS

A patent is a monopoly granted by the US Patent and Trademark Office (USPTO) for a limited time to the creator of a new invention. According to the Patent Office,

A patent for an invention is the grant of a property right to the inventor, issued by the United States Patent and Trademark Office. Generally, the term of a new utility or plant patent is twenty years from the date on which the application for the patent was filed in the United States or, in special cases, from the date an earlier related application was filed, subject to the payment of maintenance fees. Design patents are granted for ornamental designs used for nonfunctional aspects of manufactured items; design patents last fourteen to fifteen years from the date the design patent is granted, depending on when it was filed.

US patent grants are effective only within the United States, US territories, and US possessions. Under certain circumstances, patent term extensions or adjustments may be available.

The right conferred by the patent grant is, in the language of the statute and of the grant itself, "the right to exclude others from making, using, offering for sale, or selling" the invention in the United States or "importing" the invention into the United States. What is granted is not the right to make, use, offer for sale, sell, or import, but the right to exclude others from making, using, offering for sale, selling, or importing the invention. Once a patent is issued, the patentee must enforce the patent without aid of the USPTO.

There are three types of patents:

1. **utility patents** may be granted to anyone who invents or discovers any new and useful process, machine, article of manufacture, or composition of matter, or any new and useful improvement thereof;
2. **design patents** may be granted to anyone who invents a new, original, and ornamental design for an article of manufacture; and
3. **plant patents** may be granted to anyone who invents or discovers and asexually reproduces any distinct and new variety of plant.

An inventor must meet very strict standards before the Patent Office will grant a patent for his or her invention; then, the inventor can stop everyone else from manufacturing the invention without permission or even importing an infringing invention into the United States, even if the infringer of the patent independently came up with the same invention.

No product name is protectable by patent law; a product name is a trademark and trademark protection is earned in the marketplace rather than being awarded like a patent. And no song, story, painting, or play can be patented; copyright gives writers and artists the right to keep others from copying their works, but not a complete monopoly on the creation or importation of similar works.

(For a more detailed discussion of patent law, see *The Patent Guide*, by Carl Battle, from Allworth Press, and consult the US Patent and Trademark Office website at www.uspto.gov/patents-getting-started/general-information -concerning-patents.)

REQUIREMENTS FOR COPYRIGHT PROTECTION

Under the US copyright statute a work must satisfy three conditions to qualify for copyright protection. All three of these requirements must be met in order for the work to come under the copyright umbrella.

The three statutory prerequisites for protection are (1) the work must be "original" in the sense that it cannot have been copied from another work; (2) the work must embody some "expression" of the author, rather than consisting only of an idea or ideas; and (3) the work must be "fixed" in some tangible medium of expression.

Originality

The originality condition for protection leads to the apparent anomaly that two works identical to each other may be equally eligible for copyright protection. So long as neither of the two works was copied from the other, each is considered "original." In the sense that it is used in the copyright statute, "originality" means simply that a work was not copied from another work rather than that the work is unique or unusual. Judge Learned Hand, a jurist who decided many copyright cases, summarized the originality requirement with a famous hypothetical example: "If by some magic a man who had never known it were to compose anew Keats's *Ode on a Grecian Urn*, he would be an 'author,' and, if he copyrighted it, others might not copy that poem, though they might of course copy Keats's." For copyright purposes, the similarities between two works are immaterial so long as they do not result from copying.

This is reflected in Copyright Office practices and publications: "The Copyright Office does not compare deposit copies or check registration records to determine whether works submitted for registration are similar to any material for which a copyright has already been registered. The records of the Copyright Office may contain any number of registrations for works describing or illustrating the same idea, method, or system."

Anyone who feels her copyright has been infringed by a similar work created by someone else must look to the courts for a remedy, in the form of a suit for copyright infringement, rather than to the Copyright Office, which makes no judgment as to originality of any work for which registration is sought.

Expression

The current copyright statute restates the accepted rule, often enunciated in copyright decisions, that copyright subsists only in the expression embodied in a work and not in the underlying ideas upon which the work is based. The statute says: "In no case does copyright protection for an original work of authorship extend to any idea, procedure, process, system, method of operation, concept, principle, or discovery, regardless of the form in which it is described, explained, illustrated, or embodied in such work." This rule plays an important role in copyright infringement cases, because a judge often must determine whether the defendant has taken protected expression from the plaintiff or merely "borrowed" an unprotectable idea (or "procedure, process, system," etc.).

Fixation

The US copyright statute protects works eligible for protection only when they are "fixed in any tangible medium of expression . . . from which they can be perceived, reproduced, or otherwise communicated, either directly or with the aid of a machine or device." The statute deems a work fixed in a tangible medium of expression "when its embodiment in a copy or phonorecord, by or under the authority of the author, is sufficiently permanent or stable to permit it to be perceived, reproduced, or otherwise communicated for a period of more than transitory duration."

This third requirement for copyright protection sometimes surprises people, who may not realize, for instance, that a new song performed at an open mike "writers' night" or a dance routine presented in a talent show, although it is both original and contains a high proportion of protectable expression, is not protected by copyright until it is "fixed" within the definition of the copyright statute and that it can be legally (although not ethically) copied, word for word or move for move, by anyone who witnesses its performance. A song can be "fixed" by recording any intelligible version of its music and lyrics in any form or by reducing its melody to written musical notation that also includes its lyrics. Any piece of choreography can be "fixed" by videotaping it in sufficient detail to record the movements of the dancers or by use of a written system of choreographic notation.

WHAT IS PROTECTED

Most people realize that copyright protects works of art like poems and short stories, photographs, paintings and drawings, and musical compositions. It may be less obvious that copyright also protects more mundane forms of expression, including such diverse materials as advertising copy, instruction manuals, brochures, logo designs, computer programs, term papers, home movies, cartoon strips, and advertising jingles. Artistic merit has nothing to do with whether a work is protectable by copyright; in fact, the most routine business letter and the most inexpertly executed child's drawing are just as entitled to protection under our copyright statute as bestselling novels, hit songs, and blockbuster movies.

However, copyright does not protect every product of the imagination, no matter how many brain cells were expended in its creation. In fact, any discussion of copyright protection must be premised on an understanding of what copyright *does not* protect.

IDEA VERSUS EXPRESSION

It is such an important principle of copyright law that it bears repeating: copyright protects only particular *expressions* of ideas, not the ideas themselves. This means, of course, that if the guy sitting behind you on the bus looks over your shoulder and sees, comprehends, and remembers your sketches for a necklace formed of links cast in the shape of sunflowers, he is legally free to create his own sunflower necklace so long as it isn't a copy of yours. It may be *unethical* for him to steal your idea, but it's neither illegal nor actionable in court. Although this may seem unjust, if you think about it, it's logical. Our Constitution empowered Congress to pass a copyright statute granting the creators among us property rights in the products of their imaginations so that American society could gain the benefit of their creations. Because ideas are the building blocks for creations of any sort, and because one idea may lead to thousands of expressions of that idea, granting control over an idea to any one person would have the effect of severely limiting creative expression; no one else would be able to use that idea as the basis for a new creation.

Therefore, copyright protects only your particular *expression* of an idea, *not* the idea itself. Similarly, copyright protection is denied to procedures, processes, systems, methods of operation, concepts, principles, or discoveries because these products of the imagination are really all particular varieties of ideas.

This means that your *idea* of printing grocery coupons right on the brown paper bags used in your supermarket can be copied by anyone, even a competing grocery store, although the particular expression of your idea—your copy and artwork for the bags and the advertisements publicizing the promotion—may not.

And your *system* of giving your customers double the face-value discount of any coupon if they use it to buy two product items at the same time is not protectable by your copyright in your coupon-promotion materials and can be employed at any time by anyone, without your permission.

Further, if you print recipes on your grocery bags in addition to discount coupons, you cannot, of course, stop anyone from using the *method* outlined in the Low-Fat Meatloaf recipe to create a low-fat meatloaf. Nor can you stop anyone, even a competitor, from employing your *concept* of using a low-fat meatloaf recipe to sell the food products used in the recipe or from employing the marketing *principle* behind your promotion—that food shoppers are likely to purchase particular brands of food products that are specified by name in an interesting recipe. And even if you were the first person in the universe to come up with a technique for diminishing the fat content of the finished dish, once you disclose your *discovery* to the public, you can't stop anyone from recounting it to anyone else.

You can't even stop anyone from using the *information* outlined in your meatloaf recipe to create his or her own recipe for low-fat meatloaf. (See the discussion of functional works below.)

UNPROTECTABLE ELEMENTS

There are a few categories of products of the imagination that are too close to being mere unembellished ideas for copyright protection to apply. In other words, these categories of "creations" lack sufficient expression to be granted copyright protection. There are several commonly occurring, unprotectable elements of various sorts of works from which the copyright statute or courts have withheld protection, including the following:

- literary plots, situations, locales, or settings;
- *scènes à faire*, which are stock literary themes that dictate the incidents used by an author to express them;
- literary characters, to the extent that they are "types" rather than original expressions of an author;[1]
- titles of books, stories, poems, songs, movies, etc., which have been uniformly held by courts not to be protected by copyright;[2]
- short phrases and slogans, to the extent that they lack expressive content;[3]
- the rhythm or structure of musical works;
- themes expressed by song lyrics;
- short musical phrases;
- arrangements of musical compositions, unless an arrangement of a musical composition really amounts to an alternate version of the composition;[4]
- social dance steps and simple routines, which are not copyrightable as choreographic works because they are the common property of the culture that enjoys them;

---

1   The visual representation of *pictorial characters* adds considerable protectable expression to the characters.
2   However, a title may gain protection under the law of unfair competition if it becomes well known and associated in the public mind with one author.
3   The determination of expressive content is aided by the length of the phrase or slogan, very short phrases and slogans being more likely to constitute the equivalent of an unprotectable idea than long phrases or slogans.
4   An arrangement infringes the underlying composition unless it was written with the permission of the owner of copyright in that composition. The exception to this is an arrangement of a public domain song. Since you can use a public domain composition any way you want, it's legal to make a detailed arrangement of such a song, and the arrangement is protectable.

- uses of color, perspective, geometric shapes, and standard works of the visual arts;[5]
- jewelry designs and other creations that merely mimic the structures of nature (such as a jeweled pin that accurately replicates the form of a honeybee), since the natural forms on which such "creations" are based are in the public domain, the property of all humankind;[6]
- names of products, services, or businesses;[7]
- pseudonyms or professional or stage names;[8]
- mere variations on familiar symbols, emblems, or designs, such as typefaces (this includes typefonts, letterforms, and the like)[9], numerals or punctuation marks, and religious emblems or national symbols;
- information, research data, and bare historical facts;[10]
- works produced by nature, animals, or plants;[11]

---

5 However, an artist's *arrangement* of these elements may be protectable expression.
6 Works based on nature may enjoy some copyright protection if there are elements of the work that were not determined by the form and characteristics of the natural object that gave rise to the work. In other words, a creation based on any natural object is protectable by copyright only to the extent it departs from the natural form. Works based on nature are in the public domain just like works for which copyright protection has expired (see below). Although they get there by different routes, neither sort of work can be "retrieved" from the unprotectable state that is public domain.
7 However, these are protected under trademark law from use without permission on similar products or services.
8 These may also be protected under trademark law or the law of unfair competition.
9 In drafting the current copyright statute, Congress considered the question of the suitability of typefaces for copyright protection and concluded that the design of typeface is not a copyrightable "pictorial, graphic, or sculptural work" within the meaning of the copyright statute.
10 However, many compilations of such information or data and extended expressions based on historical facts are protectable by copyright.
11 Examples of such works are a photograph taken by a monkey; a mural painted by an elephant; a registration claim based on driftwood that has been shaped and smoothed by the ocean; a registration claim based on cut marks, defects, and other qualities found in natural stone; an application for a song naming the Holy Spirit as the author of the work. Similarly, the office will not register works produced by a machine or mere mechanical process that operates randomly or automatically without any creative input or intervention from a human author.

- blank forms, such as account ledger page forms, diaries, address books, blank checks, restaurant checks, order forms, and the like;[12]
- measuring and computing devices like slide rules or tape measures, calendars, height and weight charts, sporting event schedules, and other assemblages of commonly available information that contain no original material.

UTILITARIAN ASPECTS OF DESIGN

Protection is specifically denied in the copyright statute to "utilitarian elements of industrial design." The statute provides that design of a useful article is protected under copyright "only if, and only to the extent that, such design incorporates pictorial, graphic, or sculptural features that can be identified separately from, and are capable of existing independently of, the utilitarian aspects of the article." While pictorial, graphic, and sculptural works are, of course, protectable, but only insofar as their forms, the "mechanical or utilitarian aspects" of such designs are not protected. The reasoning behind this provision is that if such aspects of otherwise decorative objects are to be protected at all, they must meet the rigorous requirements for a utility patent.

The question of what features of utilitarian objects copyright protects is most prevalent in the case of objects that have little ornamentation and consist mostly of a simple design that is largely determined by the function of the object. For instance, in the case of a ceramic lamp base decorated with a painted paisley design, the paisley design has nothing to do with the function of the base—that of elevating the bulb and shade of the lamp to a height sufficient to illuminate the area surrounding the lamp—and is protectable by copyright.

However, a design consisting of a cylindrical brass lamp base fixed to a square marble foundation would embody no elements that were not primarily functional and would be unprotectable under the copyright statute. If a marble caryatid were substituted for the lamp's cylindrical brass base, the sculpture of the draped female figure would be protectable because of its

---

12 These record information rather than conveying it. To be protected by copyright, a work must contain a certain minimum amount of original literary, pictorial, or musical expression.

more decorative and less utilitarian nature, even though it would still serve to elevate the lamp's bulb and shade. This principle of copyright law is easier to remember if you consider the general rule of copyright that the more elaborate and unusual the expression embodied in the work, the more protection the work is given (provided, of course, that the work is not copied from any other work).

FUNCTIONAL WORKS

Similarly, courts treat functional works such as recipes, rules for games and contests, architectural plans, and computer programs somewhat differently from works that have no inherent functional aspects. Although functional works are eligible for copyright protection, protection for them is somewhat narrower than for other sorts of works because the intended function of such a work dictates that certain standard information, symbols, etc., be included in the work and certain protocols be followed for the ordering and presentation of the information such works contain.

For example, copyright in recipes is very limited. Copyright law does not protect recipes that are mere lists of ingredients. Such lists consist of information only and embody no protectable expression. A particular expression of recipe instructions *may* be protectable, at least from word-for-word copying, but probably only to the extent that the explanation of the steps in making the dish embodies expression that is not dictated by the necessary technique or inherent chemistry of the process. Substantial literary expression such as a description, explanation, or illustration that accompanies a recipe or a combination of recipes (as in a cookbook) would be protectable. Courts have also held the view that very short explanations of concepts, such as game rules and recipes, are *not* copyrightable because granting copyright to them would effectively prevent any other recounting of such rules or recipes.

The forms of fashion, such as those of garments, are in the same unprotectable category because of their performance as objects useful for wearing. For example, a blouse is a blouse is a blouse, so to speak; no matter how it is cut or adorned its primary function is covering the upper part of the female body. Therefore, a garment is considered functional and not subject to copyright protection. Although a drawn and written-down clothing pattern *is* protectable by copyright, its product (the garment) is not. However, aspects of a garment, such as fabric designs or unusual forms for sleeves or collars, may be individually protectable to the extent those designs or forms are non-functional and separable from the overall garment design.

COPYRIGHT IN REAL LIFE

All this has a practical application. It may be that anyone is free to use the beautiful new typeface design that you worked nights and weekends to perfect, even though you intended it to be used only in a hand-lettered story you wrote for your niece's birthday. Or that great new slogan that you came up with to advertise your company's product may soon be on everyone's lips, in contexts that don't help your sales at all.

The good news is that if you design a poster calendar for your sporting goods company, you may copy all the information you need concerning the days of the week on which the dates fall and the dates of holidays from any other calendar. You may also copy any information about the year's sporting events from schedules published in newspapers or by colleges, sports magazines, or anyone else. And when you compose the copy for ads for your business, you can make free use of slogans and catchphrases from popular culture without obtaining permission from the copyright owner of the work from which the slogan was taken; otherwise, you'd have to call up Edgar Rice Burroughs's heirs to use "Me Tarzan, you Jane," or George Lucas to use "May the Force be with you," in an ad. (However, a famous phrase or slogan of this sort may become so associated in the public's mind with its originator that it may not be used to sell products or services without the real threat of a suit for unfair competition. This means that the originator of a famous phrase or slogan could sue on the ground that your use of that phrase or slogan to market your product or service could cause consumers to associate your product or service with the originator of the phrase or slogan. Be very careful in employing a well-known phrase or slogan in any manner that displays it more prominently than, say, a line of text from a book or fragment of dialogue from a movie.)

Copyright law treats facts of all sorts like ideas; the only thing relating to facts that is protectable under copyright law is the particular expression of those facts. You may write a movie script based on the historic facts surrounding the battle of the Alamo; those facts are free for use by anyone who cares to gather them at the library or from other sources. However, if you believe that it's time for another movie about the Alamo and that Hollywood will buy your script, you may want to think twice before you mention your project to your cousin the screenwriter, since she is free to recognize your idea as a good one and write her own competing script based on the very facts you planned to use.

The same is true of plots. Shakespeare's *Romeo and Juliet* has spawned many works based on the plot of his play: the play *Abie's Irish Rose* and the movie *The Cohens and the Kellys*, now both forgotten except for the well-known copyright infringement suit concerning their similar plots; the famous musical *West Side Story*; the old television series *Bridget Loves Bernie*; and the 1969 Zeffirelli film *Romeo and Juliet*, which was only one in a long line of movies based on the Shakespeare play.

And if you think of the innumerable love songs written about heartbroken, jilted lovers, you will realize themes are not protectable by copyright either; each of the 2,438,954 songs written about somebody's broken heart is a perfectly legitimate use of that theme. No doubt there will be more songs about a broken heart as long as popular music exists.

PUBLIC DOMAIN MATERIAL

The largest category of literary and artistic work not protected by copyright is "public domain" material. Most public domain material is material for which copyright protection has expired, such as the works of "dead poets"—literary gentlemen who have been dead a long time, like Shelley, Keats, and Shakespeare. Figuring out if a work is in the public domain is not simply a matter of determining whether the author has been dead a while, however, since the creators of many still-valid copyrights expired a long time before their copyrights will. The trick is to make sure the author whose work you want to use has been dead long enough.

Herman Melville died in 1891, which obviously means his books were written before 1891, so any rights Melville or his heirs had in them expired some time ago. This means you may freely use Melville's *Moby-Dick* characters and story in your screenplay. The same is not true of Tennessee Williams, for example; even though he is just as dead as Melville, his plays are still protected. Williams's estate owns the copyrights in those plays and collects royalties from performances of them. All this applies to painters and composers too, as well as to lesser mortals like you and me whose creations are not quite great literature or art but are valuable to us nonetheless.

Unless you know for sure that the copyright in a work has expired, you must investigate the copyright status of the work before reprinting it or adapting it or otherwise exercising any right reserved to the owners of valid copyrights. And remember that this book deals with US copyright only—every country has its own copyright law and those laws may vary significantly from the US copyright statute.

Anything showing a copyright date before 1923 is safe to use without permission, as it has passed into the public domain. In recent years, the duration of US copyright protection was extended to expire seventy years after the death of an author (as opposed to the life-plus-fifty years provided before the passage of the 1998 Sonny Bono Copyright Term Extension Act, which amended the US copyright statute). This change was made in order to bring the United States into conformity with the longer term adopted by the countries of the European Union. This recent extension of the term of US copyrights was challenged in court by people who believed that extending the term of copyright rewarded rich copyright owners like entertainment giant the Walt Disney Company. However, the Supreme Court recognized that Congress had the power to grant longer protection to copyright owners and that it was immaterial that some of them were rich companies that had acquired, rather than created, the copyrights they own. Justice Ruth Bader Ginsburg said, from the bench, that the Constitution "gives Congress wide leeway to prescribe 'limited times' for copyright protection and allows Congress to secure the same level and duration of protection for all copyright holders, present and future." In other words, she knew that US copyright law protects all copyright creators and other owners equally: the starving songwriter who owns only his guitar as well as the giant corporation that has acquired libraries of famous movies. (We will consider the duration of US copyright protection at greater length in chapter 3.)

The best way to begin to determine whether a work is still protected by copyright is to consult the Copyright Office pamphlet called *How to Investigate the Copyright Status of a Work*. (This pamphlet is reprinted in chapter 4. See the Resources section of this book for information about this and other Copyright Office publications). This pamphlet will give you the information you need to either figure out the copyright status of a work yourself or get help in doing so.

US GOVERNMENT WORKS

There is one other category of public domain works of which you should be aware: works created by officers or employees of the US government as a part of their government jobs. Copyright protection is not available for "any work of the United States Government," regardless of whether it is published or unpublished. This includes legislation enacted by Congress, decisions issued by the federal judiciary, regulations issued by a federal agency, or any other work prepared by an officer or employee of the US federal government while acting within the course of his or her official duties. It also includes works prepared by an officer or employee of the government of the District of Columbia, the Commonwealth of Puerto Rico, or the organized territories under the jurisdiction of the federal government. These works are in the public domain because in 1895 Congress decided not to claim copyright in works created at the taxpayers' expense.

This means that you may quote in your handbook for consumers the entire text of a government publication on how to buy a car without any special permission from the government. However, if your end creation consists preponderantly of material produced by the government, your copyright notice should acknowledge the fact, as in, "Copyright 2018 Wilson St. Charles, except material reproduced on pages 21–40 and 64–89, which was taken from US Government Publications 306A, 'New Car Buying Guide,' and 303A, 'Buying a Used Car.'"

The only precaution necessary before using material from government publications is to make sure that the material you want to use was prepared by the US government proper and not by some private or semiprivate agency of the government or a government contractor. (Works prepared by officers or employees of the US Postal Service, the Corporation for Public Broadcasting, the Public Broadcasting Service, National Public Radio, or the Smithsonian Institution are not considered works of the US government.) You can probably do this by simply looking at the title page of the government publication or by calling the department or organization that published it. Anything published by the US Government Publishing Office is almost certainly public domain material; such publications are listed in the Catalog of US Government Publications, which may be found at https://catalog.gpo.gov/F?RN=112773287.

COPYRIGHT NOTICE

Copyright notice is an important tool in copyright protection. It is like a "No Trespassing" sign—notice to the world that you claim ownership of the copyright in the work to which it is affixed.

The form of the copyright notice used for "visually perceptible" copies—that is, copies that can be seen or read, either directly (such as books) or with the aid of a machine (such as films)—differs from the form used for phonorecords of sound recordings (such as compact discs or cassettes).

Visually Perceptible Copies

The notice for visually perceptible copies should contain all three elements described below. They should appear together or in close proximity on the copies.

1. The symbol © (letter C in a circle); the word "Copyright"; or the abbreviation "Copr."
2. The year of first publication. If the work is a derivative work or a compilation incorporating previously published material, the year date of first publication of the derivative work or compilation is sufficient. Examples of derivative works are translations or dramatizations; an example of a compilation is an anthology. The year may be omitted when a pictorial, graphic, or sculptural work, with accompanying textual matter, if any, is reproduced in or on greeting cards, postcards, stationery, jewelry, dolls, toys, or useful articles.
3. The name of the copyright owner, an abbreviation by which the name can be recognized, or a generally known alternative designation of owner.[13]

Phonorecords of Sound Recordings

The copyright notice for phonorecords embodying a sound recording is different from that for other works. Sound recordings are defined as "works that result from the fixation of a series of musical, spoken or other sounds, but not including the sounds accompanying a motion picture or other audiovisual work." Copyright in a sound recording protects the particular series of

---

13 (Example: © 2018 Jane Doe) The "C in a circle" notice is used only on "visually perceptible" copies. Certain kinds of works, such as musical, dramatic, and literary works, may be fixed not in "copies" but by means of sound in an audiorecording. Since audiorecordings such as audiotapes and phonograph discs are "phonorecords" and not "copies," the "C in a circle" notice is not used to indicate protection of the underlying musical, dramatic, or literary work that is recorded.

sounds fixed in the recording against unauthorized reproduction, revision, and distribution. This copyright is distinct from the copyright of the musical, literary, or dramatic work that may be recorded on the phonorecord. Phonorecords can be phonograph records (such as LPs and 45s), audiotapes, cassettes, or discs. The notice should contain the following three elements appearing together on the phonorecord:

1. The symbol ℗ (the letter P in a circle).
2. The year of first publication of the sound recording
3. The name of the copyright owner of the sound recording, an abbreviation by which the name can be recognized, or a generally known alternative designation of the owner. If the producer of the sound recording is named on the phonorecord label or container, and if no other name appears in conjunction with the notice, the producer's name will be considered a part of the notice.[14]

Contributions to Collective Works

A "collective work" is one in which contributions that are separate and independent works in themselves are assembled into a collective whole. Examples of collective works include periodicals (such as magazines and journals), encyclopedias, and anthologies. A single copyright notice applicable to the collective work as a whole serves to indicate protection for all the contributions in the collective work, except for advertisements, regardless of who owns copyright in the individual contributions or whether they were published previously.

However, a separate contribution to a collective work can bear its own notice of copyright, and it is sometimes advantageous to use a separate notice. A separate notice informs the public of the identity of the owner of the contribution. For works first published before March 1, 1989, there may be additional reasons to use a separate notice. If the owner of the collective work is not the same as the owner of an individual contribution that does not bear its own notice, the contribution is considered to bear an erroneous notice. In addition, if an individual author of contributions to a periodical wants to make a single registration for a group of contributions published within

---

14 (Example: ℗ 2018 X.Y.Z. Records Inc.)

a twelve-month period, each contribution must carry its own notice. For details, see Form GR/CP, available on the Copyright Office website at www .copyright.gov/forms. A notice for the collective work does not serve as notice for advertisements inserted on behalf of persons other than the copyright owner of the collective work. Such advertisements should each bear a separate notice in the name of the copyright owner of the advertisement.

So, the three elements of copyright notice, which should appear together in close proximity, are as follows:

1. The word *copyright* (that is C-O-P-Y-R-I-G-H-T, *not* "copy-write"), the abbreviation *copr.*, or the © symbol (or, in the case of a sound recording, the ℗ symbol).[15] Because the word *copy-*

---

15 Some variants on the symbols © or ℗ or the word *copyright* may be acceptable and the use of such variants may not result in a defective copyright notice. By contrast, an unacceptable variant will be treated as an omission of the notice.

Variants for the © Symbol
A variant of the symbol © is acceptable only if it resembles the © closely enough to indicate clearly that the variant is intended to be the copyright symbol.
Acceptable variants include the following:
- The letter c with a parenthesis over the top
- The letter c with a parenthesis under the bottom
- (c
- c)
- (c)
- The letter c with an unclosed circle around it
Examples of unacceptable variants on the © symbol include the following:
- CO
- C
- C/O
- @ (i.e., the letter *a* in a circle)
- The letter c with a circle attached to the bottom of the letter
- The letter c in a square
- [c]
Variants for the ℗ Symbol
A variant of the symbol ℗ is acceptable only if it resembles the ℗ closely enough to indicate clearly that the variant is intended to be the symbol for a sound recording copyright.
Acceptable variants include the following:
- The letter P with a parenthesis over the top

(Continued on next page)

right and the abbreviation *copr.* are not recognized as valid elements of copyright notice in some countries, it is preferable to use the © symbol if your work will or may be distributed outside the United States.

2. The year of "first publication" of the work. For compilations or derivative works, the year of first publication of the compilation or derivative work should be used. "Publication" is "the distribution of copies of a work to the public by sale or other transfer of ownership, or by rental, lease, or lending." However, the year-date of first publication may be omitted from copyright notice when a pictorial, graphic, or sculptural work, with any accompanying text, is reproduced on greeting cards, postcards, stationery, jewelry, dolls, toys, or other useful articles.

3. The name of the owner of the copyright or an abbreviation or alternate name by which that copyright owner is generally recognized. For example, International Business Machines,

---

- The letter P with a parenthesis under the bottom
- (P
- P)
- (P)
- The letter P with an unclosed circle around it

Variants for the Word *Copyright*

A misspelled or variant form of the word *copyright* or the abbreviation *copr.* may be accepted if it is clear that the term is intended to be *copyright.*

Acceptable variants include the following:

- Copyrighted
- Copywrite
- Copywritten
- Copyright Pending
- Copyright Applied For
- Copyright and Registered
- Registered U.S. Copyright Office
- Copy
- Copyr.

The term *All Rights Reserved* or the like is not an element of the notice prescribed by US law, and it is not an acceptable variant or substitute for the word *copyright* or the abbreviation *copr.* The same is true for similar statements in other languages, such as "Todos los Derechos Reservados." However, the use of such terms in juxtaposition with an acceptable notice is permitted.

Incorporated, can call itself "IBM" for purposes of copyright notice. However, when in doubt, employ the legal form of your name that you commonly use for other formal purposes—e.g., "Aaron L. Bowers" rather than "Sonny Bowers." If two or more people or other entities own the copyright, use all their names: "© 2018 Charles Dennis Wile and Christopher Lawrence Fort." Further, bear in mind that the *author* of the work may no longer be the *owner* of copyright in it.

Occasionally copyright owners will also add to the title page of a book or magazine something like this:

No portion of this publication may be reproduced or transmitted in any form or by any means, electronic or mechanical, including by photocopying, recording, or use of any information storage and retrieval system, without express written permission from Bifocal Book Publishers.

Besides scaring off some potential copyright infringers who may not know or appreciate the full significance of copyright notice, added language of this sort has no effect and *is not a substitute* for proper copyright notice. However, there is also nothing in copyright law that says you cannot use some language of this sort near your copyright notice to make your claim of ownership of copyright in your work.

The important thing to remember is that *there is no legal substitute for proper copyright notice.* It costs nothing, and you don't need permission from anyone to use it. Not using copyright notice on any work that leaves your hands is foolish.

When Notice Is Required

Foolish though it may be to fail to use copyright notice, it must be said that copyright notice is not *required* for any work published after March 1, 1989. That is the date the United States' entry into the Berne Convention became effective. The Berne Convention is a very old and widespread copyright treaty, but for a variety of complicated reasons, the United States became a signatory to it only in late 1988. One reason is that Berne Convention signatory countries may not require as a condition to copyright protection any "formalities," such as using copyright notice.

However, confusingly enough, the copyrights in works published before January 1, 1978, the effective date of the current copyright statute, may be *lost* in the United States if notice is not used.

Finally, copyright notice has never been required for unpublished works. The US Copyright Office will register an unpublished work that does not bear a notice, regardless of whether the work was created before or after March 1, 1989.

Benefits of Using Notice

The short of this long story is that you cannot now lose copyright protection for any work published after March 1, 1989, by failing to use copyright notice. However, in order to encourage the use of copyright notice in the United States, the law provides a valuable procedural advantage in infringement lawsuits to copyright owners who do use it. Specifically, an infringer cannot successfully claim that he or she did not know that his or her act constituted copyright infringement if the copyright owner has used proper copyright notice. Being able to prove that a defendant willfully ignored such clear evidence that the plaintiff's work was protected by copyright has the effect of increasing the potential damages award available to a plaintiff, since courts are typically much harder on defendants who have intentionally violated the rights of plaintiffs.

That takes care of people dishonest enough to ignore copyright notice. Using copyright notice also precludes the possibility that honest people, seeing no copyright notice, will believe that your work is free for anyone to use. Even after Berne, copyright notice remains one of the most useful tools for protecting your copyright.

Placement of Copyright Notice

Copyright notice does not have to be obtrusive. Copyright Office regulations specify only that notice be placed, in a durable form affixed in a permanent manner, in a location on the work where it is reasonably easy to discover. The notice should be permanently legible to an ordinary user of the work under normal conditions of use and should not be concealed from view upon reasonable examination. The Copyright Office has issued regulations, summarized below, concerning the position of the notice and methods of affixation. The following locations and methods of affixation are examples of appropriate position of notice. These examples are not exhaustive.

Works Published in Book Form

- The title page
- The page immediately following the title page
- Either side of the front or the back cover
- The first or the last page of the main body of the work

Single-Leaf Works

- The front or the back

Works Published as Periodicals or Other Serials

- Any location acceptable for books
- As part of, or adjacent to, the masthead or on the page containing the masthead
- Adjacent to a prominent heading, appearing at or near the front of the issue, containing the title of the periodical and any combination of the volume and issue number and the date of the issue

Separate Contributions to Collective Works

For a separate contribution reproduced on only one page:

- Under the title or elsewhere on the same page

For a separate contribution reproduced on more than one page:

- Under a title appearing at or near the beginning of the contribution
- On the first page of the main body of the contribution
- Immediately following the end of the contribution
- On any of the pages where the contribution appears if the contribution consists of no more than 20 pages, the notice is reproduced prominently, and the application of the notice is reproduced prominently, and the application of the notice to the particular contribution is clear

Works Reproduced in Machine-Readable Copies

- With or near the title or at the end of the work, on visually perceptible printouts
- At the user's terminal at sign-on

- On continuous display on the terminal
- Reproduced durably on a gummed or other label securely affixed to the copies or to a container used as a permanent receptacle for the copies

Motion Pictures and Other Audiovisual Works

A notice embodied in the copies by a photomechanical or electronic process so that it ordinarily would appear whenever the work is performed in its entirety may be located:

- With or near the title
- With cast, credits, and similar information
- At or immediately following the beginning of the work
- At or immediately preceding the end of the work

The notice on works lasting 60 seconds or less, such as untitled motion pictures or other audiovisual works, may be located:

- In all the locations specified above for longer motion pictures, and
- If the notice is embodied electronically or photomechanically, on the leader of the film or tape immediately preceding the work

For audiovisual works or motion pictures distributed to the public for private use, the locations include the above, and in addition:

- On the permanent housing or container

Pictorial, Graphic, and Sculptural Works

For works embodied in two-dimensional copies, a notice may be affixed directly, durably, and permanently to:

- The front or the back of the copies
- Any backing, mounting, framing, or other material to which copies are durably attached, so as to withstand normal use

For works reproduced in three-dimensional copies, a notice may be affixed directly, durably, and permanently to:

- Any visible portion of the work
- Any base, mounting, or framing or other material on which the copies are durably attached

For works on which it is impractical to affix a notice to the copies directly or by means of a durable label, a notice is acceptable if it appears on a tag or durable label attached to the copy so that it will remain with it as it passes through commerce.

For works reproduced in copies consisting of sheet-like or strip material bearing multiple or continuous reproductions of the work, such as fabrics or wallpaper, the notice may be applied:

- To the reproduction itself
- To the margin, selvage, or reverse side of the material at frequent and regular intervals
- If the material contains neither a selvage nor a reverse side, to tags or labels attached to the copies and to any spools, reels, or containers housing them in such a way that the notice is visible in commerce

Further and more detailed information concerning copyright notice and placement is available in the free Copyright Office pamphlet *Copyright Notice*, and in the Copyright Office circulars, also free, *Methods of Affixation and Positions of the Copyright Notice on Various Types of Works* and *Copyright Notice*. Information on accessing all three of these short publications is given in the Copyright Office Resources section of this book, appendix A.

GEOGRAPHIC LIMITS OF PROTECTION

All rights of US copyright owners are granted to them by the US copyright statute, which is a federal law, that is, a law passed by Congress that governs copyright matters throughout the United States. The provisions of the federal copyright statute are interpreted by court decisions. These decisions become another segment of United States copyright law because they are used by other courts in deciding later copyright cases.

It is important to realize that all this law skids to a halt at the geographic boundaries of the United States because, of course, US laws have no jurisdiction outside the fifty states and the possessions of the United States other than the more or less reciprocal recognition other countries grant US copyrights under the various copyright treaties to which the United States is a party.

There are two situations in which geography and copyright combine to concern average creators or copyright owners. These are situations involving the protection of US copyrights outside the United States and the circumstances under which the work of foreign nationals working in the United States are granted copyright protection by the US copyright statute.

INTERNATIONAL COPYRIGHT RELATIONS

Most other countries have their own copyright laws, the provisions of which may diverge considerably from those of our statute. There is no such thing as an "international copyright" that will automatically protect an author's writings throughout the world. Protection against unauthorized use in a particular country depends on the national laws of that country. However, most countries offer protection to foreign works under certain conditions that have been greatly simplified by international copyright treaties and conventions. For example, the terms of copyright in other countries are not necessarily the same as that in the United States. Copyright treaties get around the fact that no country's law has any effect outside that country by documenting the agreements between countries that each will give the same recognition to the others' copyrights that it gives to its own citizens.

The United States is now a signatory to the principal copyright treaties. These treaties are basically agreements among several nations that each treaty signatory will accord the same respect to the rights of copyright owners who are citizens of the other signatory countries as it does to those of its own citizens. In addition to the Berne Convention, which is the most important copyright treaty and offers the most protection to copyright owners, the United States is also a signatory to the Universal Copyright Convention (UCC) and the Buenos Aires Convention. Most industrialized nations are signatories to one or more of the principal copyright treaties. To ensure protection for US copyrights in countries that have not signed any of these copyright treaties or that ignore the rights of US copyright owners, the United States has, where possible, entered into bilateral treaties—that is, the treaties are signed only by the United States and the other nation.

The United States became a member of the Berne Convention on March 1, 1989. It has been a member of the UCC since September 16, 1955. Generally, the works of an author who is a national or domiciliary of a country that is a member of these treaties or works first published in a member country or published within thirty days of first publication in a Berne Convention country can claim protection under the treaties. There are no formal requirements in the Berne Convention. Under the UCC, any formality in a national law can be satisfied by the use of a notice of copyright in the form and position specified in the UCC. A UCC notice should consist of the symbol © (C in a circle) accompanied by the year of first publication and the name of the copyright proprietor (example: © 2006 John Doe). This notice must be placed in such a manner and location as to give reasonable notice of the claim to copyright. Since the Berne Convention prohibits formal requirements that affect the "exercise and enjoyment" of the copyright, the United States changed its law on March 1, 1989, to make the use of a copyright notice optional. US law, however, still provides certain advantages for use of a copyright notice; for example, the use of a copyright notice can defeat a defense of "innocent infringement."

Even if a work cannot be brought under an international convention, protection may be available in other countries by virtue of a bilateral agreement between the United States and other countries or under specific provision of a country's national laws.

Copyrighted works such as books, movies, television shows, and computer programs are important exports of the United States. Protection against unauthorized use of copyrighted works in any particular country depends basically on the laws of that country; where the law is lax or nonexistent or is not enforced, US companies suffer. In some countries, domestic problems of poverty, disease, or war take precedence over the intellectual property rights of citizens of other countries and intellectual property rights are given little or no respect. And in Russia and China and several other countries where the infringement of US copyrights (and trademarks) has spawned whole industries of pirates, enforcement of existing law (or the deficiencies of existing law) is a problem. Infringers worldwide have cost US companies many *billions* of dollars annually in recent years, largely as a result of pirated movies, books, music, software, and electronic games.

Perhaps these problems will be solved or ameliorated as a result of the United States' efforts to normalize trade relations with such renegade countries—better trade relations may bring those nations into the world intellectual property community and increase their observance of the copyright rights of US citizens. The leaders of countries that make an industry of infringing US copyrights are yielding to pressure from the United States to stop counterfeiters, who previously may have operated openly and without government interference. Increasingly, the US government has enforced its citizens' copyright rights (as well as other intellectual property rights, such as trademark and patent rights) by means of trade sanctions to punish nations that ignore US intellectual property rights. Like the eight-hundred-pound canary, the United States wields considerable clout. Some of this clout comes from provisions affecting the recognition of intellectual property rights in trade agreements with those countries. Most of the United States' ability to coerce cooperation from other countries stems from the power of its collective pocketbook; many countries produce goods—or want to—for the US market.

Such cooperation is necessary because no US copyright owner can sue in the United States for copyright infringement that occurs elsewhere. If an American CD is counterfeited in China and sold there or in another country, the only recourse the US copyright owner may have is to lobby the US government to impose trade sanctions on China to compel it to shut down the infringer's operation. Similarly, some developing countries, even though they are signatories to one or more of the world's copyright treaties, do not impose meaningful penalties on infringers of foreign copyrights. This can make suing in one of these countries expensive and futile, because the only law that applies to infringements in other countries is the law of the country where the infringement occurs.

But if a foreign company brings its infringement to the United States, the US copyright owner can sue here. For example, a US copyright owner cannot sue profitably in Somalia to stop the manufacture of infringing products because Somalia is not a signatory to any copyright treaty with the United States. Even if a country does not respect US copyrights, if it imports infringing products into the United States, a US copyright owner can sue and can ask for seizure and destruction of the infringing products, as well as other remedies available under the US copyright statute.

FOREIGN NATIONAL AUTHORS

A related question is that of the copyright status of authors who are not US citizens. Under certain conditions, the copyright statute limits the right of some foreign nationals to enjoy the protection of US copyright law even if they create their otherwise copyrightable works within the United States.

The copyright statute says that published works are eligible for copyright protection in the United States if any one of the following conditions is met:

- on the date of first publication, one or more of the authors is a national or domiciliary, or sovereign authority of a treaty party (a foreign nation that is a party to a copyright treaty to which the United States is also a party) or is a stateless person wherever that person may be domiciled; *or*
- the work is first published in the United States or in a foreign nation that, on the date of first publication, is a treaty party. For purposes of this condition, a work that is published in the United States or a treaty party within thirty days after publication in a foreign nation that is not a treaty party shall be considered to be first published in the United States or such treaty party, as the case may be; *or*
- the work is a sound recording that was first fixed in a treaty party; *or*
- the work is a pictorial, graphic, or sculptural work that is incorporated in a building or other structure, or an architectural work that is embodied in a building and the building or structure is located in the United States or a treaty party; *or*
- the work is first published by the United Nations or any of its specialized agencies, or by the Organization of American States; *or*
- the work is a foreign work that was in the public domain in the United States prior to 1996 and its copyright was restored under the Uruguay Round Agreements Act (URAA). (See the Copyright Office Circular 38b, *Highlights of Copyright Amendments Contained in the Uruguay Round Agreements Act (URAA-GATT)*, for further information.); *or*
- the work comes within the scope of a presidential proclamation.

Any unpublished work is protected by US copyright law so long as it remains unpublished, regardless of the citizenship of the author or in what country he or she resides.

US citizens may register their copyrights in other countries, but such registration is not usually necessary. Protection for any US work—to the same extent as is given to works of citizens of that country—is, by operation of law, granted to US works by any country that is a signatory to one of the copyright treaties to which the United States is a party.

The publication *International Copyright Relations of the United States*, available from the Copyright Office website (see appendix A, the Copyright Office Resources section of this book), contains general information about the treaties to which the United States is a signatory and specifies to what treaties each country of the world is a party. However, because copyright relations between the many countries of the world and the United States are in a constant state of flux and because new government regimes in some countries can create changed policies toward US copyrights, if you are planning to market a valuable copyrighted work in a particular country or countries, it is a very good idea to consult a copyright lawyer before you publish the work.

CHAPTER 2

Copyright Ownership

Nobody can tell you what your copyright is worth. You may create a photograph today that you allow someone to use to illustrate a magazine article in return for payment of a few hundred dollars, only to find that, years from now, your photograph is worth thousands as a piece of art, or because of its subject matter, or because of the growth of your fame as a photographer. And this invisible thing called a copyright can be subdivided and sold to as many people as you choose for long or short periods and you can, in the end, still own it after profiting from these exploitations of it. An author who understands the infinitely divisible nature of copyright can more easily profit from his or her work by paring off and selling, one at a time, the rights to use the work. If you can conceive of a division of copyright and convince someone to acquire the portion of your copyright that you offer for sale, you can turn your creation into money in your pocket.

EXPLOITING COPYRIGHTS

The "exploitation" of copyrights is like the cultivation of a garden. Although a copyrighted work may become very valuable, its earning power is only speculative until someone sells it or the right to use it. Some authors exploit their own copyrights; this is typical of graphic designers and freelance writers. Some depend on others to turn their copyrighted works into cash flow; for example, songwriters and book authors depend on music and book publishers to create income for them. Sometimes authors are lucky enough to find professionals who will help them sell their works. This is what literary agents, artists' reps, and gallery owners do, for a share of any proceeds. If you depend on the services of someone else to help you exploit your copyrights—

and especially if you exploit your own copyrights—you need a thorough understanding of the three ways copyright rights are owned and change hands. If you are someone who acquires copyrights for exploitation, good business practice dictates that you acquire ownership rights that are valid, since enforceable ownership is a prerequisite to any exploitation of a copyright. The three ways that copyright ownership is transferred are work for hire, assignment of copyright, and license of copyright.

Works Made for Hire

In ordinary circumstances, the author of any work eligible for copyright protection owns the copyright in that work from the creation of the work. This is not true when an employee creates a work as a part of his or her job; in that case, the work is a "work made for hire," which means that the employer is considered both the copyright owner and the author of the work from the inception of the work. Any full-time employee of a newspaper who writes a news story has created that story as a work made for hire. The same is true of a graphic artist who creates an illustration for a client of the advertising agency that employs him or a staff composer who writes the soundtrack for an industrial training film produced by the production company she works for.

Works created on or after January 1, 1978, by freelance artists cannot be works made for hire unless certain requirements are met. There must be a written document in which both the creator of the work and the person commissioning it agree that it is to be considered a work made for hire *and* it must fall into one of the nine classes of works enumerated in the copyright statute as kinds of works that may be works made for hire if specially ordered or commissioned from an independent contractor, that is, a freelancer who is not a regular employee of the commissioning party.

The present copyright statute endeavors through the use of very specific language to clarify the confusion that formerly surrounded works made for hire. However, although the new, improved statutory language has helped matters, it has not entirely eliminated the confusion—and misunderstandings and lawsuits—that have sometimes arisen over the question of ownership of copyright in works created by one person at the behest of another. Because this is such an important issue, a detailed discussion of the circumstances that result in the work made for hire status is appropriate.

The threshold determination that must be made in deciding whether a work is or can be a work made for hire is whether the creator of the work is an employee or an independent contractor. This determination is often not as simple as it would seem. Of course, anyone who shows up five days a week at the same workplace, is issued regular paychecks, and receives a W-2 form every January from the company that issues those paychecks is an employee of that company. Any work created by that employee *within the scope of his or her duties as an employee* is a work made for hire. For instance, it is clear that the employer of a man who is employed full time as a computer software designer does *not* own the copyright in the novel that man writes in his spare time. Unfortunately, it is not always so clear whether a worker is an employee.

Who Is an Employee?

The Supreme Court has identified factors that make up an "employer-employee" relationship. The factors fall into three broad categories.

1. Control by the employer over the work. For example, the employer determines how the work is done, has the work done at the employer's location, and provides equipment or other means to create the work.
2. Control by employer over the employee. For example, the employer controls the employee's schedule in creating the work, has the right to have the employee perform other assignments, determines the method of payment, or has the right to hire the employee's assistants.
3. Status and conduct of employer. For example, the employer is in business to produce such works, provides the employee with benefits, or withholds tax from the employee's payment.

These factors are not exhaustive. The court left unclear which of these factors must be present to establish the employment relationship under the work-for-hire definition. Moreover, it held that supervision or control over creation of the work alone is not controlling. However, all or most of these factors characterize a regular, salaried employment relationship, and it is clear that a work created within the scope of such employment is a work made for hire (unless the parties involved agree otherwise). Therefore, generally speaking, the more control the commissioning party has over the duties, work hours, and workplace of the person who creates a copyrightable work, the more likely that person is an employee.

Assuming that a worker does not qualify as an employee of someone who commissions the creation of a copyrightable work, that worker is what the law calls an "independent contractor." Many independent contractors who work in the arts call themselves "freelancers." Any writer, artist, composer, or other author who works for many clients in his or her own office or studio, is paid only on a fee basis, and receives 1099 forms in January from those who pay for his or her services is probably a freelancer. If you find yourself in a situation where your status—i.e., whether you are an employee or an independent contractor—is indeterminate, don't guess who owns the copyrights in the products of your labor. Seek advice from a lawyer to clarify the nature of your arrangement if any part of your work involves the creation of anything that is copyrightable. In the case of independent contractors, the question then becomes, What works created by a freelancer are or may be works made for hire?

Which Works May Be Works Made for Hire?

The copyright statute is specific in naming the sorts of works that may be agreed to be works made for hire. The statute says that a work created by an independent contractor may be a work made for hire if it:

> is specially ordered or commissioned for use as a contribution to a collective work, as a part of a motion picture or other audiovisual work, as a translation, as a supplementary work, as a compilation, as an instructional text, as a test, as answer material for a test, or as an atlas, if the parties expressly agree in a written instrument signed by them that the work shall be considered a work made for hire. For the purpose of the foregoing sentence, a "supplementary work" is a work prepared for publication as a secondary adjunct to a work by another author for the purpose of introducing, concluding, illustrating, explaining, revising, commenting upon, or assisting in the use of the other work, such as forewords, afterwords, pictorial illustrations, maps, charts, tables, editorial notes, musical arrangements, answer material for tests, bibliographies, appendixes, and indexes, and an "instructional text" is a literary, pictorial or graphic work prepared for publication and with the purpose of use in systematic instructional activities.

The meaning of this statutory language is easier to grasp with concrete examples of the sorts of works that are deemed to be appropriate works made for hire. Examples of the statute's enumerated categories are:

- works commissioned for use as contributions to collective works (such as an article prepared specifically to be included in an encyclopedia);
- works that are a part of motion pictures or other audiovisual works (such as a musical composition written to be used as the soundtrack for a television spot or a sales presentation);
- works that are translations (such as the English translation of the works of the French poet Jean Nicholas Arthur Rimbaud);
- works that are supplementary works (such as a chart or graph used to illustrate a chapter in a book);
- works that are compilations (such as research results compiled from several surveys for publication as a reference book);
- works that are instructional texts (such as a pamphlet instructing the consumer in the proper method for assembling a bicycle or other product);
- works that are tests (such as standardized tests given schoolchildren to gauge their progress);
- works that comprise answer material for tests (the correct answers to a test, to be used in grading individual students on their responses); or
- a work that is an atlas (such as a road atlas of the United States).

Each of these sorts of works may be a work made for hire even if it is prepared by a freelancer. Many freelancers object to work-for-hire agreements. They feel that in most circumstances work-for-hire agreements are unfair to freelancers. This problem stems in part from lack of information; quite often, the person commissioning a work from a freelancer does not realize that it is not necessary to acquire the work as a work made for hire in order to secure the right to use the work as planned. There are other ways to acquire the right to use a copyrighted work.

ASSIGNMENT OF COPYRIGHT

An "assignment" of copyright is like a sale of the copyright; the author and original copyright owner sells all or some of his or her exclusive rights of copyright for the entire term of copyright or a shorter period. Copyright assignments are also called "transfers" of copyright. Anyone who acquires any right of copyright by assignment can, in turn, sell that right to someone else.

An assignment of copyright makes a commissioning party the owner of the copyright in a work in just about the same way that a work-for-hire agreement does. The major pertinent difference is that with an assignment the freelancer can elect to terminate the transfer of copyright rights between the thirty-fifth and thirty-sixth year of the term of copyright. Under a work-for-hire agreement, the commissioning party is considered the "author" of the work from its creation and owns the copyright for the full term of copyright (ninety-five years from creation), with no possibility that the freelancer can terminate ownership after thirty-five years.

In the case of many works, thirty-five years is as good as forever. For these works, acquiring an assignment of the copyright in the work is sufficient to protect the interests of the commissioning party.

However, an assignment, or sale, of copyright does not have to be for the full term of copyright. Perfectly valid assignments can be made for one year or three years or twenty-five years—for as long as you wish, up to and including the full term of copyright. This fact gives a freelancer the option of agreeing that the copyright in a work belongs to the commissioning party for the full period of time that the commissioning party believes it will want to use the work or needs to restrict any such use by any other party with whom the freelancer might otherwise contract. At the end of that period, all rights in the creative work automatically revert to the freelancer.

Often freelancers object to transferring ownership of their copyrights to those who will use them almost as much as they object to work-for-hire agreements. This is because many commissioning parties routinely ask for an assignment of all the exclusive rights of copyright for the full term of copyright. This leaves the author of the work with no further control over use of the work for the period of time the transfer is effective. In cases like this, the best solution is a license of copyright tailored to the client's needs. Unfortunately, clients are sometimes greedy. For example, clients often do not distinguish between payment for the services of a freelancer and payment for the right to use the copyrighted work the freelancer's services produce. Their attitude can be *What do you mean I've only paid for your work writing this article? For* that *amount of money, I want to* own *it.*

Freelancers also must be wary of clients who try to extort copyright ownership from them by trying to make payment for their services conditional on the transfer of the copyright in the work produced. It is not unheard of for a commissioning party to insert language somewhere on the check sent in payment for a freelancer's services that purports to transfer "all rights" to the commissioning party when the freelancer endorses the check for deposit. Since the terms of an agreement must be actually consented to by both parties to the agreement before there is a legally binding contract, and because legitimate transfers of copyright typically mention "all rights of copyright" specifically and at length in very unambiguous language, the effect of such trickery is dubious. However, if you have signed such a document, the only way to prove that you did *not* mean to assign the copyright in your work to the person who paid to have it produced may be in the course of a lawsuit, which is a tedious and expensive way to prove anything. The same is true of purchase orders that contain language that transfers copyrights; the American Society of Media Photographers says that it has seen "many" examples of such purchase orders. A photographer who signed one would be faced with a battle to prove that no transfer of copyright was intended.

Never sign any document unless you understand it completely. And mark out any language that seems out of place on a check in payment for your work, writing your initials in the margin beside the deleted language. This probably won't have any effect on whether the check will be honored by the client's bank, but it may keep you out of a lawsuit to prove that you still own the copyright in the work you produced.

LICENSES OF COPYRIGHT

A "license" to use a copyrighted work is like a lease of the copyright or of part of it; a copyright owner can grant as many licenses, or permissions, to use the copyright as he or she wants. These licenses may overlap or may divide the rights of copyright among several people. The copyright owner maintains ownership of the copyright because, although he or she has agreed to allow the work to be used by someone else, no transfer of ownership of the copyright is made.

Nonexclusive licenses are permissions to use a work in a specified way that may be granted to more than one user. *Exclusive* licenses grant to only one licensee at a time the right to use a work in a specified way.

Nonexclusive License

If a freelancer does not sign any written agreement regarding a work he or she creates, even if it is specially commissioned, the only right conveyed by the freelancer's action in delivering the work to the commissioning party is the right to use that work under a nonexclusive license. That is, the freelancer is under no obligation to refrain from granting a similar license or even selling the copyright in the work to someone else.

Nonexclusive licenses are also created when a copyright owner permits another person or company to use a work for a stated period of time, for specified purposes, and within a stated area but does not agree to avoid permitting the same or overlapping uses by others who request and pay for similar nonexclusive licenses in the work. For example, a photographer could agree to give an advertising agency the right to use her landscape photograph within the United States for ads for a client during a period of five years but could reserve the right to also license the photo to others, such as a travel magazine or a publisher of nature posters. In most nonexclusive licenses, no specific reservation-of-rights language is used; rather, the license provides merely that the licensee may make a certain use of the copyrighted work but does *not* state that the license is granted solely to that licensee.

The law does not require a nonexclusive license to be in writing. However, a verbal nonexclusive license is terminable at will by the copyright owner.

Exclusive Licenses

In the case of an *exclusive* license, the copyright owner grants to another person (called the "licensee") the sole right (i.e., that person is the *only* person who has the right) to exercise some or all of her or his exclusive rights of copyright for a specified time. Again, this right may be granted for as long or as short a period of time, for all or only certain specified purposes, and everywhere or within only a stated geographic area, depending on the terms of the agreement reached between the copyright owner and the licensee. For example, a photographer could agree to give an advertising agency the exclusive right to use his landscape photograph within the United States for ads for a client corporation during a period of five years but could reserve the right to sell the photo in Europe (to a magazine, perhaps) during that five-year period and to anyone anywhere for any use thereafter.

While assignments of copyright usually give the person or company to whom the assignment is made (called the "assignee") the right to use a free-lancer's creative work in any way the assignee sees fit during the period of assignment, exclusive licenses usually specify a more limited scope of permitted use. For example, a painter could grant to a publisher the exclusive right to prepare and sell within the United States prints of one of her paintings, other publishers could be granted similar rights in other countries, and other people entirely could be given the right to reproduce the painting on tin cookie containers or calendars.

Like assignments, copyright licenses can ordinarily also be sold to someone else unless the written license prohibits such a sale. Any time a copyright owner assigns or licenses to someone else an exclusive right of copyright there must be a written agreement to that effect, signed by the copyright owner, for the exclusive assignment or license to be valid.

BENEFITS OF RECORDATION

Any written assignment or exclusive license agreement may be recorded in the Copyright Office in order to document that the particular right(s) transferred or licensed exclusively are owned for the specified period by someone other than the person who created the copyrighted work. In the case of any creative work of more than temporary significance, recording an assignment or license is a very good idea. The Copyright Office maintains accurate copies of recorded documents and makes them available for public inspection. The public catalog, which is available on the Internet for documents recorded after 1977, includes a description of each recorded document, including party names, titles of works, registration numbers (when available), heading notes, and other information. The Copyright Office does not enforce agreements that are reflected in recorded documents. Although the Copyright Office has minimum requirements that must be satisfied for a document to be recorded, such as the document being complete by its own terms, the office does not determine whether documents satisfy legal requirements that are necessary for the documents to be effective or enforceable.

Recording an assignment or exclusive license of copyright confers several benefits that are similar to those real property owners enjoy when they record deeds to land and buildings. However, since a copyright is intangible and because rights in copyright can be transferred merely by signing a document, recording the documents that transfer ownership of all or part of a copyright is, perhaps, even more important than with real property.

The first and maybe the most important benefit of recording a copyright transfer or license is that such recordation creates a public record of ownership of the copyright or part of it. This can be very important in the case of a dishonest or completely uninformed copyright owner. If a copyright owner transfers ownership of a copyright to one person and subsequently signs a document that purports to transfer the same copyright to another person, the recordation of the first transfer document by the first buyer will establish that buyer's priority with regard to ownership of the copyright. More than a few lawsuits have arisen from just such situations.

Secondly, recording assignments or exclusive licenses of copyright creates a public record of ownership of the copyrights concerned. Recordation creates the records necessary to allow someone searching for the owner of a copyright to find the *current* owner, and allows those who are considering buying copyrights to search Copyright Office records to verify ownership of the copyrights.

The Copyright Office will record just about any document pertaining to a copyright that you feel should be recorded. In addition to the written assignment or exclusive license document, *signed by the person making the assignment or license*, you should fill out and send a Document Cover Sheet, with the proper fee, to the Documents Recordation Section of the Copyright Office. If you want to record a document that pertains to a copyright, access Circular 12, *Recordation of Transfers and Other Documents* on the Copyright Office website, read it carefully, follow the instructions it gives, and use the Document Cover Sheet included in it. (See appendix A of this book for information on this and other Copyright Office publications.)

CHOICE OF METHOD

Now that you understand the differences between copyright licenses and assignments and work-for-hire agreements, you can gauge which is appropriate and fair in a given situation. It's simply a matter of considering the rights conveyed by each in light of the practical aspects of the situation.

In the case of a specially commissioned work, an assignment is like a sales contract by which a freelancer transfers all copyright rights in a creative work to a commissioning party; in the assignment, the freelancer can negotiate a "sales price" that adequately compensates him or her for the services rendered in creating the work and for the sale of the copyright for the period of time agreed upon. If the assignment transfers rights in an existing work, that is, a work not specially commissioned, the freelancer's compensation may be less.

With an exclusive license, the freelancer also negotiates both the duration of the license (which is like a lease period) and a fair price for giving up the rights of copyright for that time period, but further bases his or her price on the scope of the exclusive license; that is, he or she considers the rights retained as well as those bargained away. A copyright owner who grants a nonexclusive license will consider the same factors, but the fee paid for a non-exclusive license will probably be much smaller than that for an exclusive license, since the copyright owner who grants an nonexclusive license doesn't give up the right to grant the same permission to use the work—to one or a hundred other people.

It is to the advantage of an assignee or licensee to include language in an assignment or license agreement that allows the editing or other modification of the work to accommodate its intended use. It is to the author's advantage that the assignment or license agreement includes language that provides for a reuse fee whenever the work is used.

A work-for-hire agreement, which should be used only in situations that fit the copyright statute's requirements for works for hire, is the most exhaustive way of vesting rights in a commissioning party. This is because in a work-for-hire agreement a freelancer forfeits not only any ownership of the copyright in the work but also any right to further payment for any use of the work. He or she has no say as to how the work is used and cannot even demand credit if the work is displayed or published. Fair-minded business people will demand work-for-hire agreements only when they are really necessary and will be prepared to pay the freelancer enough to compensate him or her appropriately under all the circumstances of the situation.

In any business situation involving intangible properties like copyrights, it's smart for all parties to have a very good idea, in advance, of their respective rights and obligations. In the past, the law accommodated the assumption that any specially commissioned work was prepared as a work made for hire. This is not now the case, and anyone whose business involves the creation or use of copyrights must now leave less to unvoiced assumptions.

CHAPTER 3

Copyright Duration

Creative people often believe that copyright law is a dark mystery, accessible only to lawyers, and that the mechanisms of copyright protection are incredibly complex. Fortunately, they're wrong.

"Copyright protection" means the protection the law gives copyright owners from unauthorized use of their works. As a general rule, the US copyright statute protects all varieties of literary, musical, dramatic, choreographic, pictorial, graphic, sculptural, and audiovisual works and sound recordings as soon as they are fixed in what the statute calls any "tangible medium of expression." Copyright protection lasts a very long time. Copyrights in works created today may not expire until well into the next century, and many copyrights in works dating from the early decades of the twentieth century are still valid. The period of time during which the law offers copyright protection to a particular work is called the "term of copyright."

DETERMINING COPYRIGHT DURATION

There are two primary reasons that you may want to determine the copyright status of a work. They are (1) that you want to determine whether the copyright in the work has expired, thereby transforming the work into a public domain work, which means that you may use the work in any way without permission from anyone; and (2) that you want to contact the owner of copyright in a work which is still protected to ask permission to use the work.

Determining the term of copyright for a work is not hard if you know a few things about when, by whom, and under what circumstances the work was created. The initial question to ask in determining the copyright status of any work is whether the work was created before or after January 1, 1978.

Copyright protection for any work created *before* that date, which is the date the current United States copyright statute went into effect, is governed by the provisions of the previous copyright statute, the Copyright Act of 1909. Protection for any work created on or after January 1, 1978, is governed by the present copyright statute, the Copyright Act of 1976. Various amendments to the basic statute have been passed by Congress in the intervening years. You can read the current US copyright statute, including all additions and amendments, at www.copyright.gov/title17/.

Copyright protection for any eligible work created on or after January 1, 1978, commences at the moment the work is first "fixed" in any tangible form. This protection is automatic; no action by the author of the work is necessary to begin it; the mere act of creating a work that qualifies for copyright triggers protection. How long copyright protection endures for any such work depends largely upon its author or authors. For purposes of determining the duration of copyright, the copyright statute divides works into basic categories and specifies a term for each category of work. These categories of works and their corresponding terms are discussed below.

Works Created by Individual Authors

Copyright in a work created by an individual author vests in that author from the inception of the work. The copyright in a work created by an individual author will endure until seventy years after his or her death. This rule for determining the duration of copyright protection for a work by an individual author applies even if the author assigns or licenses the copyright in the work to someone else.

The Copyright Office maintains records concerning the deaths of authors of copyrighted works. In addition, in order to make the determination of the expiration dates of copyrights easier, the copyright statute provides that "any person having an interest in a copyright" may notify the Copyright Office that the author of the work embodying that copyright has died or is still living. Information is also gathered from Copyright Office records and from other sources.

Anyone seeking information about an old copyright in a work by an obscure author may be able to obtain a certified report from the Copyright Office that there is nothing in the records of the Copyright Office to indicate that the author is living or died within the previous seventy years. Anyone who uses a work that, in reliance on such a report, he or she in good faith believes to have fallen into the public domain may use the report as a defense if the author of the work, or the author's heirs, bring suit for copyright infringement on the ground that the copyright in the work is still valid.

Under the present statute, all copyright terms expire at the end of the calendar year. This means if you write a short story in 2017, copyright protection begins as soon as you have written your story, whether it is handwritten, typed into a computer, or recorded on a disc. Copyright protection for your story will expire at the end of the seventieth year after your death; if you die in January of 2058, your story will be protected by copyright through December 31, 2128.

Joint Works

The copyright statute says that if two or more people create a work "with the intention that their contributions be merged into inseparable or interdependent parts of a unitary whole," those people are "joint authors" and the work they create is a "joint work." To qualify as one of the joint authors of a work, a person must contribute copyrightable expression to the work; someone who contributes only an unembellished idea to a work is not a joint author of the work.

Joint authors of a work share equally in any profits created by an exploitation of the work unless the authors agree otherwise at the time of the creation of the work. With the limitation that he or she may not grant an exclusive license to use a work without permission from the other author or authors of the work, a joint author may exploit the work without the permission of any other joint author. However, the exploiting author must share the profits derived from any such exploitation with the other joint author or authors. The copyright in a joint work endures until seventy years after the death of the last surviving author.

Anonymous or Pseudonymous Works

The copyright statute says that an anonymous work is a "work on the copies or phonorecords of which no natural person is identified as author." A pseudonymous work is defined as a "work on the copies or phonorecords of which the author is identified under a fictitious name." Even if the identity or, in the case of pseudonymous works, the real identity, of the author of an anonymous or pseudonymous work is known, unless the real name of the author appears on the copies or phonorecords of the work, the work will be treated as an anonymous or pseudonymous work. The status of a work as an anonymous or pseudonymous work has an important effect on the duration of copyright protection for the work.

The term of copyright for an anonymous or pseudonymous work is ninety-five years from the year of first publication of the work, or one hundred and twenty years from the year of its creation, whichever expires first. However, the copyright statute also provides that any person having an interest in the copyright in an anonymous or pseudonymous work may convert the term of copyright protection for the work to a term measured by the life or lives of the author or authors of the work plus seventy years. This is accomplished by simply filing with the Copyright Office, at any time before ninety-five years after the work's publication or one hundred twenty years after its creation, a statement that identifies the authors or one of the authors of the work. This has the effect of converting the term of copyright for the work to the life-plus-seventy-years measurement that applies to individual works.

The Copyright Act of 1976 has not been in effect long enough to allow the heirs or assigns of any anonymous or pseudonymous author who disclosed his or her real name to the Copyright Office during his or her lifetime to determine whether, by that action, the term of copyright in the formerly anonymous or pseudonymous work was enlarged. However, depending upon the age at which an author creates an anonymous or pseudonymous work and how many years the author lives thereafter, disclosing the author's name to the Copyright Office may, indeed, have the effect of prolonging copyright protection for the work. Therefore, this provision of the copyright statute is something that any anonymous or pseudonymous author and anyone who acquires the copyright in an anonymous or pseudonymous work should keep in mind.

Although most authors are proud to affix their names to their works, there are some circumstances when the anonymity of an author is desirable. Perhaps the most common example of this is the ghostwritten celebrity "autobiography." Anyone who thinks about it will readily realize that the movie star or rock star or statesman whose autobiography is the newest addition to the best-seller list probably did not personally spend six months of eight-hour days in front of a computer and that the hard work of researching and writing the book was performed by someone else. However, it is often the case that the celebrity's name is the only name that appears on the book's dust jacket or copyright page. The ghostwriter for the book may be mostly responsible for the book's appeal and cohesiveness and may be contractually entitled to a fat fee for writing the book and/or a generous share of the royalties produced by its sale, but, in the same contract that entitles him or her to be paid, may have agreed to keep his or her role in creating the book a secret.

Works Made for Hire

Works made for hire are the only category of work the copyrights to which do not initially vest in the creators of those works. The most common variety of works made for hire are works prepared by employees within the scope of their employment. The present copyright statute also specifies nine categories of specially commissioned works created by independent contractors that are appropriate for works made for hire, provided that the person or company who commissions the work and the freelancer who creates it agree in writing that the work is to be considered a work made for hire. (See chapter 2 for a more detailed discussion of works made for hire.)

The term of copyright for a work made for hire is ninety-five years from the year of first publication of the work, or one hundred and twenty years from the year of its creation, whichever expires first.

Pre-1978 Works

Determining whether a work created before January 1, 1978, (while the 1909 copyright statute was still in effect) is protected by copyright may be a complicated undertaking.

Under the 1909 copyright statute, a work was entitled to an initial twenty-eight-year term of copyright protection. This initial term was measured from the date the work was first published with copyright notice. At the end of the first twenty-eight-year term of protection, copyright could be renewed for an additional twenty-eight years, for a total of fifty-six years of copyright protection. If renewal was not made, the copyright in the work was lost and the work fell into the public domain. This sometimes led to the unfortunate result that some authors earned nothing in old age from their years of creative labor because the copyrights in their works had expired.

In drafting the present copyright statute, our legislators tried to remedy this situation by eliminating the renewal concept for works created on or after January 1, 1978. In addition, they extended copyright protection for works created under the previous copyright statute that were still protected by copyright (under the old statute) when the new statute went into effect. Copyright protection for works that were in their renewal terms on January 1, 1978, was extended by nineteen years; this meant that the term of protection for those works was enlarged to a total of seventy-five years. Works that were in their initial twenty-eight-year term of protection on January 1, 1978, still had to be renewed at the end of that term; they, too, were granted extended renewal terms (of forty-seven years) for a total of seventy-five years of protection.

In spite of this bonanza for the owners of pre-1978 copyrights, many of these older copyrights continued to be lost because of the failure to renew them. A very large percentage of pre-1978 works therefore entered the public domain after only twenty-eight years of copyright protection.

To even things up a bit between the owners of pre-1978 copyrights and copyrights created under the present statute, the law was changed in 1992. The Copyright Renewal Act of 1992 made renewal automatic for pre-1978 works first published between January 1, 1964, and December 31, 1977. With the passage in late 1998 of the Sonny Bono Copyright Term Extension Act, which generally increased copyright terms twenty years across the board, the renewal term for pre-1978 copyrights was increased to sixty-seven years (twenty-eight plus nineteen plus twenty years). Owners of pre-1978 copyrights may still file renewal forms and, in fact, are encouraged to do so, but no such action is *required* to secure the forty-seven additional years of protection granted to these older works. Certain benefits, such as the presumption that the statements made in the renewal certificate are valid, accrue to those who do file timely renewal certificates.

If no renewal was made for works published *before* 1964, those works have fallen into the public domain, which is an irrevocable state of copyright outer darkness that no one can alter.

Unpublished Works

Unpublished works created before January 1, 1978, fall into a special class of works as regards the term of copyright protection.

The current copyright statute provides that works created prior to 1978 that have neither been published nor registered for copyright will be protected in the same way that post-1977 works are protected. That is, the term of copyright protection for such a work created by an individual is the life of the author plus seventy years (or the life of the last surviving author plus seventy years, for joint works). If the work is anonymous, pseudonymous, or a work made for hire, the term of protection is ninety-five years from the year of first publication of the work, or one hundred and twenty years from the year of its creation, whichever expires first.

The present copyright statute provides that protection for works created prior to 1978 but published only *after* January 1, 1978, could not expire before December 31, 2002. Further, if such a pre-1978 work was published before December 21, 2003, its copyright cannot expire before December 31, 2047. These periods of protection are not affected by the dates of death of the authors of such works.

This provision has interesting implications for anyone who has an ancestor who kept a diary or was a novelist or composer. Old manuscripts and other works that would have become public domain many years ago had they been published prior to 1978 may be eligible for copyright protection for several decades to come.

Using the Works of Others

Once you have definitely determined the copyright status of a work, there are two avenues open to you.

If you are certain that the copyright in the work has expired, you may safely use the work in any way, including exercising any of the rights reserved to owners of valid copyrights. The copyright in the work has fallen into the "public domain," which means it is no longer owned by any one person or company but is now available for use by anyone, its protection under copyright law having expired. This means that you can adapt Charlotte Brontë's novel *Jane Eyre* for a screenplay; set Ben Jonson's poem "Though I Am Young and Cannot Tell" to music; reprint all or any portion of Ralph Waldo Emerson's essay "Self-Reliance"; adapt and record Johann Pachelbel's *Canon* for use as a film soundtrack; print and sell reproductions of Leonardo da Vinci's famous painting *Mona Lisa*; create a poster from a photograph by the very early photographer Julia Margaret Cameron; or create and sell copies of Michelangelo's sculpture *David*—all without permission from anyone.

If you find that the copyright in the work you want to use is still valid, you must respect the fact that the owner of that copyright still owns the exclusive rights of copyright in it. This means that you must request permission to use the work in the manner you have planned from the owner of copyright in that work. Finding the owner of copyright in a work (as opposed to the *author* of the work, who may no longer own the copyright in the work) may be easy or difficult, depending on the circumstances. More information on getting the permissions you need is given in chapter 8.

CHAPTER 4

Determining Copyright Status

As you may have guessed, determining the copyright status of a work isn't always a straightforward undertaking. Luckily, there are some shortcuts. One of the easiest ways to reliably determine whether a work is still protected by copyright is to consult a copyright duration chart. There are several available online; the best ones are offered by colleges and universities. Cornell University offers a very good one at http://copyright.cornell.edu/publicdomain. The University of North Carolina offers a shorter copyright duration chart at www.unc.edu/~unclng/public-d.htm. If you consult one of these charts and study the Copyright Office pamphlet *How to Investigate the Copyright Status of a Work* (reprinted below), you should be able to decide correctly whether the work you want to use is still protected by copyright or has fallen into the public domain. Don't get distracted by information you don't need—you can speed your perusal of the pamphlet by skipping the subheads that offer information on topics that are not applicable to your situation. The reprinted Copyright Office pamphlet begins below.

How to Investigate the Copyright Status of a Work

There are several ways to investigate whether a work is under copyright protection and, if so, the facts of the copyright. These are the main ones:

1. Examine a copy of the work for such elements as a copyright notice, place and date of publication, author and publisher. If the work is a sound recording, examine the

disc, tape, cartridge, or cassette in which the recorded sound is fixed, or the album cover, sleeve, or container in which the recording is sold.

2. Search the Copyright Office catalogs and other records.
3. Have the Copyright Office conduct a search for you.

A FEW WORDS OF CAUTION ABOUT COPYRIGHT INVESTIGATIONS

Copyright investigations often involve more than one of these methods. Even if you follow all three approaches, the results may not be conclusive. Moreover, as explained in this circular, the changes brought about under the Copyright Act of 1976, the Berne Convention Implementation Act of 1988, the Copyright Renewal Act of 1992, and the Sonny Bono Copyright Term Extension Act of 1998 must be considered when investigating the copyright status of a work.

This circular offers some practical guidance on what to look for if you are making a copyright investigation. It is important to realize, however, that this circular contains only general information and that there are a number of exceptions to the principles outlined here. In many cases, it is important to consult with a copyright attorney before reaching any conclusions regarding the copyright status of a work.

HOW TO SEARCH COPYRIGHT OFFICE CATALOGS AND RECORDS

Catalog of Copyright Entries

The Copyright Office published the *Catalog of Copyright Entries* (*CCE*) in printed format from 1891 through 1978. From 1979 through 1982, the *CCE* was issued in microfiche format. The *CCE* is divided into parts according to the classes of works registered. Each *CCE* segment covers all registrations made during a particular period of time. Renewal registrations made from 1979 through 1982 are found in section 8 of the catalog. Renewals prior to that time are generally listed at the end of the volume containing the class of work to which they pertained.

A number of libraries throughout the US maintain copies of the *CCE*, and this may provide a good starting point if you wish to make a search yourself. There are some cases, however, in which a search of the *CCE* alone will not be sufficient to provide the needed information. For example:

- Because the *CCE* does not include entries for assignments or other recorded documents, it cannot be used for searches involving the ownership of rights.
- The *CCE* entry contains the essential facts concerning a registration, but it is not a verbatim transcript of the registration record. It does not contain the address of the copyright claimant.

Effective with registrations made since 1982 when the *CCE* was discontinued, the only method of searching *CCE* volumes outside the Library of Congress is by using the Internet to access the online catalog. The online catalog contains entries from 1978 to the present. Information on accessing the catalog via the Internet is provided below. The Copyright Office has been digitizing the 660 volumes of the *CCE* and many are now available at www.archive.org/details/copyrightrecords/.

Individual Searches of Copyright Records

The Copyright Office is located in the Library of Congress, James Madison Memorial Building, 101 Independence Avenue SE, Washington, DC 20559.

Most Copyright Office records are open to public inspection and searching from 8:30 am to 5:00 pm, eastern time, Monday through Friday, except federal holidays. The various records freely available to the public include an extensive card catalog, an automated catalog containing records from 1978 forward, record books, and microfilm records of assignments and related documents. Other records, including correspondence files and deposit copies, are not open to the public for searching. However, they may be inspected upon request and payment of a search fee.

For current fees, please check the Copyright Office website at www.copyright.gov, write the Copyright Office, or call (202) 707-3000 or (877) 476–0778.

If you wish to do your own searching in the Copyright Office files open to the public, you will be given assistance in locating the records you need and in learning procedures for searching. If the Copyright Office staff member actually makes the search for you, a search fee must be charged. The search will not be done while you wait.

In addition, Copyright Office records in machine-readable form cataloged from January 1, 1978, to the present, including registration and renewal information and recorded documents, are available for searching from the Copyright Office website at www.copyright.gov.

The Copyright Office does not offer search assistance to users on the Internet.

Searching by the Copyright Office in General

Upon request and at the statutory rate for each hour or fraction of an hour used, the Copyright Office staff will search the records of registrations and other recorded documents concerning ownership of copyrights and will provide a written report. If you request a cost estimate, the Copyright Office will provide one. Estimates for searches are based on the information you furnish and are provided for a set fee that is applied toward the cost of the search and report. Fees for estimates are nonrefundable and may be applied to a search for up to one year from the date of the estimate. Requests must include an address and telephone number where you may be reached during business hours and an email address if available.

Certification of a search report is available for an additional fee. Certified searches are frequently requested to meet the evidentiary requirements of litigation.

Preferred payment is by personal check or credit card. Contact the Copyright Office for information regarding payment with money orders or by overseas banking institutions.

For information, correspondence, or payment, contact:

Copyright Office GC/I&R/RRC
Attn: RCC
PO Box 70400
Washington, DC 20024
phone: (202) 707–6850 (M–F, 8:30–5:00 eastern time)
fax: (202) 252–3485
email: copysearch@loc.gov

What the Fee Does Not Cover

The search fee does not include the cost of additional certificates, photocopies of deposits, or copies of other office records. For information concerning these services, see Circular 6, *Obtaining Access to and Copies of Copyright Office Records and Deposits.*

Information Needed

The more detailed information you furnish with your request, the less expensive the search will be. Please provide as much of the following information as possible:

- the title of the work, with any possible variants;
- the names of the authors, including possible pseudonyms;
- the name of the probable copyright owner, which may be the publisher or producer;
- the approximate year when the work was published or registered;
- the type of work involved (book, play, musical composition, sound recording, photograph, etc.);
- for a work originally published as a part of a periodical or collection, the title of that publication and any other information, such as the volume or issue number, to help identify it; and
- the registration number or any other copyright data.

Motion pictures are often based on other works, such as books or serialized contributions to periodicals or other composite works. *If you want a search for an underlying work or for music from a motion picture, you must specifically request such a search. You must also identify the underlying works and music and furnish the specific titles, authors, and approximate dates of these works.*

Searches Involving Assignments and Other Documents Affecting Copyright Ownership

For the standard hourly search fee, the Copyright Office staff will search its indexes covering the records of assignments and other recorded documents concerning ownership of copyrights. The reports of searches in these cases will state the facts shown in the office's indexes of the recorded documents but will offer no interpretation of the content of the documents or their legal effect.

Limitations on Searches

In determining whether or not to have a search made, you should keep the following points in mind:

No Special Lists—The Copyright Office does not maintain any lists of works by subject or any lists of works that are in the public domain.

Contributions Not Listed Separately in Copyright Office Records— Individual works such as stories, poems, articles, or musical compositions that were published as contributions to a copyrighted periodical or collection are usually not listed separately by title in our records.

No Comparisons—The Copyright Office does not search or compare copies of works to determine questions of possible infringement or to determine how much two or more versions of a work have in common.

Titles and Names Not Copyrightable—Copyright does not protect names and titles, and our records list many different works identified by the same or similar titles. Some brand names, trade names, slogans, and phrases may be entitled to protection under the general rules of law relating to unfair competition. They may also be entitled to registration under the provisions of the trademark laws. Questions about the trademark laws should be addressed to: *Commissioner for Patents, PO Box 1450, Alexandria, VA 22313–1450*. Possible protection of names and titles under common law principles of unfair competition is a question of state law.

No Legal Advice—The Copyright Office cannot express any opinion as to the legal significance or effect of the facts included in a search report.

Some Words of Caution

Searches Not Always Conclusive

Searches of the Copyright Office catalogs and records are useful in helping to determine the copyright status of a work, but they cannot be regarded as conclusive in all cases. The complete absence of any information about a work in the office records does not mean that the work is unprotected. The following are examples of cases in which information about a particular work may be incomplete or lacking entirely in the Copyright Office:

- Before 1978, unpublished works were entitled to protection under common law without the need of registration.
- Works published with notice prior to 1978 may be registered at any time within the first twenty-eight-year term.
- Works copyrighted between January 1, 1964, and December 31, 1977, are affected by the Copyright Renewal Act of 1992, which automatically extends the copyright term and makes renewal registrations optional.
- For works under copyright protection on or after January 1, 1978, registration may be made at any time during the term of protection. Although registration is not required as a condition of copyright protection, there are certain definite advantages to registration.
- For further information, see Circular 1, *Copyright Basics*.
- Since searches are ordinarily limited to registrations that have already been cataloged, a search report may not cover recent registrations for which catalog records are not yet available.
- The information in the search request may not have been complete or specific enough to identify the work.
- The work may have been registered under a different title or as part of a larger work.

Protection in Foreign Countries

Even if you conclude that a work is in the public domain in the United States, this does not necessarily mean that you are free to use it in other countries. Every nation has its own laws governing the length and scope of copyright protection, and these are applicable to uses of the work within that nation's borders. Thus, the expiration or loss of copyright protection in the United States may still leave the work fully protected against unauthorized use in other countries. For further information, see Circular 6; Circular 15, *Renewal of Copyright*; and Circular 15a, *Duration of Copyright*.

Impact of the Copyright Act on Copyright Investigations

On October 19, 1976, the president signed into law a complete revision of the copyright law of the United States (title 17 of the *United States Code*). Most provisions of this statute came into force on January 1, 1978, superseding the Copyright Act of 1909. These provisions made significant changes in the copyright law. Further important changes resulted from the Berne Convention Implementation Act of 1988, which took effect March 1, 1989; the Copyright Renewal Act of 1992 (P.L. 102–307) enacted June 26, 1992, which amended the renewal provisions of the copyright law; and the Sonny Bono Copyright Term Extension Act of 1998 (P.L. 105–298) enacted October 27, 1998, which extended the term of copyrights for an additional twenty years.

If you need more information about the provisions of either the 1909 or the 1976 law, write or call the Copyright Office. Both laws are available on the Copyright Office website. For information about renewals, see Circular 15. For paper copies of the law, order Circular 92, *Copyright Law of the United States*, from:

US Government Printing Office
PO Box 979050
St. Louis, MO 63197–9000
web: bookstore.gpo.gov
phone: (202) 512–1800 [toll free: (866) 512–1800]
fax: (202) 512–2104
email: contactcenter@gpo.gov

Or go to the Copyright Office website at www.copyright.gov/title17.

For copyright investigations, the following points about the impact of the Copyright Act of 1976, the Berne Convention Implementation Act of 1988, and the Copyright Renewal Act of 1992 should be considered.

A Changed System of Copyright Formalities

Some of the most sweeping changes under the 1976 Copyright Act involve copyright formalities, that is, the procedural requirements for securing and maintaining full copyright protection. The old system of formalities involved copyright notice, deposit, and registration; recordation of transfers and licenses of copyright ownership; and US manufacture, among other things. In general, while retaining formalities, the 1976 law reduced the chances of mistakes, softened the consequences of errors and omissions, and allowed for the correction of errors.

The Berne Convention Implementation Act of 1988 reduced formalities, most notably making the addition of the previously mandatory copyright notice optional. It should be noted that the amended notice requirements are not retroactive.

The Copyright Renewal Act of 1992, enacted June 26, 1992, automatically extends the term of copyrights secured between January 1, 1964, and December 31, 1977, making renewal registration optional. Consult Circular 15 for details. For additional information, contact the Copyright Office by phone at (202) 707–3000 or (877) 476–0778 (toll free).

Automatic Copyright

Under the present copyright law, copyright exists in original works of authorship created and fixed in any tangible medium of expression, now known or later developed, from which they can be perceived, reproduced, or otherwise communicated, either directly or indirectly with the aid of a machine or device. In other words, copyright is an incident of creative authorship and is not dependent on statutory formalities. Thus, registration with the Copyright Office generally is not required, but there are certain advantages that arise from a timely registration. For further information on the advantages of registration, see Circular 1.

Copyright Notice

The 1909 Copyright Act and the 1976 Copyright Act as originally enacted required a notice of copyright on published works. For most works, a copyright notice consisted of the symbol ©, the word *Copyright* or the abbreviation *Copr.*, together with the name of the owner of copyright and the year of first publication. For example: "© Joan Crane 2004" or "Copyright 2008 by Abraham Adams."

For sound recordings published on or after February 15, 1972, a copyright notice might read "℗ 1994 XYZ Records, Inc." See below for more information about sound recordings.

For mask works, a copyright notice might read "Ⓜ SDR Industries." See Circular 100, *Federal Statutory Protection for Mask Works*, for more information.

As originally enacted, the 1976 law prescribed that all visually perceptible published copies of a work, or published phonorecords of a sound recording, should bear a proper copyright notice. This applies to such works published before March 1, 1989. After March 1, 1989, notice of copyright on these works is optional. Adding the notice, however, is strongly encouraged and, if litigation involving the copyright occurs, certain advantages exist for publishing a work with notice.

Prior to March 1, 1989, the requirement for the notice applied equally whether the work was published in the United States or elsewhere by authority of the copyright owner. Compliance with the statutory notice requirements was the responsibility of the copyright owner. Unauthorized publication without the copyright notice, or with a defective notice, does not affect the validity of the copyright in the work.

Advance permission from, or registration with, the Copyright Office is not required before placing a copyright notice on copies of the work or on phonorecords of a sound recording. Moreover, for works first published on or after January 1, 1978, through February 28, 1989, omission of the required notice, or use of a defective notice, did not result in forfeiture or outright loss of copyright protection. Certain omissions of, or defects in, the notice of copyright, however, could have led to loss of copyright protection if steps were not taken to correct or cure the omissions or defects. The Copyright Office has issued a final regulation (37 CFR 201.20) that suggests various acceptable positions for the notice of copyright. This regulation is available on the Copyright Office website at www.copyright.gov/title37/201/index.html. For further information, see Circular 3, *Copyright Notice*.

Works Already in the Public Domain

In general, once a work enters the public domain, copyright protection cannot be restored. However, certain exceptions apply to works of foreign origin. For eligible foreign works, copyright protection is automatically restored under the provisions of the Uruguay Round Agreements Act (URAA) and section 104(a) of the copyright law. Previous to the URAA, the North American Free Trade Agreement Implementation Act contained copyright restoration provisions for certain Canadian and Mexican works.

Under the copyright law in effect prior to January 1, 1978, copyright could be lost in several situations. The most common were publication without the required notice of copyright, expiration of the first twenty-eight-year term without renewal, or final expiration of the second copyright term. The Copyright Renewal Act of 1992 automatically renews first term copyrights secured between January 1, 1964, and December 31, 1977.

Scope of Exclusive Rights Under Copyright

The present law has changed and enlarged in some cases the scope of the copyright owner's rights. The new rights apply to all uses of a work subject to protection by copyright after January 1, 1978, regardless of when the work was created.

Duration of Copyright Protection

Works Originally Copyrighted on or After January 1, 1978

A work that is created and fixed in tangible form for the first time on or after January 1, 1978, is automatically protected from the moment of its creation and is ordinarily given a term enduring for the author's life plus an additional seventy years after the author's death. In the case of "a joint work prepared by two or more authors who did not work for hire," the term lasts for 70 years after the last surviving author's death. For works made for hire and for anonymous and pseudonymous works (unless the author's identity is revealed in the Copyright Office records), the duration of copyright will be 95 years from publication or 120 years from creation, whichever is less.

Works created before the 1976 law came into effect but neither published nor registered for copyright before January 1, 1978, have been automatically brought under the statute and are now given federal copyright protection. The duration of copyright in these works will generally be computed in the same way as for new works: the life-plus-70 or -95/120-year terms will apply. However, all works in this category were guaranteed at least twenty-five years of statutory protection.

Works Copyrighted Before January 1, 1978

Under the law in effect before 1978, copyright was secured either on the date a work was published with notice of copyright or on the date of registration if the work was registered in unpublished form. In either case, copyright endured for a first term of twenty-eight years from the date on which it was secured. During the last (twenty-eighth) year of the first term, the copyright was eligible for renewal. The copyright law extends the renewal term from twenty-eight to sixty-seven years for copyrights in existence on January 1, 1978.

However, for works copyrighted prior to January 1, 1964, the copyright still must have been renewed in the twenty-eighth calendar year to receive the sixty-seven-year period of added protection. The amending legislation enacted June 26, 1992, automatically extends this second term for works first copyrighted between January 1, 1964, and December 31, 1977. For more detailed information on the copyright term, see Circular 15a.

Works First Published Before 1978: The Copyright Notice

General Information About the Copyright Notice

In investigating the copyright status of works first published before January 1, 1978, the most important thing to look for is the notice of copyright. As a general rule under the 1909 law, copyright protection was lost permanently if the notice was omitted from the first authorized published edition of a work or if it appeared in the wrong form or position. The form and position of the copyright notice for various types of works were specified in the copyright statute. Some courts were liberal in overlooking relatively minor departures from the statutory requirements, but a basic failure to comply with the notice provisions forfeited copyright protection and put the work into the public domain in this country.

Absence of Copyright Notice

For works first published before 1978, the complete absence of a copyright notice from a published copy generally indicates that the work is not protected by copyright. For works first published before March 1, 1989, the copyright notice is required, but omission could have been cured by registration before or within five years of publication and by adding the notice to copies published in the United States after discovery of the omission. Some works may contain a notice, others may not. The absence of a notice in works published on or after March 1, 1989, does not necessarily indicate that the work is in the public domain.

Unpublished Works—No notice of copyright was required on the copies of any unpublished work. The concept of "publication" is very technical, and it was possible for a number of copies lacking a copyright notice to be reproduced and distributed without affecting copyright protection.

Foreign Editions—In the case of works seeking ad interim copyright, copies of a copyrighted work were exempted from the notice requirements if they were first published outside the United States. Some copies of these foreign editions could find their way into the United States without impairing the copyright. "Ad interim copyright" refers to a special short term of copyright available to certain pre-1978 books and periodicals. For further information on ad interim copyright, see the discussion below.

Accidental Omission—The 1909 statute preserved copyright protection if the notice was omitted by accident or mistake from a "particular copy or copies."

Unauthorized Publication—A valid copyright was not secured if someone deleted the notice and/or published the work without authorization from the copyright owner.

Sound Recordings—Reproductions of sound recordings usually contain two different types of creative works: the underlying musical, dramatic, or literary work that is being performed or read and the fixation of the actual sounds embodying the performance or reading. For protection of the underlying musical or literary work embodied in a recording, it is not necessary that a copyright notice covering this material appear on the phonograph records or tapes on which the recording is reproduced. A special notice is required for protection of the recording of a series of musical, spoken, or other sounds that were fixed on or after February 15, 1972. Sound recordings fixed before February 15, 1972, are not eligible for federal copyright protection. The Sound Recording Act of 1971, the present copyright law, and the Berne Convention Implementation Act of 1988 cannot be applied or be construed to provide any retroactive protection for sound recordings fixed before February 15, 1972. Such works, however, may be protected by various state laws or doctrines of common law.

The Date in the Copyright Notice

If you find a copyright notice, the date it contains may be important in determining the copyright status of the work. In general, the notice on works published before 1978 must include the year in which copyright was secured by publication or, if the work was first registered for copyright in unpublished form, the year in which registration was made. There are two main exceptions to this rule.

1. For pictorial, graphic, or sculptural works (Classes F through K under the 1909 law), the law permitted omission of the year date in the notice.
2. For "new versions" of previously published or copyrighted works, the notice was not usually required to include more than the year of first publication of the new version itself. This is explained further under Derivative Works below.

The year in the notice usually (though not always) indicated when the copyright began. It is, therefore, significant in determining whether a copyright is still in effect; or, if the copyright has not yet run its course, the year date will help in deciding when the copyright is scheduled to expire. For further information about the duration of copyright, see Circular 15a.

In evaluating the meaning of the date in a notice, you should keep the following points in mind:

Works Published and Copyrighted Before January 1, 1978—A work published before January 1, 1978, and copyrighted on or after January 1, 1923, may still be protected by copyright in the United States if a valid renewal registration was made during the twenty-eighth year of the first term of the copyright. If renewed by registration or under the Copyright Renewal Act of 1992 and if still valid under the other provisions of the law, the copyright will expire ninety-five years from the end of the year in which it was first secured.

Therefore, the US copyright in any work published or copyrighted prior to January 1, 1923, has expired by operation of law, and the work has permanently fallen into the public domain in the United States. For example, on January 1, 1997, copyrights in works first published or copyrighted before January 1, 1922, expired; on January 1, 1998, copyrights in works first published or copyrighted before January 1, 1923, expired. Unless the copyright law is changed again, no works under protection on January 1, 1999, will fall into the public domain in the United States until January 1, 2019.

Works First Published or Copyrighted between January 1, 1923, and December 31, 1949, but Not Renewed—If a work was first published or copyrighted between January 1, 1923, and December 31, 1949, it is important to determine whether the copyright was renewed during the last (twenty-eighth) year of the first term of the copyright. This can be done by searching the Copyright Office records or catalogs as explained previously. If no renewal registration was made, copyright protection expired permanently at the end of the twenty-eighth year from the year date it was first secured.

Works First Published or Copyrighted between January 1, 1923, and December 31, 1949, and Registered for Renewal—When a valid renewal registration was made and copyright in the work was in its second term on December 31, 1977, the renewal copyright term was extended under the latest act to sixty-seven years. In these cases, copyright will last for a total of ninety-five years from the end of the year in which copyright was originally secured. Example: copyright in a work first published in 1925 and renewed in 1953 will expire on December 31, 2020.

Works First Published or Copyrighted between January 1, 1950, and December 31, 1963—If a work was in its first twenty-eight-year term of copyright protection on January 1, 1978, it must have been renewed in a timely fashion to have secured the maximum term of copyright protection. If renewal registration was made during the twenty-eighth calendar year of its first term, copyright would endure for ninety-five years from the end of the year copyright was originally secured. If not renewed, the copyright expired at the end of its twenty-eighth calendar year.

Works First Published or Copyrighted between January 1, 1964, and December 31, 1977—If a work was in its first twenty-eight-year term of copyright protection on June 26, 1992, renewal registration was optional. The term of copyright for works published or copyrighted during this time period was extended to ninety-five years by the Copyright Renewal Act of 1992 and the Sonny Bono Term Extension Act of 1998. There was no need to make the renewal filing to extend the original twenty-eight-year copyright term to the full ninety-five years.

However, there were several advantages to making a renewal registration during the twenty-eighth year of the original term of copyright. If renewal registration was made during the twenty-eighth year of the original term of copyright, the renewal copyright vested in the name of the renewal claimant on the effective date of the renewal registration; the renewal certificate constitutes prima facie evidence as to the validity of the copyright during the renewed and extended term and of the facts stated in the certificate; and, the right to use the derivative work in the extended term may be affected. See Circular 15 for further information.

Unpublished, Unregistered Works—Before 1978, if a work had been neither "published" in the legal sense nor registered in the Copyright Office, it was subject to perpetual protection under the common law. On January 1, 1978, all works of this kind, subject to protection by copyright, were automatically brought under the federal copyright statute. The duration of copyright for these works can vary, but none of them expired before December 31, 2002.

Derivative Works

In examining a copy (or a record, disc, or tape) for copyright information, it is important to determine whether that particular version of the work is an original edition of the work or a "new version." New versions include musical arrangements, adaptations, revised or newly edited editions, translations, dramatizations, abridgments, compilations, and works republished with new matter added. The law provides that derivative works, published or unpublished, are independently copyrightable and that the copyright in such a work does not affect or extend the protection, if any, in the underlying work. Under the 1909 law, courts have also held that the notice of copyright on a derivative work ordinarily need not include the dates or other information pertaining to the earlier works incorporated in it. This principle is specifically preserved in the present copyright law. Thus, if the copy (or the record, disc, or tape) constitutes a derivative version of the work, these points should be kept in mind:

- The date in the copyright notice is not necessarily an indication of when copyright in all the material in the work will expire. Some of the material may already be in the public domain, and some parts of the work may expire sooner than others.
- Even if some of the material in the derivative work is in the public domain and free for use, this does not mean that the "new" material added to it can be used without permission from the owner of copyright in the derivative work. It may be necessary to compare editions to determine what is free to use and what is not.
- Ownership of rights in the material included in a derivative work and in the preexisting work upon which it may be based may differ, and permission obtained from the owners of certain parts of the work may not authorize the use of other parts.

The Name in the Copyright Notice

Under the copyright statute in effect before 1978, the notice was required to include "the name of the copyright proprietor." The present act requires that the notice include "the name of the owner of copyright in the work, or an abbreviation by which the name can be recognized, or a generally known alternative designation of the owner." The name in the notice (sometimes in combination with the other statements on the copy, records, disc, tape, container, or label) often gives persons wishing to use the work the information needed to identify the owner from whom licenses or permission can be sought. In other cases, the name provides a starting point for a search in the Copyright Office records or catalogs, as explained at the beginning of this circular.

In the case of works published before 1978, copyright registration is made in the name of the individual person or the entity identified as the copyright owner in the notice. For works published on or after January 1, 1978, registration is made in the name of the person or entity owning all the rights on the date the registration is made. This may or may not be the name appearing in the notice. In addition to its records of copyright registration, the Copyright Office maintains extensive records of assignments, exclusive licenses, and other documents dealing with copyright ownership.

Ad Interim

Ad interim copyright was a special short-term copyright that applied to certain books and periodicals in the English language that were first manufactured and published outside the United States. It was a partial exception to the manufacturing requirements of the previous US copyright law. Its purpose was to secure temporary US protection for a work, pending the manufacture of an edition in the United States. The ad interim requirements changed several times over the years and were subject to a number of exceptions and qualifications.

The manufacturing provisions of the copyright act expired on July 1, 1986, and are no longer a part of the copyright law. The transitional and supplementary provisions of the act provide that for any work in which ad interim copyright was subsisting or capable of being secured on December 31, 1977, copyright protection would be extended for a term compatible with the other works in which copyright was subsisting on the effective date of the new act. Consequently, if the work was first published on or after July 1, 1977, and was eligible for ad interim copyright protection, the provisions of the present copyright act will be applicable to the protection of these works. Anyone investigating the copyright status of an English-language book or periodical first published outside the United States before July 1, 1977, should check carefully to determine:

- whether the manufacturing requirements were applicable to the work, and
- if so, whether the ad interim requirements were met.

For Further Information

By Internet

Circulars, announcements, regulations, other related materials, and all copyright application forms are available from the Copyright Office website at www.copyright.gov. To send an email communication, click on Contact Us at the bottom of the home page.

By Telephone

For general information about copyright, call the Copyright Public Information Office at (202) 707–3000 or (877) 476–0778 (toll free). Staff members are on duty from 8:30 am to 5:00 pm, eastern time, Monday through Friday, except federal holidays. Recorded information is available twenty-four hours a day. Or, if you know which application forms and circulars you want, request them twenty-four hours a day from the Forms and Publications Hotline at (202) 707–9100. Leave a recorded message.

By Regular Mail

Write to:
Library of Congress
Copyright Office–COPUBS
101 Independence Avenue SE
Washington, DC 20559

CHAPTER 5

Copyright Registration

You probably don't need a lawyer to help you register your copyright properly, but you do need to educate yourself about registration in order to avoid mistakes.

THE COPYRIGHT OFFICE

The Copyright Office in Washington, DC, is the federal agency that has the responsibility for administering the registration of copyrights and performing other government functions relating to copyrights, such as maintaining records of copyright registrations and creating and disseminating regulations interpreting sections of the copyright statute. The Copyright Office is a division of the Library of Congress; copies of works registered for copyright may end up in the collections of the library, depending on the work and the needs and collections policies of the library.

There is no such thing as a state copyright law. That means that there is no state agency anywhere in the United States that grants copyright registrations or otherwise has anything to do with copyrights. All US copyright registrations are granted by the Copyright Office; whether it is a child's poem or a hit song or the screenplay for a blockbuster movie, if it is registered for copyright in the United States, it is registered in the Copyright Office in Washington.

"Poor Man's Copyright"

A short discussion concerning a persistent piece of folklore called "poor man's copyright" is in order. "Poor man's copyright" is a homemade and virtually worthless would-be substitute for copyright registration. It supposedly works like this: you finish your novel (or song or computer program), seal the manuscript (or CD or flash drive) in an envelope, and mail it to yourself. You then preserve the postmarked envelope, unopened, until the day that you dramatically rip it open in court, where you use the dated, sealed envelope to demonstrate that your work existed in a certain form on a certain date, thereby proving either that any similarities between your work and the work of the person who has sued you for infringement are coincidental, since your work existed before the plaintiff's work. It never happens this way in real life. In real life, there is no legal substitute for copyright registration, which is the only event that courts recognize as sufficient to accomplish what copyright registration accomplishes.

Other similar repositories for unpublished creative works, such as that operated by the Writers Guild of America (a screenwriters' union) and other organizations for creative people working in a particular medium, are no more worthwhile as *substitutes* for copyright registration, whatever else they may accomplish. (For example, to protect themselves from accusations that they have stolen material from scripts that they have not bought, many studios and producers will not read a script *unless* it is registered with the Writers Guild.) Spend your money and time to register your copyright with the Copyright Office. It won't hurt to mail a copy of your work to yourself or place it in some registry *in addition to* registering your copyright, but nothing can substitute legally for copyright registration. Depositing a copy of your work with a reliable registry can be a pretty good cheap substitute for the full-term retention of a copy of your work by the Copyright Office (discussed below), even though it is probable that, periodically, you will need to renew your deposit contract with any such registry.

COPYRIGHT REGISTRATION TODAY

Under current US copyright law, a work of authorship is protected by copyright from the moment it is created, provided that the work is original and has been fixed in a tangible medium of expression.

Although registration is not required for a work to be protected by copyright, there are many advantages to registering your copyright, among them:

- A registration creates a public record that includes key facts relating to the authorship and ownership of the claimed work, as well as information about the work, such as title, year of creation, date of publication (if any), and the type of authorship that the work contains (e.g., photographs, text, sound recordings).
- Registration is a prerequisite to filing a lawsuit for copyright infringement involving a US work. Although a copyright owner has property rights in his or her copyright without registration, both the registration certificate and the original work must be on file with the Copyright Office before a copyright owner can sue for infringement.
- To claim statutory damages or attorney's fees in a copyright infringement lawsuit, a work must be registered before the infringement began or within three months after the first publication of the work. (See Chapter 10 for a discussion of statutory damages.)
- A registration constitutes prima facie evidence of the validity of the copyright and the facts stated in the certificate of registration, but only if the work is registered before or within five years after the work is first published.
- A registration provides information to prospective licensees, such as the name and address for obtaining permission to use the work.
- A document that has been recorded with the US Copyright Office may provide constructive notice of the facts stated therein, but only if the document specifically identifies a work of authorship and only if that work has been registered.
- The deposit copy(ies) submitted with an application for registration of a published work may satisfy the mandatory

    deposit requirement, provided that the applicant submitted the best edition of the work.

- The US Customs and Border Protection Service may seize foreign pirated copies of a copyright owner's work, provided that the work has been registered with the US Copyright Office and the certificate of registration has been recorded with the US Customs and Border Protection Service.

- A registration is required to claim royalties under the compulsory license for making and distributing phonorecords. See 17 U.S.C. § 115(c)(1).

It is best to register a copyright promptly, but it's never too late to apply for registration. You can register any copyright that has not entered the public domain, even at the very end of the term of copyright protection. And if you make a mistake in filling out your registration form, the worst that will happen is that the Copyright Office will request corrections or clarification. You will be given plenty of time to respond. Then, when the application is granted, a certificate will be issued that gives, for the effective date of your registration, the date all the elements of your application were received by the Copyright Office. The vast majority of applications for copyright registration are granted, but if yours is denied for any reason, you will be notified.

Varieties of Copyrightable Works

Copyright can be registered in the following varieties of works:

Literary Works—Fiction, nonfiction, poetry, serial publications (e.g., newspapers, magazines, etc.), articles, advertising copy, written communications (e.g., letters, email messages), reference works, directories, catalogs, compilations of information, computer programs, databases, ebooks, audiobooks, online textual works (e.g., blogs, website text), and similar types of textual works.

Pictorial Works—Paintings, drawings, photographs, prints, art reproductions, maps, technical drawings, diagrams, applied art (i.e., two-dimensional pictorial artwork applied to a useful article), artistic crafts (e.g., textiles, table service patterns, wall plaques), online or digital artwork (e.g., computer-aided artwork, digital imaging, pixel art), and similar types of pictorial works.

Graphic Works—Drawings, prints, art reproductions, maps, technical drawings, diagrams, applied art (i.e., two-dimensional graphic artwork applied to a useful article), artistic crafts (e.g., textiles, table service patterns, wall plaques), online or digital artwork (e.g., computer-aided artwork, digital imaging, pixel art), and similar types of graphic works.

Sculptural Works—Sculptures, globes, models, applied art (i.e., three-dimensional artwork applied to a useful article), artistic crafts (e.g., jewelry, glassware, toys, dolls, stuffed toy animals, models), and similar types of sculptural works.

Musical Works—Songs, song lyrics, symphonies, concertos, advertising jingles, and similar types of musical works.

Dramatic Works—Plays, musicals, operas, scripts, screenplays, and similar types of dramatic works.

Choreographic Works—Ballet, modern dance, and similar types of complex dances.

Motion Pictures—Films, television shows, videogames, videos, online videos, motion picture soundtracks, and similar types of audiovisual works.

Audiovisual Works—Videogames, slide presentations, online audiovisual works (e.g., smartphone and tablet applications, online courses and tutorials, website content), and similar types of audiovisual works.

Sound Recordings—A recording of a song, a recording of a vocal performance, a recording of a musical performance, a recording of a literary work (e.g., an audiobook), a digital file of a performance, and similar types of recordings.

Architectural Works—Buildings, architectural plans, and architectural drawings.

Remember that these categories are interpreted broadly—notice, for example, that computer programs fall into the category of "literary works." Remember, too, that a copyright registration covers the copyrightable authorship that the author contributed to the work rather than the medium in which the work has been fixed. The Copyright Office recognizes that there is a fundamental distinction between the "original work," which is the product of authorship, and the multitude of material objects in which it can be embodied. Thus, when completing an application, the applicant should describe the *copyrightable authorship* (i.e., "the full text of the novel" or "the lyrics of the musical composition") that the author contributed to the work, rather than the *medium* (the full text of the novel may be written in a paper manuscript, documented on a disc, printed in a book, or recorded in an audiobook) that the author used to create that work.

REGISTRATION REQUIREMENTS

The Copyright Office publishes helpful circulars and factsheets explaining registration procedures for most kinds of works, including *Copyright Registration for Pictorial, Graphic, and Sculptural Works* (Circular 40), *Copyright Claims in Architectural Works* (Circular 41), *Copyright Registration for Motion Pictures Including Video Recordings* (Circular 45), *Copyright Registration for Musical Compositions* (Circular 50), *Copyright Registration for Multimedia Works* (Circular 55), *Copyright Registration for Computer Programs* (Circular 61), *Copyright Registration of Poetry* (Factsheet FL106), *Copyright Registration of Photographs* (Factsheet FL 107), *Copyright Registration of Books, Manuscripts, and Speeches* (Factsheet 109), and so on.

The best way to figure out the requirements for any particular copyright registration is to download and print the free Copyright Office publications that correspond to the sort of work you want to register. To access these publications, go to the Copyright Office home page at www.copyright.gov and select "Circulars" or "Factsheets" from the menu under "Publications" in the navigation bar. This will take you to a page that will allow you to select and print out any of the useful publications the Copyright Office offers. (A list of these publications is also reprinted in appendix A, the Copyright Office Resources section of this book.) You can also access and print out registration forms from this menu.

After reading the Copyright Office circular that pertains to the registration of your sort of work, you are ready to begin the registration process. Any registration of copyright requires a completed registration form, a registration fee, and a deposit of "identifying material" to specify the character and content of the registered work. The registration form you use depends on whether you register online, as does the registration fee you must pay. The material you deposit with the Copyright Office when you apply for registration is determined by Copyright Office requirements and the character of the work you want to register. The form, fee, and deposit requirements are accomplished in different ways in each of the three basic ways the Copyright Office now accepts registration applications: online registration, registration with a fill-in online form, and registration with a paper form.

1. Registration Online

The Copyright Office strongly encourages applicants for copyright registration to use the online application whenever possible. The benefits to filing an online application include:

- **Lower filing fees for online applications:** The filing fee for an online application is lower than the filing fee for a paper application.
- **Faster processing:** The office typically processes electronic claims three to six months sooner than nonelectronic claims.
- **Multiple options for paying the filing fee:** An applicant may pay the filing fee for an online application by credit card, debit card, electronic check, or with a US Copyright Office deposit account, while in most cases an applicant may pay the filing fee for a paper application only by check, money order, or deposit account.
- **Easier submission of the deposit copy(ies):** For certain types of works, the applicant may upload deposit copy(ies) directly to the online system as an electronic file, instead of having to submit physical deposit copies through the mail.
- **The ability to track the status of the application:** After submission, the online system allows the applicant to log in and see whether the online application is still pending or whether it has been registered and closed.

The online registration process is, for most applicants, easier and less cumbersome than the paper registration process. In many cases, and especially if you have reviewed the registration process in advance by reading about how to register your particular type of work and studied the Copyright Office's tutorial about the registration process, online registration can be accomplished in less than half an hour.

Before you start to fill out the online copyright registration form, access and study the PDF of the *eCO (electronic Copyright Office) Single Application Tutorial* located at www.copyright.gov/eco/eco-tutorial-single.pdf. Run through this tutorial a couple of times and note any information that you must collect before filing your actual application. Then review the FAQs at the eCO Help Desk at www.copyright.gov/eco/help/. When you are familiar with the application form and process and the FAQs that apply to your application, go to www.copyright.gov/registration/ and click on the bar that says "Log in to the Electronic Copyright Office (eCO) Registration System." First-time users of the site will have to choose a user ID and a password. Once in the system, answer the questions and follow the prompts. You will be asked to pay the registration fee and send a deposit copy of your work at the end of the process and will receive a receipt for your filing by email.

2. Registration with a Fill-in Form

The Copyright Office offers fill-in versions of its forms on the Copyright Office website. To register a copyright or record a document, select the proper form online and key information directly onto the form instead of filling it in by hand or on a typewriter. You must print your application after you have filled it in online and mail it together with the deposit and the filing fee to the Copyright Office. You can find the information you will need about fill-in forms at www.copyright.gov/fls/sl08.pdf and locate the forms themselves by selecting "Forms" under "Publications" on the Copyright Office website at www.copyright.gov. Choose either of five forms, depending on the nature of your work: Literary (Form TX); Visual (Form VA); Single Serials (Form SE); Performing Arts (Form PA); or Sound Recording (Form SR). Each form consists of a detailed instructions section followed by a series of questions that may be answered by filling them in on your computer.

3. Registration by Mail with Paper Forms

Applications for copyright registration for groups of published works *must* be completed on paper and mailed to the Copyright Office with the appropriate fee and deposit. The group registration categories are:

- Form GR/CP w/instructions: For groups of literary works published as contributions to periodicals

- Form GR/CP w/instructions: For groups of performing arts works published as contributions to periodicals
- Form GR/CP w/instructions: For groups of visual art works published as contributions to periodicals
- Form GR/PPh/CON: For groups of published photographs
- Form SE/Group: For groups of serial publications, such as newspapers, magazines, newsletters, journals, etc.
- Form G/DN: For groups of daily newspapers or newsletters

Forms for group registrations are available on the Copyright Office website. From the Copyright Office home page at www.copyright.gov, click on the subhead "Forms" under the "Publications" heading. The forms for group registration are accessible under the "Group Registration Forms" subhead.

There are additional forms used to register the copyrights in more obscure sorts of works. They also must be completed on paper and mailed to the Copyright Office with the appropriate fee and deposit. They are:

- Form D-VH for registration of vessel hull designs
- Form MW for three-dimensional patterns fixed on a semiconductor chip (not for theatrical facial masks)
- Form PRE for certain works that have had a history of prerelease infringement (such as movies and recorded music that are subject to widespread pirating)
- Electronic Form PRE
- Document Cover Sheet Form DCS for use when submitting transfers and other documents
- Form GATT for restored works

(If you want to know what "vessel design" or "mask work" or "GATT" registrations are, search the Copyright Office website for definitions of those terms.) These rarely used registration forms are available on the Copyright Office website. From the Copyright Office home page at www.copyright.gov, click on the subhead "Forms" under the "Publications" heading. These forms can be found under the "Additional Forms" subhead.

For any paper registration application, you can download paper applications from the Copyright Office's website at www.copyright.gov/forms/, or request the forms from the Copyright Office. Once completed, you can mail the paper application, along with the required deposit copy(ies) and filing fee, to the Copyright Office.

If you know which paper application forms you want, request them twenty-four hours a day from the Forms and Publications Hotline at (202) 707–9100. Leave a recorded message. In order to encourage online registration, the Copyright Office limits the number of forms it will mail to two of each kind.

Registration Fees

Whatever method you use to register your work, you must pay a fee for processing. Go to www.copyright.gov/fls/sl04.pdf for a list of fees charged. As of this writing, online registration costs $35, while paper registrations cost $85.

Registration Deposits and Mandatory Deposits of Copies of Works

The US Copyright Act provides for two separate sets of deposit requirements: deposits submitted in connection with registration applications (registration deposits) and those submitted in accordance with the mandatory deposit provisions of the law (mandatory deposits). The Copyright Office administers both sets of provisions.

Registration Deposits

The Register of Copyrights specifies by regulation the form of deposit that must accompany a copyright registration application. In specific instances, the deposit copy(ies) may be submitted in digital or physical format. The deposit copy(ies) must conform to certain requirements depending on the type of work, the deposit requirements, and whether the work is published or unpublished. As a general rule, the deposit copy(ies) should be clear and should contain all the authorship that the applicant intends to register. An application submitted with an incomplete or unclear deposit copy(ies) will be delayed until the Copyright Office receives a complete and/or clear copy, and delays due to incomplete and/or unclear deposit copy(ies) may affect the effective date of registration. Once the Copyright Office receives the registration materials, a registration specialist will examine the deposit copy(ies) to determine if the work is eligible for registration. For information on deposit copies for works of the visual arts, see *Deposit Requirements for Registration of Claims to Copyright in Visual Arts Material* (Circular 40A) at www.copyright.gov/circs/circ40a.pdf. Deposit requirements for other sorts of works are explained in the "Help" section of the Copyright Office website at www.copyright.gov/eco/help-deposit.html.

Mandatory Deposits

Mandatory deposit is a statutory requirement for the benefit of the collections of the Library of Congress; the copyright statute provides that the owner of copyright or the owner of the exclusive right of publication in a work *that has been published* in the United States must deposit two copies or phonorecords of the work within three months after publication. (Works first published in a foreign country are subject to mandatory deposit at the point at which they are distributed in the United States in the form of copies that are imported or are part of an American edition.)

All works under copyright protection that are published in the United States are subject to the mandatory deposit provision of the copyright law. Generally, for works other than published electronic works available only online, the law requires that two copies of the "best edition" of every copyrightable work published in the United States be sent to the Copyright Office within three months of publication of the work. In most cases, a deposit submitted with a copyright registration application may be used to satisfy the mandatory deposit requirement, if the work deposited has been published and provided that the applicant submits two complete copies or two phonorecords of the best edition of the work, which is probably the published version of it. In such cases, there is no need to submit additional copies or phonorecords for the purpose of mandatory deposit. The double application of best edition formats to both the registration and mandatory deposit provisions was designed to minimize the number of necessary submissions to the Copyright Office and therefore the cost of compliance. (Go to www.copyright.gov/help/faq/mandatory_deposit.html for FAQs about mandatory deposits.) The mandatory deposit requirements of the copyright statute are also explained in *Mandatory Deposit of Copies or Phonorecords for the Library of Congress* (Circular 7D) at www.copyright.gov/circs/circ07d.pdf.

Help from the Copyright Office

You can call the Copyright Office to help you fill out a registration form correctly or to answer any question relating to any function of the Copyright

Office.[1] To speak to a Copyright Office staff member, call (202) 707–3000 or (877) 476–0778 (toll free). Staff members are on duty from 8:30 am to 5:00 pm, eastern time, Monday through Friday, except federal holidays. Recorded information is available twenty-four hours a day. The assistance of the Copyright Office is authoritative and, best of all, it's free!

The Uses of Lawyers

That lawyer that you didn't need in the first paragraph of this chapter? Well, he or she actually might come in handy. If you have a complicated ownership situation with your copyright or if it's worth a lot to you, either in terms of money or artistic worth, consider hiring a lawyer to register it. You can consult a lawyer at any point during the process of registration, even after your application has been denied. Ask your lawyer to take a look at your situation and quote you a flat fee for handling your registration. And be careful with online registration services. They are not lawyers and really are not equipped to handle any but the simplest registration situation. If your application is that simple, you probably won't have any trouble handling it yourself.

---

1   Copyright Office staffers are not able to give any opinions about possible infringements or settle disputes between copyright owners or answer any specific questions about your copyright, but they can offer assistance navigating the Copyright Office and its services.

CHAPTER 6

Copyright Infringement

The only thing worse than having to sue someone for copyright infringement is being sued yourself. If you create any sort of work—and especially if you license or assign your work to someone else or prepare it for an employer —you must know not only how to protect your own rights but also how to avoid trampling those of others. To determine whether your rights have been infringed or your work infringes someone else's work, you must first have a good understanding of what rights copyright gives to copyright owners: only the person who created the copyrighted work (or someone to whom he or she has given permission to use the work) is legally permitted to reproduce, perform or display it, distribute copies of it, or create variations of it.

DEFINING INFRINGEMENT

The federal copyright statute defines copyright infringement with a simple statement: "Anyone who violates any of the exclusive rights of [a] copyright owner . . . is an infringer of . . . copyright." Because it is a violation of rights granted under federal law, copyright infringement is actionable in federal court; that is, any copyright infringement lawsuit must be filed in one of the federal district courts distributed throughout the country.

The question of just *what* actions are sufficient to violate the rights of a copyright owner is left for courts to answer as they evaluate the circumstances in each case of claimed infringement. The body of law made up of court decisions in copyright infringement cases is called copyright "case law." Copyright case law is the source for the test for copyright infringement and the standard for applying the test to the facts in particular copyright infringement cases.

Although any of the exclusive rights of copyright may be infringed, as a practical matter copyright infringement suits usually claim that the defendant copied the plaintiff's work without permission. Sometimes an infringer *has* intentionally copied the copyright owner's song or book or painting in an effort to steal the successful features of that work and profit from them. However, many copyright infringement lawsuits are brought because the plaintiff wrongly believes that someone who has created a *somewhat* similar work has infringed the plaintiff's copyright by copying. Understanding copyright infringement means understanding the standard courts generally use in evaluating whether accusations of copyright infringement are true.

THE INFRINGEMENT TEST

Assuming that the copyright in the work that is said to have been infringed is valid and that the work was created *before* the work accused of infringing it, and in the absence of any admission by the defendant author that he or she *did* copy the plaintiff's work, courts ordinarily judge copyright infringement by a circumstantial evidence test. The circumstantial evidence test for copyright infringement has three parts:

1. Did the accused infringer have *access* to the work that is said to have been infringed, so that copying was possible?
2. Is the defendant actually guilty of *copying* part of the plaintiff's protectable expression from the plaintiff's work? and
3. Is the accused work *substantially similar* to the work the plaintiff says was copied?

If you can remember and understand these three parts of the test for copyright infringement—"access," "copying," and "substantial similarity"— you should always be able to decide correctly for yourself whether a work of yours infringes someone else's work or whether someone else has infringed your copyright.

Access to the "Infringed" Work

"Access" simply means what it says. Did the accused infringer have access to the "infringed" work before creating the "infringing" work? It's very important to remember that the action for which the copyright statute prescribes penalties is *copying,* not the mere *coincidental creation* of a work that is similar or even nearly identical to a preexisting work. In most cases, access is not presumed but must be proved before the questions of copying and substantial similarity even enter the equation.

This means that if you write a piece for a local alternative newspaper on the continuing economic fallout from the closing of a major manufacturer in your city and some other journalist writes an article on the same subject for an issue of a regional magazine that hits the newsstands only days after your piece is published, *each* of you owns a valid copyright in your own article, even if the magazine article addresses all the same issues as your newspaper piece does and comes to the same conclusions.

This is easier to understand if you remember that our copyright statute rewards the act of creation. You own the copyright in a product of your own imagination so long as your imagination—and not that of another author— really is the source of your work. This is true regardless of what anybody else in the world comes up with before, at the same time as, or after you create your work.

If you are a freelancer, the obvious implication of the access requirement in proving copyright infringement is that good documentation of your attempts to sell your novel or song or screenplay to those who are in a position to exploit it can be critically important in the event someone decides your work is good enough to steal. If you know where your manuscript or demo tape or script has been, you may be able to prove that an infringer had "reasonable opportunity" (which is usually sufficient proof of access) to copy your work.

Copying of the Protectable Expression

The circumstantial evidence test for copyright infringement is like a three-legged stool. All three legs of the test are necessary to support a claim of copyright infringement, and the absence of proof of one of the three parts of the test means an infringement suit will fail. Proving the second element of copyright infringement, copying of protected subject matter, is just as important as proving access and substantial similarity, but would-be plaintiffs often gloss over this requirement in the mistaken assumption that *any* copying is sufficient to support an infringement suit.

To understand what constitutes copying of protected expression, you must consider what elements of your work are *not* protected. The copyright statute specifically excludes from protection "any idea, procedure, process, system, method of operation, concept, principle, or discovery." And, as we discussed in chapter 1, there are several categories of elements of copyrightable works, some of them important to the overall quality of a work, that are not protected by copyright.

If you review the list of *exceptions* to the general rule that copyright protects what you create, you can better apply the second part of the test for copyright infringement. It is *Does the material suspected to have been copied from the "infringed" work include protectable expression?* If your answer is "yes" and it can be proved that the accused infringer had access to the work that is said to have been infringed, you must then evaluate whether the theft was substantial.

Substantial Similarity

The third part of the test for copyright infringement is determining whether the "infringing" work is "substantially similar" to the "infringed" work. Substantial similarity is hard to define. Even the courts have never been able to come up with a hard-and-fast test for determining substantial similarity. This may be because no such test is possible—each copyright infringement case must be decided entirely on the facts of *that* case, and what happened in a similar suit has no real bearing on the question whether *this* defendant did create a work that is substantially similar to that of *this* plaintiff. The test for copyright infringement is like the system one Supreme Court justice once said he used for determining whether a work was obscene: "I can't define it," he said, "but I know it if I see it."

Although it's not possible to pinpoint the border between infringing and noninfringing similarity, a map of the danger zone between the two exists in the form of copyright case law. Courts do not require plaintiffs to demonstrate that their defendants' works are almost identical to their own works to prove substantial similarity. However, courts will not interpret even several small, unimportant similarities between the works in question as substantial similarity. In short, "substantial similarity" is just that: substantial. The sort of similarity between two works is just as important as the degree of similarity—the judgment of substantial similarity is both *qualitative* and *quantitative*.

Further, although plaintiffs in copyright infringement suits routinely hire expert witnesses—usually people who are very familiar with the sort of work that is the subject of litigation—to testify as to what similarities exist between the works at issue, courts judge whether those similarities are substantial by the "ordinary observer" test, which is a sort of "man on the street" view of the effect of those similarities. Courts try to decide whether an ordinary observer, reading or hearing or seeing two similar works for the first time, would believe that the "infringing" work and "infringed" work are the same. If so, substantial similarity exists. This means that you probably have the equipment you need—your own eyes and ears—to decide for yourself whether someone's work infringes yours.

CREATOR BEWARE

Copyright infringement is an area of real danger for creative people. Consequently, anyone who aspires to earn a living by exploiting the products of his or her imagination needs to know enough about copyright infringement to stay out of danger. People often think that writing plays or songs or advertising copy is a nice, safe job that can't get anyone in trouble. In reality, what you do with your computer or guitar or pad and pencil in your own little workspace can land you in federal court, where you will be asked to explain just *what* you did and *why* and *when* you did it.

IS IT INFRINGEMENT?

Q. You want to use Grant Wood's famous painting *American Gothic* in a magazine ad for your travel agency ("Bored at Home?"), so you shoot a copy of it from an Art Institute of Chicago guidebook, blow it up a little, add copy, and run the ad in the travel section of the Sunday paper. *Is it infringement?*

A. Yes. You are in trouble with this ad. Grant Wood painted *American Gothic* in 1930. Although he died in 1942, the copyright in the painting will endure through the end of 2025 if it was renewed after the first twenty-eight-year term of copyright protection and is owned by his estate. You need permission from Wood's estate to use a copy of his painting in your ad. (See chapter 3 for a more detailed discussion of the duration of copyright in older works.)

Q. Your boss put you in charge of writing the sales training manual that will be sent out to all the branch offices of your company. You are a fan of Mark McCormack's book *What They Don't Teach You at Harvard Business School* and decide to paraphrase two chapters of this bestseller as sections of your training manual. You proudly present the finished manual to your boss, who takes it home to read over the weekend. You are chagrined and surprised when he demands to see you first thing Monday morning. It seems that your boss is also a fan of Mr. McCormack and has recognized the source material for the two paraphrased sections of the manual. He says that you and your company could be sued by McCormack's estate and by his publisher. You are almost sure that paraphrasing McCormack's material is all it takes to eliminate the threat of any lawsuit. *Is it infringement?*

A. Yes, of the most blatant sort. While it is permissible to quote authorities in any field ("McCormack believes that . . .") or even to cite their theories without attribution ("Many business theorists hold that . . ."), use of whole chunks of their writings is a violation of their rights and the rights of their publishers, to whom they have assigned the exclusive right to reproduce and disseminate their works. When you paraphrased Mr. McCormack's chapters, you followed them line by line and simply changed the way his ideas were expressed. While no one's *ideas* are protected by copyright, their expressions are protected. Your paraphrasing was a bodily theft of Mr. McCormack's expressions of his ideas. The fact that you changed Mr. McCormack's words makes little difference since the sections of your training manual based on his chapters are simply reworded duplications of his statements. That's copying of protected expression. *And* substantial similarity. Your boss is also right that both you *and* your employer can be sued for copyright infringement. As a full-time employee, you are an agent of your company. Any action that you take during the course of performing your duties as an employee is attributable to your company. Your boss is one smart guy. Maybe that's why he's the boss. Next time, if you can't come up with your own material, either hire someone on a work-for-hire basis to write your manual or copy *The Prince* by Niccolo Machiavelli, written in 1513, or *The Art of War* by Sun Tzu, written more than 2,500 years ago. But stay strictly away from the work of anyone who ever saw an electric light bulb.

Q. You reprint the entire text of Martin Luther King Jr.'s famous "I Have a Dream" speech on "parchment" paper in a form suitable for framing for your alma mater, a small and struggling but well-regarded liberal arts college, which sells the printed speeches for twenty dollars each to raise money for a new library. *Is it infringement?*

A. Almost certainly. Any use of the full text for Dr. King's 1963 speech without the permission of his estate constitutes infringement, especially if that use is made for commercial gain, as in this situation. It is possible that you could successfully argue that your otherwise infringing use of the speech is actually a "fair use" because it was made on behalf of and for the benefit of a nonprofit educational institution, but it is more likely that a court would, at the very least, require your college to pay a royalty on each copy of the King speech sold. The King estate could also ask the court to stop the sale of the speech, to compel the destruction of all unsold copies of it, and to make your alma mater pay it the profits from all sales made. Even national heroes have copyright rights.

Q. On the cover of your corporation's annual report, you use a photo of a small segment of a *Wall Street Journal* article that contains a twenty-five-word quotation naming your corporation as an innovator in its field. *Is it infringement?*

A. No. Your use of the *Wall Street Journal* quotation is a fair use of that publication's copyrighted story in two ways: it is a properly attributed short quote used in a First Amendment context, since the annual report is the corporation's way of informing its stockholders about the corporation, and you used only a small portion of the *Journal* story, not enough to constitute "substantial similarity" between the text of the annual report and the *Journal* story. Reprinting the whole story without permission for distribution to stockholders would be a different matter.

Q. You own an auto dealership and advertise yourself as "The Super-Dealer." In your newest ads, which you dreamed up yourself, you use a photo of yourself dressed in blue long johns, a red cape, and a wide gold belt, standing shoulder-to-shoulder with those other superheroes, Batman and Superman, who appear as their original cartoon-figure, comic-book selves. *Is it infringement?*

A. Yes, of two kinds. You infringed the copyright rights of the publishers from whose comic books you copied the cartoon figures you used, and you infringed their trademark rights by using the well-known superheroes to attract attention to your ads. You are in more trouble for your trademark transgression than for your copyright infringement. Duck into a phone booth and disguise yourself as a smarter person.

Q. Armed with a brand-new diploma in hotel-restaurant management, you go to work for your Uncle Vito, helping him run his restaurant, Vito's. Driving to the restaurant on your second day of work, you hear on your favorite oldies station the Billy Joel standard "My Italian Restaurant." You get the great idea to use the song as the background for the new radio and television spots you talked your uncle into the day before. You buy a copy of the Billy Joel album that includes "My Italian Restaurant," get your uncle to narrate the spots, and rush to get them on the air. Your uncle loves the spots and you begin to think about asking for a raise. Then one morning your uncle receives by certified mail a "cease and desist letter" from a New York law firm representing Billy Joel's record company and music publishing company. The letter informs your uncle that his use of the Billy Joel recording of the song "My Italian Restaurant" in ads for Vito's is an infringement of the copyright rights of both the record company, which owns the copyright in the recording of the song, and the music publishing company, which owns the copyright in the song itself. Your uncle calls you and wakes you up to ask *Is it infringement?*

A. Yes. The New York lawyers are right. They demand that your Uncle Vito immediately "cease" use of the recording or song and "desist" from any additional use of either and offer to forego filing suit if your uncle pays a settlement of twenty thousand dollars within thirty days, in lieu of the licensing fees they would have charged had he contacted them before using the song and recording. The lawyer you and your uncle consult brushes aside your arguments that, since no more than sixty seconds of the recording were used in any spot, your use of the song and recording does not constitute infringement and that, in any event, your uncle shouldn't be sued, since neither you nor he *intended* to trespass on anyone's rights. He says that any broadcast of any recording of a copyrighted song in a *commercial* context is infringement if it is made without the permission of the owners of the copyrights in the recording and in the song because it is a violation of the copyright owners' exclusive right to control performances of their copyrighted recording and song. He says that using sixty seconds or thirty seconds or even ten seconds of a three-minute recording is more than sufficient to eliminate any argument that Vito's use of "My Italian Restaurant" was merely an incidental, "fair" use of the song and recording. He tells you that it is immaterial that you did not realize that your actions amounted to infringement, since copyright infringement is judged by evaluating the quantity, quality, and context of the use of the copyrighted work, *not* by gauging the wrongful intent of the accused infringer. When you make your brilliant argument that you know for a fact (because you once had a summer job as a deejay) that radio stations do not call up record companies and music publishing companies to ask permission before playing each recording they broadcast, your lawyer reminds you that radio stations (and other users of copyrighted recordings) pay license fees each year to the performing rights organizations that collect such fees on behalf of songwriters and publishers. Uncle Vito settles. You are out of bright ideas. And out of a job.

PLAINTIFF VERSUS DEFENDANT

The only thing worse than being a plaintiff in a lawsuit is being a defendant. A plaintiff at least has the choice of filing the suit or not and can choose, to some extent, when and where the suit is filed and what issues are involved. A defendant has none of these choices. In a suit brought on meritorious grounds, a plaintiff has some justifiable hope of winning the suit, collecting an award of damages and, possibly, an award of the attorneys' fees and costs he or she has incurred in pursuing the suit.

If someone sues you for copyright infringement, the best that you can hope for is to have the court rule in your favor, in which case you can pay your own (perhaps enormous) legal fees and go home (although since 1994, courts may in their discretion award attorney fees and costs to a prevailing defendant in copyright infringement suits). And even if the case is settled before it goes to trial, you still may have to pay a cash settlement to the plaintiff, as well as your lawyer's fees for handling the case to the point of settlement. If the court finds that an infringement took place, the court may award the plaintiff an injunction to halt further sales, distribution, or dissemination of the infringing work, and you could be forced to pay a substantial judgment, including any profits you have made from the infringement and, possibly, the plaintiff's attorneys' fees and costs. The lawyers' fees you will incur in defending a copyright infringement suit through trial can be, in themselves, huge, even if the judgment against you isn't. Finding yourself on the receiving end of these remedies for infringement will make you regret that you were ever so foolish as to trifle with the plaintiff's copyright. Sometimes plaintiffs come out ahead in lawsuits; defendants almost never do, even if the judgment is in their favor.

In determining whether your work infringes someone else's copyright, let your conscience be your guide; if you think that you have taken more than inspiration from another, copyrighted work, you could very well have stepped over the meandering boundary between permissible use of another's work and "substantial similarity."

And don't forget that registration of your copyright provides very good protection if you are accused of having infringed someone else's copyright. Registration of your copyright establishes a public record that your copyrighted work existed in a certain form at least as early as the date of registration. This is all the proof necessary to prove that you are not guilty of infringement if the copyright you are accused of infringing was created later than yours, even if your work is very similar to that of the person who accuses you of infringement.

THEORY VERSUS PRACTICE

Our judicial system is, in theory, one of the best ever invented. In practice, it often leaves a great deal to be desired. Some disputes cannot be settled out of court and must be litigated to avoid injustice, but too often litigation is commenced because someone is trying to prove a point or holds a grudge or gets greedy. Copyright infringement suits in particular can make even the lawyers involved tired. This is because the issues involved in any copyright infringement suit are usually highly technical and because the egos of the parties to the suit may be more involved in the litigation than in, say, a suit where one insurance company is suing another.

In evaluation any potential lawsuit, remember that, while it is important to be right, what you really want is to be right *out* of court. That means careful attention to the rights of others.

CHAPTER 7

Other People's Copyrights

As in any civil or criminal litigation, the defendant in a copyright infringement suit may offer various arguments to demonstrate either that his or her actions did not infringe the plaintiff's work or, if they did, that there are good reasons why the court should not punish him or her. These arguments that a defendant makes in self-defense are called "defenses." Many defenses to charges of copyright infringement are technical in nature. Others are rarely used. The most important and the most commonly used of such defenses is the defense of "fair use." There are situations in which you may use parts of another person's copyrighted work without that person's permission and without infringing that person's copyright; this sort of use is called "fair use." The fair use defense can render otherwise infringing actions noninfringing.

COPYRIGHT FAIR USE

Fair use is a kind of public policy exception to the usual standard for determining copyright infringement; that is, there is an infringing use of a copyrighted work but because of a countervailing public interest, that use is permitted and is not called infringement. Any use that is deemed by the law to be "fair" typically creates some social, cultural, or political benefit, which outweighs any resulting harm to the copyright owner. In one fair use decision, the US Supreme Court characterized fair use as a "breathing space within the confines of copyright." Courts often view a fair use defense with some suspicion—after all, it contravenes the instincts of most lawyers and judges to accept that there are situations in which it is legal and even societally useful for one person to use the property of another without the consent of the owner.

Courts consider a long list of factors in determining whether a use is "fair." The factors that courts must weigh in determining whether a use of a copyrighted work is a fair use are set out in section 107 of the US copyright statute. It's worth quoting this short section in its entirety to set out exactly what the copyright statute has to say about fair use. Here it is:

§ 107. Limitations on exclusive rights: Fair use

Notwithstanding the provisions of sections 106 and 106A,[1] the fair use of a copyrighted work, including such use by reproduction in copies or phonorecords or by any other means specified by that section, for purposes such as criticism, comment, news reporting, teaching (including multiple copies for classroom use), scholarship, or research, is not an infringement of copyright. In determining whether the use made of a work in any particular case is a fair use the factors to be considered shall include—

1. the purpose and character of the use, including whether such use is of a commercial nature or is for non-profit educational purposes;[2]
2. the nature of the copyrighted work;[3]
3. the amount and substantiality of the portion used in relation to the copyrighted work as a whole;[4] and

---

1 Section 106 gives copyright owners the exclusive rights of copyright; section 106A gives visual artists certain "rights of attribution and integrity" in their works.
2 Nonprofit educational, research, criticism, and news reporting uses are almost always fair; commercial uses, such as uses in advertising, are seldom fair uses.
3 The permissible uses that may be made of informational works are considerably broader than permissible uses of creative works. However, courts have yet to permit the fair use defense to infringement in a case involving an *unpublished* work, where the private nature of the work is ordinarily protected.
4 This is the "substantial similarity" question again. It is quantitative and qualitative; that is, did you quote the twelve-page climactic scene of a mystery novel, thereby disclosing the identity of the killer, or did you quote only a three-paragraph section that describes the city where the detective works?

4. the effect of the use upon the potential market for or value
   of the copyrighted work.[5]

The fact that a work is unpublished shall not itself bar a finding of fair use if such finding is made upon consideration of all the above factors.

---

5   This evaluation is often determinative in a court's decision whether the use constitutes infringement. It is undoubtedly the most important of the four factors to be weighed in determining fair use. If the market for the copyrighted work is significantly diminished because of the purported fair use, then it is not a fair use. Fewer readers will want to buy a book if its most sensational and newsworthy sections have been previously excerpted in a magazine. A related factor that is considered is the effect of the purported fair use on any of the rights in the copyright of the work said to be infringed. If, without permission, one person writes and sells a screenplay based on another person's copyrighted novel, the right to prepare and sell a screen adaptation of the novel may have been lost to the author of that novel.

The House Report that accompanied the 1976 Copyright Act is also informative because it illustrates the scope of the fair use section of the statute with several examples of fair use:

Quotation of excerpts in a review or criticism for purposes of illustration or comment; quotation of short passages in a scholarly or technical work, for illustration or clarification of the author's observations; use in a parody of some of the content of the work parodied; summary of an address or article, with brief quotations, in a news report; reproduction by a library of a portion of a work to replace part of a damaged copy; reproduction by a teacher or student of a small part of a work to illustrate a lesson; reproduction of a work in legislative or judicial proceedings or reports; incidental and fortuitous reproduction, in a newsreel or broadcast, of a work located in the scene of an event being reported.

AVOIDING CLAIMS OF INFRINGEMENT

Whenever you encounter or consider using someone else's work, you should take action to protect yourself from false claims of infringement. The best way to do this is to take care to ensure that any use you make of another person's copyrighted work falls into one of the fair use exceptions to infringement. Creators and business people who deal in creative works can greatly diminish the likelihood of being sued for copyright infringement by using the simple techniques outlined below.

1. Keep your notes and the progressive drafts or sketches, etc., of your creative work to prove that you created your work yourself. Date each such document when you create it in the same pen or pencil, etc., used to write or draw the draft of your work. If you do not own the books, etc., to which you referred in the process of creating your work, make sure you keep a list of any such works you used for reference to show where you got your information.

2. Parody of copyrighted works is not a permissible fair use unless the parody uses only so much of the parodied work as is necessary to "call to mind" the parodied work; this is dangerous to attempt without very careful attention to the question of infringement. Anyone who must use more than a small segment or feature of a copyrighted work to make a parody of that work effective should consider approaching the owner of the copyright in the work for permission to use whatever portion of the work is necessary. In recent years, several court decisions have applied a doctrine of fair use called "transformative use" to parody uses. A transformative use is one that uses elements of a copyrighted work to transform the existing work; this is what happens in a parody—some elements of the underlying work are used in addition to new, parodic elements created by the parodist.

3. If you are an editor or publisher, a movie producer or director, a music publisher, a writer, an artist, a songwriter, a screenwriter, a copywriter, or are in any position or profession that involves the exploitation or creation of copyrighted works, be careful what you are exposed to. Promptly return manuscripts, scripts, songs, etc., submitted to you for possible use if you cannot use them. Keep a record of what and when and to whom such materials are returned. Consider refusing

to examine any such material at all until it is registered for copyright, especially if it is unpublished, or without a release of liability from the creator. If you are a creator of copyrights, and especially if you are successful in your field, protect yourself from people who want to show you their newest work, especially if they are unknown to you. Disappointed and envious creators have been known to sue those who enjoy more success in the mistaken belief that part of that success originated with them.

4. Direct quotations should always be attributed. Quotations of short passages of copyrighted works, such as the sort of quoting found in book reviews or news stories, is generally safe in any context where the First Amendment protection of free speech can be reasonably invoked, even if the piece in which the quotation is used has a partially commercial purpose. You should also attribute closely paraphrased statements. It is very important to understand, however, that you cannot escape responsibility for copyright infringement simply by attributing the lifted portion of any work to its author; if the "borrowed" segment amounts to a substantial portion of the copyrighted work, attribution does not eradicate your sin. As indicated earlier, you should also avoid any use of even two- or three-paragraph direct quotations or close paraphrases if they embody the "meat" of the work from which they were taken or if use of them would diminish the salability of that work. And if you do paraphrase another writer's work, attribute the ideas you use to the other writer. Do your homework; use as many sources as are available for your work. Remember the old saw that "stealing from one source is plagiarism, but stealing from several sources is research."

5. Working journalists and people affiliated with nonprofit institutions such as schools and churches have more latitude in using other people's copyrighted works than the average painter or writer or composer. A professor who duplicates a poem to use as a handout in an English class is probably not going to run afoul of the copyright owner of the poem. However, the company formerly known as Kinko's encountered

big trouble, in the form of a lawsuit for copyright infringement, when it disregarded this principle of the law of fair use. Without permission from the copyright holders, Kinko's was assembling from many sources "anthologies" consisting of writings taught in university courses and selling them to students. These makeshift anthologies hurt the market for the books that legitimately contained the copied writings. Kinko's lost the suit; it has been remarkably attentive to the interests of copyright holders since.

6. Obtain permission to use any photo, letter, passage, illustration, etc., that is either unpublished or, if previously published, is possibly still protected by copyright. Save the permissions you obtain in a file. Never exceed the permission granted and never use any material for which permission to use has been denied. (A form permission letter appears in the appendix to this book.) And remember that using unpublished works without permission is especially dangerous, even if the use is minimal. A tension exists between the owners of such materials and biographers, historians, and other scholars who may want to quote from them. It is understandable that anyone who needs to reproduce in a biography or journal article long passages from the unpublished letters or manuscripts of his or her subject would dislike this restriction. However, the law protects the privacy of those who do not wish to make their writings public and does not require the owners of those copyrights to pay any attention at all to even the most valid requests for permission to reproduce and publish such works. Presently, only the narrowest uses may be made of unpublished works without the consent of the owner of copyright in them and disregarding restrictions placed on the use of unpublished materials is dangerous. Even close paraphrasing of such materials may be actionable.

FAIR USE CHECKLIST

A useful tool for evaluating whether a use is a fair use or veers too close to infringement is the Fair Use Checklist reproduced in the Resources section of this book. Notice that the checklist leaves the decision whether a use is fair or infringing up to you. However, it can help you evaluate your use on a point-by-point basis using the only binding standard that exists—the four factors of the copyright statute (and their subcategories). There is no definite boundary between fair use and infringement because no general rule defining infringement is possible—remember, the infringement evaluation must be made by weighing *particular* circumstances. Make a few photocopies of the Fair Use Checklist and use it like a worksheet the next time you have a question about how much of someone else's work you can use without permission—or whether you can use it at all without tracking down the copyright owner and asking for a license.

IS IT INFRINGEMENT?

Q. Your cousin Bridget is an avid scrapbooker. She turns out beautiful and artistic scrapbooks for every family vacation and for each of her children's school years. You especially like her latest effort, a family history scrapbook that contains old family photos as well as genealogical information about the branch of your family that you and she share. You peruse the book at a family gathering and are very impressed with her work. You like the "Irish Blessing" that she used at the beginning of the book:

> May the road rise to meet you,
> May the wind be always at your back.
> May the sun shine warm upon your face,
> The rains fall soft upon your fields.
> And until we meet again,
> May God hold you in the palm of his hand.

You like the little verse so much so that you copy it into your pocket notebook. The very next week you are readying for the printer a brochure about the tours to Ireland that are offered by the travel agency for which you work. You have assembled several great photos taken by the owner of the agency when he led last year's tour, and those photos, along with the copy about the tours the agency offers, nearly fill the space available in the brochure. But you need something else—a nice quotation of some sort for the front of the brochure that conveys the warmth of the Irish people. Then you remember the "Irish Blessing" that you copied from your cousin's family history scrapbook. You dig it out of your purse and plug the blessing into the brochure. You send the brochure to the printer and don't give the blessing another thought until your boss says that his wife, who is a lawyer, wondered whether his agency would get in trouble for using it for a brochure. You are forced to admit that you don't know the answer to his question, but you tell him you'll find out. Then you head to the library, where you hope you can find the answer to the question. What you want to know, of course, is *Is it infringement?*

A. To avoid wandering around aimlessly in the reference department of the library, you approach one of the reference librarians for help. "I need to find out about copyright infringement," you say. She helps you find a couple of books on copyright law and shows you the chapters on copyright infringement. What you read scares you. You find out that using in any way any substantial portion of the work of someone else without permission is usually copyright infringement. You read that there's something called "fair use" that is a sort of loophole to copyright infringement—that some uses of other people's work without permission are actually not copyright infringement because of the purposes of the uses. You figure that if you had used the "Irish Blessing" in a church newsletter or on a school bulletin board for St. Patrick's Day, you would have nothing to worry about. But you also read that using someone else's work for any commercial purpose is especially likely to constitute infringement. And you realize that a brochure advertising tours offered by your employer—tours for which the travel agency most certainly charges and expects to make a profit—would certainly be held by a court to be a commercial use in any evaluation of copyright infringement. You are trying to figure out just how you are going to tell your employer that his travel agency's brochure may end up in court when the helpful librarian asks if there is anything else she can help you find. "I don't think there's anything else you can do for me," you say, "unless you have a magic wand that can turn copyright infringement into fair use." "What, exactly, do you mean?" she asks. You tell her. She listens carefully to your tale of woe and then says, "Wait right here." You don't mind waiting because waiting will postpone your return to the office and your meeting with your boss. The librarian returns with a large volume called *Ireland and Its People*. She shows you a chapter on traditional Irish sayings, toasts, and blessings. You get a glimmer of hope. "What does 'traditional' mean?" you ask. "Usually, it means that the originator of a work is forgotten, that the work has been around so long in the culture that no one knows when or by whom it was created. It may even have been created by many people over many years. See, here are several versions of your blessing. It seems that you haven't infringed anyone's copyright at all because this blessing is no longer protected by copyright," she says. "Maybe you shouldn't have used it in your brochure without first determining that it was safe to do so, but you got lucky this time. No one is going to sue you." You hug the librarian, get her name so that you can send a letter to her supervisor telling him that she is a treasure, and rush out the door to return to your office. Your boss is very happy to have an answer to his wife's question and even happier that he's not going to be sued for something you did because you were pressed for time and didn't do your homework. You feel that the luck of the Irish has helped you through this dilemma and buy a copy of one of the books on copyright that you read at the library so that, next time, you won't have to depend on luck.

Q. You develop a cologne from your own unique mixture of herbal essential oils that is such a hit with your family and friends that you decide to market it. You call your cologne and the soap and bath salts of the same fragrance Love Potion No. 9. One of your first marketing efforts is setting up a website so that you can sell your products online. You hire a web designer to create a really cool site and give him a copy of the lyrics to the famous old doo-wop hit recording "Love Potion No. 9" by the Searchers, which you copy from an online song lyrics site. You figure that you need to create a certain "mystique" for your cologne and that the lyrics of the old song, describing a potion that makes a guy love everybody he encounters, will do it. You figure that women will buy the cologne because the implication is that it will make them irresistible to men. You advertise your site as widely as you can afford to and start getting orders for your products. Then, among some online orders, you get a message to call a guy who says he is the lawyer for the publishers of the song. You call, wondering what interest he has in your cologne. What you find out when you get him on the phone is that he is only interested in your cologne as a possible source of revenue to pay a federal court judgment for copyright infringement. *Is it infringement?*

A. The lawyer you call says he represents the interests of Jerry Leiber Music and Mike Stoller Music; you learn that "Love Potion No. 9" was written by Jerry

Leiber and Mike Stoller and that each writer owns half the copyright in the song, along with the copyrights in a long string of other famous late-twentieth-century hit songs. "But what has that got to do with me?" you ask. "Just this," the Leiber-Stoller lawyer replies. "I will recommend to my clients that they bring a suit against you for copyright infringement if you do not immediately stop any use of their song." "You must be joking," you say, since you are really surprised that (a) two writers and their lawyer in California have even heard of you and your fledgling personal-care products business and (b) that they have anything at all to complain about, since your business has nothing to do with music. The lawyer sets you straight. "It's not my job to educate you to the particulars of federal law, but, in the interests of saving my clients the expense of filing a lawsuit, let me give you a short course in copyright infringement," he says. "Your website posts the entire lyric for my clients' song 'Love Potion No. 9.' That, in itself, is probably sufficient to constitute copyright infringement, since you are using an undeniably 'substantial' portion of the entire work. Further, you are using the song lyrics for a commercial purpose—to advertise and promote your products. That is also infringement. And, third, you have used the title of my clients' song to name your products. There is no copyright protection available for titles of any kind, but by your use of my clients' title you may be creating a false association between my clients and your products. That's trademark infringement or, at least, unfair competition," he says. "Do you have anything to say for yourself?" he asks. "Not at the moment," you reply. "I need to talk to my lawyer." "Have your lawyer call me if he—or she—has any questions. And either you or your lawyer need to get back to me by next Friday at noon; otherwise, I'm going to start drafting the complaint for the lawsuit," he adds in an ominous tone. You call your own friendly lawyer as soon as you get off the phone with the ominous one. You don't like what your lawyer tells you, but he assures you that he can probably save you lots of money and trouble if you will authorize him to take immediate action to placate everybody in California. "You have committed one of the most common sins of entrepreneurs," he says. "You leapt before you looked. In your eagerness to sell your products, you have ignored the rights of others. I know you have a business license, because I filed for it. And I know that you have made sure that your products and their labels meet FDA standards, because I also helped you attend to those requirements. But you didn't even ask me about copyright. I'm a little hurt—I had a whole course in copyright and trademark law in law school and I got a really good grade. I could have helped you avoid this problem." "I'm so happy for you," you say. "But, counselor, cut to the chase. What do I have to do to keep myself out of court? And make it a short answer—I haven't made a nickel in profits yet." "What do you have to do? Just this—everything the Leiber-Stoller lawyer asked. And you need to do it in a hurry and with great deference toward his clients. A little kowtowing in the right direction has saved lots of potential defendants from lawsuits." "You mean he's right?" you ask. "But he's complaining about my infringing a song, and I didn't use any music at all—not even the *written* melody. And I got the lyrics off the Internet—there are lots of lyrics sites out there. What about them? Doesn't it matter that those sites have posted the song lyrics?" Your lawyer dismisses these arguments. "Using the lyrics of a song is plenty for infringement. Songs—and poems—are short and using most or all of the words to either a song or a poem without permission is infringement. And it doesn't matter how many lyrics sites there are on the Internet. First of all, you can't get away with stealing something by pointing out that other people have done it before. And secondly, if those sites don't charge for the lyrics or otherwise make money off the lyrics, the copyright owners may have decided to ignore them. But that doesn't give you the right to use the lyrics in a commercial setting." Your lawyer emphasizes that the fact that your use was for a commercial purpose destroys any possibility that you could claim your use was a "fair use." He says he's not so sure about the Leiber-Stoller lawyer's claim that naming your cologne with their song title constitutes trademark infringement, but he tells you that it is a very good rule to avoid annoying people richer than you, since they can better afford to sue you than you can afford to be sued. You say that you suppose all this means that you will have to stop using the Leiber-Stoller lyrics and rename your product. He says that if you'll promise to accomplish this before Friday, he can call the California lawyer and get you off the hook. "I'll tell him that you are *not* a 'deep-pocket' defendant," he says. "I'm more like an '*empty-pocket*' defendant," you say. "Do it." You call your webmaster and take down the website until you can redesign it and rename your product. Then you call your printer to stop the presses that are ready to roll on five thousand new Love Potion No. 9 labels. You try to feel good about having to completely redirect your marketing for your products and remind yourself that you were never happy about the sections of the song lyrics that say that Love Potion No. 9 "smelled like turpentine and looked like India ink." Then you consider renaming your products simply

Potion. But you make a note to call your lawyer first so that he can put his law-school intellectual property law course to work advising you.

Q. You are the sales manager for an auto-parts distributor. One of the toughest tasks you face is educating your salespeople. One day you have a bright idea: you start a weekly program of mailing a packet of information to each of your seventy-five sales reps. You include the spec sheets on new parts that the manufacturers of those parts furnish to you, memos that you write regarding clients, and copies of important articles from auto-industry publications and books on sales techniques. You are very pleased with the effectiveness of your campaign to keep your reps up-to-date—sales have increased and your clients seem to like and respect your salespeople. Then one day your new assistant asks a question. You ask her to prepare twenty-five photocopies of an article from *Automotive Age* and burn twenty-five CDs of one of the first sections of the audio version of *The Dale Carnegie Leadership Mastery Course: How to Challenge Yourself and Others to Greatness* and she wonders whether your directive is kosher. You try to brush off her concerns because you don't understand why she is worried—after all, your former assistant never raised any such questions. However, she is so persistent that you figure you'll investigate the issue just to shut her up. You call the company lawyer. You ask him, *"Is it infringement?"*

A. Your company lawyer is a very nice man named Nick. You have never seen him lose his cool, but you think he may be on the verge of it when you explain your question. At his insistence, you pause in your phone conversation to instruct your assistant to halt work on this week's packet of materials for your sales reps. Then, again at Nick's insistence, you take the originals of the materials you had planned to send out to him for his examination. He spends a few minutes examining the documents and then tells you that your efforts to educate your salespeople could get your company sued for copyright infringement. "I don't understand," you say. "The company has a subscription to *Automotive Age* and I paid for the set of CDs for *The Dale Carnegie Leadership Mastery Course* with my company credit card, so we own it, too. I plan to send the sales reps one or two articles from every issue of *Automotive Age* and I'm going to send one section of the Dale Carnegie course every week until the reps have heard all of it." Mild-mannered Nick is suddenly adamant. "Not if I have anything to say about it, you won't," he says. "Because if you continue with this plan, you will be jeopardizing the company. A subscriber to *Automotive Age* could make one copy of one article from one issue and put it in a file for reference purposes without problems; that would be a fair use of the publication. And you could also probably make a duplicate of a short section of one of the Carnegie course CDs for your own use after you had bought the set. But it's definitely not permissible to make twenty-five Xerox copies of the article and twenty-five duplicate CDs of part of the course and distribute them to the whole sales staff." "But why?" you ask. "The *Automotive Age* subscription is expensive, and we paid thirty-five dollars for the Carnegie course. Those guys are making money off us." "Not enough," Nick says. "First of all, you are copying substantial portions of *Automotive Age* each week and will eventually copy the entire Carnegie course. That alone is copyright infringement. And in any context where you are making copies of any copyrighted work, you have to consider the effect that your copies will have on sales of that work. It's one of the most important factors in evaluating whether a use of a copyrighted work is a fair use. If the use replaces a sale of the copyrighted work, it's almost certainly not a fair use. You're making it unnecessary for your sales reps to subscribe to *Automotive Age* or buy their own copies of the Dale Carnegie course. That alone is also infringement. You lose all the way around on this one. And I don't think your company would be very happy with you if you got it sued—remember that your actions in the course of your job are attributable to the company. *Automotive Age* and the publishers of the Carnegie course would sue the company, not you." Nick doesn't let you leave his office until you promise that you will never again make copies of anything you didn't create from scratch without running it by him first. You return to the office, call *Automotive Age* to try to negotiate a group discount for subscriptions for all your sales reps, and order sets of the Dale Carnegie course for each of them as part of their Christmas bonus. Then you give your new assistant a raise.

Q. You are a reporter for the morning newspaper in Springfield, Illinois, where you live. Because you are a fan of live theatre and because you can stay free overnight with your sister, who lives there, your editor chooses you for a plum assignment in Chicago—you are to cover the opening night of a play written by your city's only famous playwright, your former high school

English teacher, Mr. Montmorency. Mr. Montmorency hasn't been home in years, but he used to teach English at your high school, and you hope he'll remember you and give you a personal interview. You write him a note and call your sister to let her know to expect you. You interview Mr. Montmorency briefly after the play; he seems to have become much grander since he became a successful playwright, but he is courteous to you and doesn't even mention that he gave you a very bad grade once for a lame term paper. Because you are grateful not to have been reminded of your adolescent ineptitude, you decide that you won't even mention that Mr. Montmorency appears to have acquired an English accent since he left Springfield. However, you feel that your credibility as a journalist is at stake when you write your review of Montmorency's play, *The Yearning Heart*, and you decide that you must call it as you see it—that is, you must give your honest opinion of the play, which stinks. You write and rewrite your review, trying to be objective and honest. To illustrate that Montmorency's dialogue has become stilted and florid and pompous since he wrote his first play, the one that allowed him to leave teaching and Springfield for the bright lights of New York and Chicago, you quote several short sections of dialogue from the notes you took the night of the play. Your editor reads the review and tells you that it takes a brave man to criticize a favorite son in print in his own hometown but that being able to occasionally say that the emperor has no clothes is a prerequisite to good journalism and that he is proud of you. You are feeling pretty good about your first effort as a theatre critic until about two weeks after your review is published, when your editor calls you into his office to tell you that the newspaper has been sued by Montmorency for copyright infringement. You listen to your editor as he tells you that you probably don't have anything to worry about. Then he asks you if you still have the notes you used to write your review—it seems that he wants to give them your story, and a copy of the play to the lawyer for the newspaper. He tells you that you and he have an appointment with that lawyer the next day. You smile bravely, dig out your notes and the copy of your story that you had laminated to give to your mom, and go back to work. But you can't concentrate on your piece about last night's city council meeting because you keep asking yourself *Is it infringement?*

A. You have always admired the man who is the lawyer for your newspaper, but after you hear what he has to say, you like him even better. As you and your editor sit in his office, he tells you that the only reason that he can come up with to explain Montmorency's lawsuit is that Montmorency was so angry that his hometown paper panned his play that he shopped around until he found a lawyer incompetent enough or greedy enough to file a copyright infringement suit that is without any real foundation in the law. "I've reviewed the portions of dialogue from Montmorency's play that you quoted in your story, I've compared them with the whole text of the play, and I've reviewed the law regarding fair use and copyright infringement, but I can't find any legitimate basis for Montmorency's accusation of infringement," he says. After you stop grinning, you ask him just how much of the dialogue from the play you would have had to quote in your review before your actions amounted to infringement. "I'm not sure that I—or any lawyer—can answer that question. Each case of accused infringement is judged on the particular fact situation of that case, and there just is no 'bright-line' standard for infringement. I can tell you that you would have to have quoted far more of the play than you did for it to amount to infringement," he says. He adds that, as a drama critic, you should know that the law presumes that any reasonable amount of quoting of the text of a play in a review is a "fair" use—that is, that such quoting is a permissible use of the copyrighted play because of society's interest in knowing about new works of art and what informed persons have to say about them. Your editor grins at you. You are smiling yourself and feel far more important when you leave the lawyer's office than when you walked in. Within a month or two, your lawyer does what he said he would be able to do—he is able to get the judge of the federal court where the lawsuit was filed to rule in favor of your newspaper even before there is a trial. He calls it a "summary judgment" and tells you that such judgments are usually awarded where there is really no basis for a suit in the first place. And you really feel vindicated when you read in a Chicago newspaper that *The Yearning Heart* has closed after only a brief run due to poor ticket sales. But you are very, very careful from that point on about what and how much you quote in any story you write because you don't like the feeling of being a defendant, even for a little while.

Q. You are a college economics professor with a special interest in the economic effects on their home communities of the migration of poor Southerners to the industrial cities of the Midwest during the mid-twentieth century. You wrote your dissertation on this topic and have since bought every scholarly treatise you have encountered that touches on it. You are excited—and a little envious—when you hear that another academic with interests similar to yours, Professor Moira Kelly, has published *her* dissertation as a book called *Sharecroppers to Autoworkers: The Displacement of Poor Southerners to Detroit's Factories*. As soon as you receive the copy you ordered, you scan it to figure out if Kelly's book has anticipated your own, which will be called *Sending Money Home: Exiled Southern Workers in the Industrial Midwest*. You are happy when you discover that her book has a somewhat different focus than yours. However, you do find that a series of three graphs in her book that compare blue-collar income in West Virginia and in Michigan during the 1940s, 1950s, and 1960s is applicable to your study of the topic. You copy the graphs for classroom use and begin displaying them via an overhead projector when you lecture. When you are selected to present a paper at an academic conference, you doctor up your classroom lecture that includes Professor Kelly's graphs and plan to present it. In order to ensure that your audience will grasp and remember your paper, you convert it to a very nice PowerPoint presentation that includes all the visuals you will use along with an outline of your points and copy the presentation to a CD, which you duplicate. You prepare a hundred CDs—one for every member of the audience for your presentation. Because it is expensive to produce the CDs, you ask the association that sponsors the conference to reimburse you for the expense you incurred in producing them; you are paid five hundred dollars—five dollars per CD. Your paper is a hit and you feel as if you are really beginning to make your mark in the field of twentieth-century American economics. You get several emails from people who heard your presentation and received a copy of it on CD. They are uniformly complimentary; two even contain job offers. You get about twenty more emails from other people who heard about the presentation and want to buy their own CD copy of it. Then you get an email message from Professor Kelly. She is livid that you have used her graphs and is threatening to file a complaint with the academic association that sponsored the conference. She says in her message that she is shocked that a fellow academic is not more sensitive to the copyright rights of other scholars. She asks you to explain your actions, telling you that she won't file her complaint until she hears what you have to say for yourself. You call the legal counsel for your university. You ask *"Is it infringement?"*

A. The university lawyer says that it wasn't infringement—and then it was. "What you have done is to exceed fair use," she says. "It's not an uncommon event. People who use the copyrights of others in their own works often forget that not all the material in the finished product is theirs. Your using Professor Kelly's original graphs to illustrate your classroom lectures was fair use—you made one copy of the graphs, displayed them to your students during your lectures. That is definitely fair use, especially since you actually purchased your copy of her book." "Then I'm in the clear?" you ask, tentatively. "No, you're not," she says, "because you didn't stop there. Using the graphs in your presentation at the academic conference was also fair use, because you used them in another classroom setting. You could even have gotten away with turning your presentation into a CD for your own use for the sake of convenience. *One* CD. But you overstepped the bounds of fair use when you had all those CD copies made of your presentation—including her graphs, when you distributed them to the other conference attendees, and especially when you charged for them." "But I was out of pocket a significant amount of money—it's not fair that I should have to bear the cost of the CDs myself," you say. "What isn't fair is that you took Professor Kelly's graphs—graphs she worked several years to research—and distributed them without her permission or that of her publisher, to the very people who are the audience for her book. Those graphs weren't the whole book, but they are separate works on their own and are important parts of her book. Did you ever consider the fact that now lots of the conference attendees will not buy her book because they already have, thanks to you, an important part of it? They may feel that they don't want to pay thirty-nine dollars for her book when they already have one of the most useful features of it—for free. Further, because you furnished the graphs to them in CD form, it's a safe bet that many of them will send one or all three graphs around to their colleagues without paying anything to you or Professor Kelly. Are you getting the picture? Do you now realize why Professor Kelly is so upset?" "What can I do," you ask. "If I were you," she replies, "I would write every single conference attendee and explain your error—that you used Professor Kelly's graphs without permission and that while academic freedom depends on free use of materials in classroom settings, you were wrong to make copies of her graphs, distribute them, and charge for them. Ask everyone you write to return their CD to you and to go out and buy her book. Then you can send another copy of your presentation to everyone, if you want, *sans* the Kelly graphs. That may be enough to forestall a lawsuit. And it may get you off the hook with the university ethics committee. And I'd sure like to be able to tell the legal counsel for Professor Kelly's college, who called me this morning, that you are doing everything you can to remedy your egregious error." You hurry back to your office to respond to Professor Kelly's email and write what you hope is not a groveling letter to everyone who got a copy of your ill-fated CD. And the next time you copy anything you didn't create yourself, you check first with the university counsel so that she won't have to save your bacon ever again.

Q. You are managing the mayoral campaign for your old college roommate. You feel that he can't help but make a big difference if he is elected, because he's smart, hardworking, and really interested in the future of the state where you both live. You also think that almost anyone would be an improvement over the incumbent, a man who was elected primarily because his father used to be governor and who has done little during his term to improve state government or the economic climate in the state. You especially loathe his habit of being out of town whenever a crisis arises—so far, during the four years he has been in office, he has traveled to six foreign countries on so-called "trade missions" that you think are really just nice trips at city expense for him and his wife and has spent a total of six months in Aspen, in his family's ski lodge, and a total of two months attending various conferences. In planning your candidate's campaign, you come up with the idea of creating a television spot from a selection of news clips of the incumbent governor waving goodbye to the press as he boards the jets that took him to his many out-of-state destinations. You get the news footage you need from the television stations who originally aired it, select the clips you need, and sync the resulting film to the old Peter, Paul and Mary recording of the John Denver song "I'm Leaving on a Jet Plane." The resulting ad is hilarious and effective. TV viewers see their governor, waving goodbye over and over, as they hear Peter, Paul and Mary sing, "I'm leaving on a jet plane. Don't know when I'll be back again . . . ." Your candidate's campaign is off to a great start. Then you get a phone call from a lawyer who represents Cherry Lane Music, the publisher of the song. It seems his client is upset because you have used the song without permission. The lawyer keeps referring to something called a "sink license." When you tell him you don't even know what a "sink license" is, he suggests that you make an appointment with a lawyer and says he is sending you a letter via FedEx that explains his complaints. You hang up and call the campaign's lawyer, who passes you off to another lawyer in his firm, a Miss Johnson, who is an intellectual property lawyer. You ask her "What is a 'sink license?'" and *"Is it infringement?"*

A.   Miss Johnson says she has seen the campaign ad that uses the Peter, Paul and Mary recording of the John Denver song. She thinks it's hilarious, too, but she tells you that it won't be on the air long if you fail to placate the lawyer for the music publisher who owns the copyright in the song. She tells you that it's a "sync license," not a "sink license," and that the word "sync" is short for "synchronization," which means combining a performance of the song with film or video footage. "Song publishers grant these licenses all the time for use in commercials," she says. "They charge whatever the traffic will bear. There are some guidelines that they use, but it really gets down to how you want to use the song and for how long and for what purpose. How popular the song is has a lot to do with how much you have to pay, too," she adds. "So we're going to have to pay to keep using our TV spot?" you ask. "Great. How much, do you think?" "More than if you had asked first," Miss Johnson says. "And lots of music publishers don't like to let their songs be used for any commercial purpose—they think it hurts the value of the composition." "But this *isn't* a commercial purpose," you protest. "It's political speech—you know, the First Amendment and everything. Doesn't that count for something?" "Not with copyright," she says. "Copyright owners can deny the right to use their copyrighted works for any reason, whether the requested use is a good one or a bad one. They pretty much have a monopoly on the use of their works, for a while, anyway. No one can use them without permission." "So will you call this guy back and negotiate the right to use the song for as little as possible?" you ask, trying not to whine as you do so. "Sure," Miss Johnson replies. "And I suppose I should call Peter, Paul and Mary's record company, too. If you didn't call the music publisher about using the song, you probably also didn't call the record company about using the recording. Am I right?" You admit that she is, and also admit that it never occurred to you that *in addition* you'd have to contact Peter, Paul and Mary's lawyers for permission to use their recording so as to avoid infringing something called their "right of publicity." "Let me get this straight," you say in an exasperated tone. "I have to get permission from the music publisher to use the song. I have to get permission from the record company to use the recording. And I have to get permission from Peter, Paul and Mary to use their performance. And I have to *pay* everybody for those permissions. Is that what you're telling me?" "Exactly," Miss Johnson says. "I can plead your ignorance [which, you think, is vast], and I can plead your small budget, but we have to get these permissions *now*—we should have had them *before* the TV spot ever aired. I'll get right on it." You feel a little better, but not much. You figure that you're going to have to spend a big hunk of your advertising budget on the "Jet Plane" TV ad to avoid being sued for copyright infringement and infringement of Peter, Paul and Mary's right of publicity. But, you think, it will be money well spent, since being sued in the middle of a campaign is definitely bad publicity, so in a way your advertising budget will go for its intended purpose—promoting your candidate. You hope your candidate will see it this way.

Q. You are a rookie high school teacher who volunteers to teach an art appreciation course as part of an extra-credit program. You minored in art history in college, so you search your old textbooks and the many art books you have collected since graduation, searching for material. You have only a small budget for your class, and you spend most of that on a set of Sister Wendy videos that you use to introduce your students to some of the more famous paintings in Western art. In order to show your students other examples of the various schools of painting, you haul a stack of your art books down to the local copy shop and make color photocopies of a bunch of significant paintings. Then you mount the color photocopies on poster board and carefully write the names of the painting and of the painter under each photocopy. You plan to pass the photocopied paintings around the room and to make a famous-paintings "art exhibit" on a bulletin board in your classroom that changes weekly. One afternoon, as you are arranging some color photocopies of Impressionist paintings on your big bulletin board, the teacher from down the hall stops in. She asks where you got the copies of the paintings; you tell her. Then she launches into a long tirade about how you are probably guilty of copyright infringement and that the school board could be held liable for your infringing actions because it employs you and that you had better destroy all the nice color photocopies of Cezanne and Matisse, Van Gogh and Monet, Degas, Morisot, and Cassatt that you were tacking to your bulletin board before the principal sees them. Even though you think she's just jealous because you were voted Coolest Teacher last year and none of the students like her, you thank her for her advice and tell her you'll look into it. You don't even mention the photocopies of the other paintings that you have stored in the closet. That night, you put in a call to your old college roommate, who is now a lawyer for a big firm in Chicago. What you want to ask her is *Is it infringement?*

A.   The first thing your roommate says, after listening closely to your tale of your art-appreciation course and the photocopied masterpieces and asking a lot of questions is, "Nobody is going to sue you because you haven't infringed anybody's copyright." You ask her why, since you want to be able to quote her accurately the next time somebody tries to make you feel like a criminal for doing your job. "Well, if the paintings you copied were created before the turn of the twentieth century, those paintings can be copied by anyone at any time, because they are in the public domain." "What a relief," you say, prematurely. "However," she adds, "more recent paintings are still protected by copyright, so you have to be careful to find out when a painting you want to copy was created." You get nervous again and you ask another question: "What about the photos in the books? Am I infringing the rights of the photographers by making copies of them?" You are happy to hear your old roommate say, decisively, "No." She continues, "There was a federal court decision a few years ago that held that exact reproductions of public domain artworks are not protected by copyright. The goal of the photographers in creating those photographs was to present the paintings as accurately as possible, so there was no original expression added that would make them subject to copyright. The court called photos like the ones you copied mere 'slavish copies' of public domain works of art." "What about Sister Wendy?" you ask. Your roommate isn't intimidated by Sister Wendy: "Showing the Sister Wendy videos to a class in a classroom is fair use. Remember, you are a teacher," she says. "How is that important?" you say, "Surely it can't keep me from being sued for copyright infringement," "Actually, it can," she says. "You won't be sued for copyright infringement because your use of the videos amounts only to something called 'fair use.' If you weren't a teacher, you would be infringing the copyright in the Sister Wendy videos by showing them publicly." You reflect that it's a good thing to find out that you're not in trouble with Sister Wendy, especially since the question of whether you had infringed anyone's rights by classroom use of those videos has never entered your head.

But you ask one more question that has confused you. "Let's say it was infringement," you say, "Could somebody really sue the school board for something I did?" you ask. Your old roommate tells you that your employer can be sued for anything you do as part of your job that violates anyone's rights of any sort but that since you have not violated anyone's rights, you and the school board are safe from suit. That weekend you call your favorite professor from college and ask about guidelines on fair use for teachers. She sends you the names of several websites about classroom use of copyrighted materials. You study them until your eyes hurt. Then you continue as you had planned with your art appreciation course. You are again voted Coolest Teacher, which makes a certain fellow teacher envious, but you are able to bear the pressure because you know it's always lonely at the top.

FAIR USE INDEX

Recently the Copyright Office has instituted the Fair Use Index. The goal of the Fair Use Index is to make the principles of fair use more accessible to the public by presenting a searchable database of court opinions.

The Fair Use Index tracks a variety of judicial decisions to help both lawyers and nonlawyers better understand the types of uses courts have previously determined to be fair—or not fair. The decisions span multiple federal jurisdictions, including the US Supreme Court, circuit courts of appeal, and district courts, although the index does not include *all* judicial opinions on fair use. The Copyright Office updates and expands the index periodically.

The Fair Use Index is designed to be user friendly. The brief table summarizing each decision includes a summary of the facts, the relevant questions presented, and the court's determination as to whether the contested use was fair. You can search for cases involving specific subject matter or categories of work, or review cases from specific courts. The index ordinarily will reflect only the highest court decision issued in a case, which means that it is the final word on that dispute. Browsing the index is enlightening and allows you, with a minimum of effort, to educate yourself as to what actions are likely to get you in trouble and what are deemed fair under the law. You can view the Fair Use Index at www.copyright.gov/fair-use/.

CHAPTER 8

Requesting Permissions

One of the realities of copyright that is often very difficult for would-be copyright users to understand is that copyright owners control almost absolutely both how and whether their works are used by others. There are only a few exceptions to this rule.

The most important exception to the rule that a copyright owner controls how her copyright is used is called a compulsory license. If your song has been recorded previously with your permission and the recording was distributed in the form of phonorecords to the public within the United States, anyone can issue another recording of the song, subject only to the obligations imposed by law to notify you in advance of releasing the new phonorecord, to pay you royalties at a prescribed rate, and to furnish you with periodic royalty statements. This provision of the copyright statute is referred to as the "compulsory [mechanical] license" provision. (There are three other, less important and more obscure, uses specified in the US copyright statute for which compulsory licensing is prescribed.)

The other exception to the rule of absolute control by the copyright owner is fair use of the copyrighted work. You can review the fair use doctrine in chapter 7.

We already know the name for any use that is made without specific permission and that is neither governed by the compulsory license provisions of the copyright statute nor a legitimate fair use of the copyrighted work—any such use is called copyright infringement. In fact, it's safe to say that many infringements result from a would-be user's inability to understand the word "No"—or the reluctance, for whatever reason, to ask for permission to use the copyrighted work in the first place. The ability to correctly ask for permission to use a copyrighted work is an art—in some situations it may approach diplomacy. That's because the more you need to obtain permission to use a work, the more you may need to call on everything you know about copyright and everything you know about diplomacy in order to make your request properly and enhance your chances of getting the permission you need.

It's important to understand that, other than in a very few instances involving musical compositions, there are no fixed fees prescribed by the copyright statute or the Copyright Office or otherwise for the right to use copyrighted works. This lack of universal standards for what is charged for permissions means that each request for a permission leads to a negotiation with almost no parameters—in some cases, the only standard for what a copyright owner can charge for a copyright license is the amount the licensee will pay.

It is also important to understand before seeking permission to use a copyrighted work that a copyright owner's agenda may not include accommodating yours. If you request the right to use a copyrighted work in the same format as that the copyright owner markets, you are likely to be denied permission to use the work. And even if the work is not presently being used in the form in which you want to use it, the copyright owner may have plans for a similar use or a more profitable license may have been offered by someone else. Never *assume* that you will be given the right to use the work in the way you want. The only way to find out what you will be permitted to do is to ask.

THE COPYRIGHT CLOCK

The first determination you must make in seeking permission to use a copyrighted work is whether the work is still protected by copyright. This seems too obvious to mention, but skipping an examination of the copyright status of the work you want to use can end up costing you whatever time you spend seeking a permission you don't need. Always devote your first efforts to figuring out whether the work is protected by copyright or has fallen into the public domain. This exercise can do more than keep you from spending time requesting permission to use a public domain work. It may be that you will be able to trump a copyright owner who is reluctant to grant permission to use a work by simply biding your time—if you find that copyright protection for the work is running out and will expire soon, perhaps you can simply wait until copyright protection expires and save yourself the effort of asking for permission to use the work. Consult chapter 3 for information on determining the copyright status of a work.

WHAT DO YOU NEED?

The second determination you must make in seeking permission to use a copyrighted work is exactly *what* rights you need. Do you want to reprint the entire scientific paper or would being able to reproduce the chart on page 11 suffice? Do you want to be able to use the photograph as the cover of your book, or is it better as an illustration in one of the chapters? Do you plan to mount a full production of the play and charge admission to those who see it, or are you planning only to recite one of the monologues in a one-night free-admission talent contest? Attention to this question can even eliminate the need for a permission altogether—perhaps the portion of the copyrighted work that you really need to use is so small as to qualify your proposed use as a fair use of the work. For example, maybe you need to quote only two sentences from the *New York Times* review that praises your first documentary in the prospectus that you're writing to raise money for the second one—using the entire review would be superfluous and would require that you obtain the right to reprint it, but you don't need permission to quote only a very brief section of the review.

Narrowing your request to obtain only the rights you actually *need* can also save you money; using an entire musical composition as the soundtrack for your short animated film will cost you more than using only a few bars as incidental music in one scene. It may even be useful to come up with two possible approaches to using a work—what is the minimum you need and what is the maximum you could use? If the copyright owner agrees to grant permission for the minimal use of his or her work, ask what it would cost to make the maximum use of it. Or, conversely, if permission to make maximum use of the work is too expensive or is denied, find out whether it's possible to get permission to use the work minimally.

WHAT DO YOU ASK?

Your skill as a researcher can be an important factor in whether getting permission to use a copyrighted work is a relatively straightforward task or a months-long wild goose chase, because before you can ask for permission you must find where and to whom to send your request. It may be all but impossible to trace the copyright owner for an unpublished work, but a published work will almost certainly bear some information about the publisher and/ or the copyright owner. Somewhere on the physical object that embodies a published work, there will be publication information that can lead you to the owner of copyright or the owner of the exclusive right to publish the copyrighted work, which are different statuses from the viewpoint of the copyright owner but are functionally the same from the viewpoint of a would-be user of the work, like you.

With a poem or play or book or any other published literary work, write the permissions department of the publisher of the work to request permission to use it. If the publisher isn't the owner of copyright in the work, it will certainly have been licensed to publish it and, depending upon the nature of the use for which you request permission, will grant or deny your request or forward your letter to the author of the work for his or her consideration.

Copyrights in popular songs and other contemporary musical compositions are usually owned by music publishers. If you call one of the performing rights societies that collect royalties for broadcast uses of musical compositions (BMI, ASCAP, and SESAC) with the title of the composition and the name of the songwriter or composer, you can determine the name of the publisher of the composition, from whom you should request permission to use it. (Contact information for BMI, ASCAP, and SESAC is given on the University of Texas at Austin's "Getting Permission" source list, discussed below.) Record companies own the recordings of songs that they release; write the record company if you want permission to use the *recording* of the song, as opposed to the song itself, *in addition to* the publisher, who can grant permission to use the *song*.

For works of the visual arts such as paintings or sculptures you should contact the artist directly or, in the case of a deceased artist, the artist's estate. Galleries and museums may be good sources for such address information. However, don't assume that because a painting is owned by a museum or an individual collector the copyright in the painting or sculpture is also owned by the museum or collector. Although the owner of a painting or sculpture is, of course, allowed to display it, ownership of a work of art does not automatically bestow on the owner of the work the right to exercise any of the other exclusive rights of copyright. Requests to use photos should be addressed to the photographer or his or her licensing agency.

Finding the owners of copyrights in other sorts of works may be more difficult. If you can't find the information you need about the owner of a copyright, you may be able to get it online. If you know the title of the work or the name of the author, start with the Copyright Office. Go to www.copyright.gov

and select "Search Copyright Records" to search the registration and ownership records for books, music, films, sound recordings, maps, software, photos, art, multimedia works, periodicals, magazines, journals, and newspapers recorded since January 1, 1978. If the work is older, you can search the records at the Copyright Office, but the search may be tricky and you may have go to Washington or hire someone to search for you. A better method of determining the ownership of a copyright may be to hire the Copyright Office to search its records for you; at $165 an hour (with a two-hour minimum), having the Copyright Office search for you is not cheap, but the results of such a search may be more reliable than a do-it-yourself effort. For more information about searching the records of the Copyright Office consult the Copyright Office publication *How to Investigate the Copyright Status of a Work*, reprinted in its entirety in chapter 4, and Circular 23, *The Copyright Card Catalog and the Online Files of the Copyright Office*, available online (select "Circulars and Brochures" under "Publications" on the Copyright Office home page to access this circular).

Another excellent source of information is the "Getting Permission" source list maintained by the University of Texas at Austin at guides.lib.utexas .edu/copyright/permission. This site offers information about and links to organizations that can grant permission to use all sorts of copyrighted works or, if they can't grant permission, can give you the information you need to find the right person or company to ask for permission. There are other online sites that give information about copyright clearance; like the UT-Austin site, many of them are operated by universities, perhaps because universities are concerned, justly, about the liability inherent in the unauthorized use of copyrights by their faculty, staff, and students.

The age of the work can be important in determining whom to ask for permission to use it because the owner of an older work may be hard to find, even if you have a name and address for the owner. Lots of things can happen during the term of copyright in a work—publishers may be bought by other publishers, authors may sell copyrights or die and leave them to their heirs, contracts that give someone the right to use a work may expire, and so on. If you have a copy of the work you want to use that indicates a publisher or copyright owner, you may be in a better position than someone who has no leads as to where to start in a search for the owner of a copyright, but neither can you assume that the copyright owner or publisher named on the copy of an older work still controls the copyright in it. View such information as a starting place and in any situation where there may be a later edition or version of a published work, try to find the later edition so your information about the copyright owner will be as recent as possible.

The prominence or obscurity of the owner of copyright in a work can determine how difficult it will be for you to get permission to use the work. If the copyright owner is a big company or a prominent person, you won't have much trouble locating them. But that same prominence may make it harder to get permission to use the copyrighted work—a work that has been exploited by and is owned by a successful publisher or a well-known author may be more valuable than a more obscure work and less likely to be licensed for use by someone else.

ORPHAN WORKS

"Orphan" works are works for which the copyright owner cannot be located, even after an informed search. When you want to use an existing work but cannot locate the owner of the work to ask for permission to use it, you face a choice: you can proceed with your plan to use the work and risk a lawsuit when and if the copyright owner finds out about your use or you can abandon your plan to use the work. Sometimes works become "orphan" works because no one really knows who currently owns them. Changes in the copyright law over the last few decades have made it easier for copyright owners to enjoy the protections of the law without falling into technical traps (such as losing copyright for omitting copyright notice on copies of the work, which sometimes happened in the past) but, in many cases, have made it more difficult to locate the owner of a work. Protection has become more automatic, but records of copyright ownership have become less complete and one of the most important functions of our system of copyright—rewarding the authors and owners of copyrights—has been hampered.

This situation impoverishes our society. For example, in congressional hearing on the topic, representatives of the US Holocaust Museum spoke of the millions of pages of archival documents, photographs, oral histories, and reels of film that it and other museums cannot publish or digitize because ownership of these materials cannot be determined. The Copyright Office appreciates the problem: "The Office has long shared the concern with many in the copyright community that the uncertainty surrounding the ownership status of orphan works does not serve the objectives of the copyright system.

For good faith users, orphan works are a frustration, a liability risk, and a major cause of gridlock in the digital marketplace." Given the high costs of litigation and the inability of most creators, scholars, and small publishers to bear the costs of being sued for infringement, the result is that orphan works often are not used—even where there is no one who would object to the use.

Congress came very close to adopting orphan works legislation in 2008, but ultimately did not do so before adjourning. Orphan works bills were introduced in both the House and Senate, and the Senate passed its version by unanimous consent. The proposed legislation included several provisions that would make using an orphan work less perilous for a good faith user: (a) a good faith, reasonably diligent search for the copyright owner; (b) attribution to the author and copyright owner, if possible and appropriate under the circumstances; and (c) a limitation on remedies that would be available if the user proves that he or she conducted a reasonably diligent search. It is probable that any future law that is enacted will contain similar provisions.

You can read the Copyright Office's 2015 *Orphan Works and Mass Digitization: A Report of the Register of Copyrights* at www.copyright.gov/orphan/reports/orphan-works2015.pdf. Look at "Appendix A: Orphan Works Legislation Discussion Draft and Section-by-Section Analysis" for the office's recommendations for an addition to the copyright statute. And stay tuned to find out what Congress does with this issue.

CHAPTER 9

Managing Permissions

Permissions, also called licenses, do not have to take any particular form. In fact, *non*exclusive licenses, which are what most permissions are, don't even have to be in writing to be effective. However, it is a bad idea to depend on anyone's ability to recall the terms of a verbal license.

This means that you should request any permission in writing. Fortunately, permissions are simple enough documents that you may be able to secure any permission you need yourself. The simplest form for requesting a permission is a letter that includes a space for the countersignature of the person who is in a position to grant your request to use the copyrighted work. (A signature at the bottom of a letter to indicate someone's assent to the contents of the letter is called a "countersignature.") If all the terms of the proposed permission are stated unambiguously in the body of the letter, the signature of the person to whom the letter is addressed will transform the letter into a binding agreement. (Chapter 11 discusses written agreements in more depth and appendix C includes a simple permission letter that may be used as a model.)

Nothing compels anyone to grant your request for permission to use a work. Some materials such as unpublished letters and manuscripts may contain confidential or embarrassing information or comments, at least in the view of the person who wrote them or whose relative wrote them. This means that letters requesting permissions should be polite and deferential. Further, although many such requests are granted without payment, it may be that offering even a small amount in return for the requested permission will decrease your chances of being turned down. After all, if the material you want to use is important to your project, it is probably valuable enough to pay for.

PERMISSIONS LETTERS

Even if you are able to reach the owner of the copyright you want to use by phone or email, it is necessary to follow up this initial contact with a letter. You may be able to write this letter yourself, without the help of a lawyer; you can certainly gather all the information you need and negotiate the terms of your license. Whether you write the letter or hire a lawyer to do it, your request letter should include a clear statement of the details of the license you wish to acquire. The important points to cover in any request of this sort are listed below.

1. Describe the work you want to use. Give enough information that the work and the portion of it you want to use can be identified with certainty. This will entail descriptions of the following:

   - The full, correct title of the work (*The Florence King Reader*; *The Billie Holiday Collection: The Golden Greats*; *Pilgrim at Tinker's Creek*; *The Way of Zen*; W. H. Auden's *Selected Poems*, New Edition; *The Wives of Henry VIII*; *The Dead and the Living*; *The Effect of Prenatal Maternal Nutrition on a Select Population of Newborns*; the 1991 French film *Baxter*; etc.).

   - The edition of the work ("the hardback edition," "the third edition," "the revised edition," the paperback edition"). Do the best you can here; some works, such as websites or unpublished works, have no edition description. Substitute the best description available, such as "the collection of poems privately published by the author in 1976, a copy of which was deposited in the Special Collections of the University of North Carolina Library by the author's estate"; "the unpublished diary of your grandmother, a photocopy of which was given to my professor, Dr. Clare Bratten, by your father in early 1999 when Dr. Bratten was researching her master's thesis"; "currently posted on your website, at www.tennessee spelunkers.org"; and so on.

   - The publisher of the work ("published by St. Martin's Press"; "published by the fraternity's home office in

Duluth"; "published by Xlibris at the expense of the author"; "unpublished, so far as I can tell by the manuscript copy of the play I found in my attic"; "unpublished except for the short excerpts published in the local newspaper soon after the letters were received by Mr. Boyd's mother during the war"; "Backstreet Films"; etc.).

- The date of copyright ("which shows a copyright date of 1995"; "which shows copyright dates of 1985, 1989, and 1994"; "which bears a copyright notice in the name of the author that does not include a year date"; "which is unpublished and therefore bears no copyright notice or year of first publication"; etc.).

- The owner of copyright ("the book reflects that the owner of copyright is Florence King"; "the author of the collection and owner of copyright in the poems in it is the poet, Sharon Olds"; "the album insert indicates that the collection is copyrighted by Déjà Vu and that the disc was manufactured in Austria by Koch Digital Disc"; "Ms. Chapman's album is copyrighted by Elektra/Asylum Records for the United States and by WEA International Inc. for the world outside of the United States"; "the recording of Beethoven's Fifth Symphony that I want to use was recorded in 1998 by the London Symphony Orchestra; the copyright in that recording is owned by the orchestra").

2. Describe how you want to use the work. Indicate the purpose of your proposed use of the copyrighted work in as much detail as possible. This will entail descriptions of the following:

- The exact portion of the work that you want to use ("the entire essay titled 'Big Daddy' from Ms. King's previous book *Southern Ladies and Gentlemen . . .*"). (In the case of another sort of work, use whatever identifiers are available to precisely indicate the portion of the work that you want permission to use, such as "the drawings on pages 11, 17, and 49 of the aforementioned book"; "the third cut on this album, the recording of 'On the Sunny Side of the Street'"; "the entire poem 'In Memory of

W. B. Yeats'"; "chapter 6 of the book titled *The King and His Lady* from 'Part Two: Anne Boleyn'"; "the final three minutes and thirty seconds of the film"; "the 'Glossary of Looms' and 'Glossary of Weaving Terms' from pages 179 and 180"; etc.) Remember, if you are in doubt about including any information that could help precisely identify the work you want to use, include it— too much information is far preferable to too little. In cases where it is practical, attach to your letter a two-dimensional visual copy of the work—a photocopy of a drawing or photograph, an essay, a poem, a play, a letter, a diary entry, a paper, or a printout of a portion of a website, etc.

- The method by which you want to reproduce the work you want to use, such as "to be printed in the forthcoming anthology of essays I am editing"; "to be used as illustrations for the association's website listing historic Native American sites in this state"; "to be engraved on a memorial plaque that will be placed inside the library's front entrance"; "to be used as part of the soundtrack for the short I am producing"; "to be used as a clip in the instructional video I am producing"; "to be printed in a souvenir booklet that will be given, free of charge, to those who attend the awards dinner"; "to be used as an example of the free-verse form in the textbook on poetic forms that I am editing with another professor"; and so forth.

- The number of copies you expect to make using the licensed work, such as "I have a contract for the publication of my biography of Ulysses S. Grant with the University of Georgia Press; my editor tells me that the initial press run for my book will be 2,500 copies but that there may be more copies printed in future years"; "Since I am preparing my instructional video for use only in the annual night course I teach through the adult-education program of the local school board, I expect to make no more than three or four copies of the video that would embody your photographs"; "I want to use the diary of your great-aunt as the basis for a chapter in my book on early women aviators, which will be published in hardcover by William Morrow, a division of HarperCollins; the initial press run will be 100,000 copies"; "I anticipate making only seventy-five copies of your poem, one for each member of the association, and would not make any additional copies without your permission"; "I want to create a medley of mid-twentieth-century pop recordings and would use the recording you own as part of this medley, which would serve as part of the musical accompaniment to my stage play, which will be performed by a local little-theatre group here for six nights only"; and so on.

- Whether and how the copies of the licensed work will be distributed and/or sold, such as, "My textbook on American literature will be sold for use in college-level classes and will be used primarily in the United States"; "I intend to enter my short film in several independent film competitions, where it may be exhibited"; "The records of the plantation owned by your ancestors would be used as the basis for one section of my PhD dissertation, which I would like to publish as a book; however, I do not presently have a contract for any such publication and I am not sure that I will be able to obtain one, since there was a university-press book on a similar topic published last year"; "The recording that I seek permission to use would become part of a promotional CD to be given without charge to the attendees of the 2018 American Bar Association convention to encourage them to attend my company's sales presentation; while the promotional CD would not be sold, it would be distributed as part of my company's effort to boost sales of its online database product"; "Your photo would be printed on the front of 450 T-shirts that would be sold to benefit the Davidson County Humane Association"; and so forth.

All these details concerning the copyrighted work and how and for what purpose you want to use it should be specified at the beginning of your request letter, perhaps in one paragraph. These points need to be addressed first because the person who will or will not grant the permission you want needs to know at the beginning of your letter what you are asking to do—if you request the right to use a photograph to make five hundred posters to be sold for the benefit of a local animal shelter, the owner of the copyright in the photograph may be more inclined to grant your request than if you want to use the photo to produce five hundred posters supporting a controversial political candidate. This may be so even if you don't propose to pay to use the photo and even though the animal-shelter poster would create income and the political poster would not. Tell the copyright owner what you want to do before you begin discussing the terms of the permission to do it.

The terms of the permission, or license, should follow this initial description of the copyrighted work and how and for what purpose you propose to use it.

3. Request the type of license you want to acquire. Unless it is important to your project that no one else is allowed to use the copyrighted work, ask for a *nonexclusive* license to use it. A nonexclusive license will be more readily granted than an exclusive license, even an exclusive license for a short period. Further, while nonexclusive licenses are often granted free of charge (especially where the portion of the copyrighted work used is small or the use made of it is for nonprofit or charitable or educational purposes), exclusive licenses almost never are. If what you really need is to *own* the copyrighted work, you should use a transfer of copyright; see the form assignment of copyright in appendix E of this book.

4. Specify the scope of the license. How do you want to use the copyrighted work? Do you want to reproduce it in a CD? On a website? In a book or an article in a magazine or as an encyclopedia article? On a poster or a T-shirt? As the soundtrack for a slideshow presentation? In a video? In an ad or on product packaging? Be as specific as possible in your statement of the proposed use of the work. If you want to be able to edit or

adapt the copyrighted work for your project, say so because you will not have this right unless it is specifically granted by the copyright owner *in addition to* the right to use the copyrighted work. If you plan to adapt or edit the copyrighted work or prepare a derivative work from it, will the copyright owner have any right to approve the resulting product? If so, say so and say whether the license to use the copyrighted work is conditioned on the copyright owner's approval of the final product.

5. Specify the territory of the license. Is the license granted for the world, the continental United States, France, Sweden, the state of California, the Orlando television market, the county where your political candidate is running for council member, what? Again, be specific. State the territory you want as narrowly as will allow you to do what you want with the copyrighted work, but beware of confining yourself with boundaries that aren't really sufficient.

6. Specify the term of the license. How long do you need to use the copyrighted work? Forever, as in the case of an essay to be included in a book that may be reprinted numerous times? Or for a briefer time, such as through the end of a particular advertising campaign? (Remember, when negotiating the term of the license you want, to take into account the number of years remaining that the copyrighted work will be protected by copyright.) And do you want the ability to renew the license? If so, you should include language that allows you to renew for an additional period of the same length as the initial term of the license upon your payment of a stated amount of money to the copyright owner. This amount may be the same fee you paid for the initial term of the license or it may be less or more.

7. Specify the payment you propose or have agreed to make in return for the license. How much is the right to use the work worth to you? Is your project built around it? Will it be only an incidental part of the finished project? Decide what you can afford before you make the first contact with the owner of the copyright and negotiate with that figure in mind. And don't

forget that many licenses to use copyrighted works are granted by the owners of the copyrights without any compensating payment. This is especially true for scholarly uses of works that have little or no commercial value and for uses that are made for nonprofit purposes, such as those made for charity or the good of society. It is almost never true for the use of a commercially successful work.

Specify a payment schedule. This can be "one-half payment due on receipt of the countersigned permission letter and one-half due on completion of the project" or "the entire fee on receipt of the countersigned permission letter" or "five equal payments, due on the first day of each month after receipt of the countersigned permission letter," and so on. It is usually more expensive to pay in a lump sum, whenever that lump sum is due, than to pay royalties, but paying royalties involves a lot more work tracking copies incorporating the copyrighted work, as well as sales and returns, and usually involves an obligation to render an accounting to anyone who is due royalty payments, as well as allowing access to financial records that concern sales.

8. Specify the credits language that the copyright owner requires. Negotiate language to attribute the copyrighted work that you use to the creator and/or owner of the work. This language should be specified or at least approved by the copyright owner when you negotiate the license. Look at similar credit lines from similar uses of similar works to get an idea what is customary. For example, a photo that was taken by Arnold Shutterbug but is licensed by Primo Photos may carry the following credit line: "Arnold Shutterbug/Primo Photos."

9. Specify that the person who will countersign your letter has the authority to grant the license you need. In spite of your research, you need a written guarantee that the copyright owner does own the copyright in the work and has the right to grant the permission you want or that an agent of the owner has the authority to grant that permission. Sometimes the authors of works assign the copyrights in them to others and no longer have the right to dispose of any rights in the copyrights in

those works. Language similar to this should suffice: "I, Mary Sue Smith, general manager of Primo Photos, state that Primo Photos is the agent for Arnold Shutterbug and that I have the authority to grant the permission made herein to use the photo described herein." Or use a blank space after or under the space for the signature of the person who will countersign the letter; this blank space should have a caption under it that says "an authorized agent." Don't accept a signature from anyone who is not a partner or high-ranking officer of the company. Usually, asking someone to countersign a letter that asks for confirmation of his or her authority will eliminate people who really don't have the right to do what you need them to do. Of course, a dishonest person could decide to "grant" you a permission that he or she had no right to give and pocket the payment you offer; the best protection against a situation like this is to thoroughly research the ownership history of the licensed copyright and to ask enough questions of the person who appears to own it or have the right to license it to eliminate any doubt.

10. Specify the reasons why the license agreement may be terminated. Don't include any paragraph of this sort (a termination provision) in your permission letter unless the copyright owner asks for one. The copyright owner will probably not ask for a termination provision unless you have agreed to pay royalties or to make payments for use of the copyrighted work over a significant period of time. If you must include a termination provision, state that the license to use the copyrighted work may be terminated by the copyright owner if you fail to make any required payment within sixty days of the date it is due. You should make any such payment much more promptly, but give yourself a little room in case you need it.

PERMISSIONS CHECKLIST

Use the following checklist (see pages 133–134) as a tool for composing your own permission letters. Refer to the discussions above if you need help describing what you need and what you plan to do. Photocopy this checklist and use it as a worksheet—just fill in the blanks and then hook the information together in a letter in the order you have written it. Or take this worksheet to your lawyer, if you think you need help drafting a letter or agreement.

FINAL STEPS

Send two copies of your signed, finished letter—one to be signed and returned to you, one to be signed and kept by the copyright owner—along with a self-addressed, stamped envelope. If possible, attach to both copies of the finished letter a photocopy of the portion of the copyrighted work that you want to use. Specify a date by which you want to receive the countersigned permission letter even if time isn't an issue—people tend to neglect chores that have no deadline. But give the copyright owner at least two or three weeks to return the countersigned letter; the copyright owner may want to consult a lawyer or otherwise investigate the advisability of granting the permission you request. If you have agreed to pay for the license, send that payment immediately after you receive the countersigned permission letter so that you, and the copyright owner, will both know with certainty that you have an agreement.

CAVEATS

As with any agreement, unless you are absolutely confident that you understand what is going on with your permission letter, consult a lawyer. This doesn't have to cost a fortune. You can save yourself hundreds of dollars in legal fees if you research the identity of the copyright owner yourself and negotiate with the owner regarding the terms of your license agreement. If you take your (detailed) notes to a lawyer skilled in copyright law and describe to him or her, maybe in a memo, exactly what has happened so far in your quest for the permission you need, you should be able to emerge from your lawyer's office with a short agreement that you can then send to the copyright owner for execution. Use your common sense in whether to prepare your license yourself—the more important your project, the more money involved, and the longer the term of the license, the more you need to get a lawyer to advise you, even if you maintain contact with the owner of the copyrighted work yourself.

Permissions Checklist

1. Describe the work you want to use. Give enough information that the work and the portion of it you want to use can be identified with certainty. This will entail descriptions of the following:

   - the full, correct title of the work: _____
   _____
   _____

   - the edition of the work: _____
   _____

   - the publisher of the work: _____
   _____

   - the date of copyright: _____
   _____

   - the owner of copyright: _____
   _____

2. Describe how you want to use the work. Indicate the purpose of your proposed use of the copyrighted work in as much detail as possible. This will entail descriptions of the following:

   - the exact portion of the work that you want to use:
   _____
   _____
   _____

   - the method by which you want to reproduce the work you want to use: _____
   _____
   _____

   - the number of copies you expect to make using the licensed work: _____

   - whether and how the copies of the licensed work will be distributed and/or sold: _____
   _____

3. Specify the scope of the license. _____

_____

_____

4. Specify the territory of the license. _____

_____

_____

5. Specify the term of the license. _____

_____

_____

6. Specify the payment you propose or have agreed to make in return for the license. _____

_____

_____

7. Specify the credits language that the copyright owner requires.

_____

_____

_____

8. Specify that the person who will countersign your letter has the authority to grant the license you need. _____

_____

9. Specify the reasons why the license agreement may be terminated.

_____

_____

_____

And if the copyright owner sends you an agreement to sign or refers you to a lawyer, call your own—even an honest, principled lawyer for the copyright owner is looking out for his or her own client, not for you.

It is worth noting that none of the information in this chapter will do you any good at all if you forget that you *need* a permission. It happens more than it should that, in the course of researching a project, someone fails to make good notes about the source of a photo or piece of music or poem. Sometimes that photo or music or poem ends up, without even attribution, in the finished project. Faulty recordkeeping can hinder you even if you do remember you need permission to use a copyrighted work—knowing you need permission to use a work when you no longer have information about the source or owner of the work can result in your having to backtrack through all your research to find that information.

You should also remember that even if you have gone to the trouble of obtaining permission to use a copyrighted work, *it is still copyright infringement if you exceed the permission you have been granted.* This means that you need to predict your use, in all its dimensions (term of the license, territory of the license, purpose of the use, etc.), as accurately as possible, and also that you should be vigilant that the use you actually make of the copyrighted work does not stray over the boundaries of the written permission you secured. Be sure to comply with any condition that requires you to return original copies of the work to their owner or to destroy any excess copies that you make of the owner's work.

Remember that obtaining permissions takes time. Don't wait until the last minute to request the licenses you need for your project. In fact, writing permission letters should be the first or at least a very early step in any project that would use one or more copyrighted works. If you do your research and write your letters early, you will have established contact with the people you need to convince to grant your requests or will learn that you can't find those people or that they won't grant the permissions you need. In any event, you will be better positioned to adjust your project to the realities of the situation, such as that permission to use a work is unequivocally denied or that the copyright in a work has been sold and you must write another person for permission to use it. Early attention to permissions will help you avoid ending up, at the eleventh hour, without permission to use a work that comprises a big part of your nearly finished project.

One word of warning about requesting permissions: never decide to use a copyrighted work after you have been *denied* permission to do so. Your transgression will be no greater than it would have been if you had never requested such permission, but your action in defiance of the denial of permission to use the work is likely to anger the owner of the copyright in it. Anger is an important ingredient in lawsuits. Further, your earlier request for permission to use the work may be used against you in court as evidence that the claimed infringement was not an innocent blunder.

A far better course if you are denied permission to use a work that is critical to your own project is to write again to the person who can grant that permission. In this second letter, if you think that doing so would help your case, recount your credentials as a scholar, journalist, artist, critic, or the like. Describe your project in detail and emphasize the value of the copyright you want to use to the project as a whole. Finally, acknowledge the reservations of the copyright owner, but politely ask him or her to reconsider your request. You may even ask your publisher, if you have one, or someone who is noted in your field to write a similar letter. This sort of second assault may not produce the permission you want, but it can't hurt; the worst that can happen is that the copyright owner will say no again or won't reply to your letter. All that means is that you're still where you were. However, as mentioned above, it also means that you should restructure your project, substituting another work for the one you wanted to use. Or, if your project is really dependent on the work you have been denied permission to use, you may have to abandon it. An unfinished project, no matter how brilliantly conceived, is preferable to a lawsuit for copyright infringement any day.

CHAPTER 10

If You Want to Sue

People who believe that their copyrights have been infringed often have no idea how complicated copyright infringement lawsuits are, and they have exaggerated ideas about how much money they can recover if they bring suit against the suspected infringer. Unfortunately, the contemplation of the large amounts of money you feel certain you'll be awarded is often the most satisfying stage of a copyright infringement suit. As with most civil litigation, copyright infringement suits are more fun for plaintiffs to think about than to participate in. For defendants, lawsuits are no fun at all.

LITIGANTS AND LAWYERS

Every ancient mapmaker knew that his very own country was the center of the world, but most were confused as to what lay over the horizon. They prudently decided that what they didn't know could hurt them and sometimes marked these vast terra incognita areas with the warning "Here Be Dragons" to warn explorers of the perils there. If you have never been involved in a civil lawsuit, this is a wise attitude to cultivate toward suing and being sued, because today in the United States the dragons are Litigants and Lawyers.

This doesn't mean that there are no issues worth going to court over—litigation is sometimes the only way to settle some disputes or to pursue that elusive goal, justice. However, and especially with regard to business disputes of any sort, litigation should be viewed as a last resort. In civilized countries, if your neighbor offends you, you do not engage him and his clan in a feud; rather, you file your complaint in a court of law and let a judge decide the dispute. Unfortunately, the US judicial system is so complex that a lawsuit can leave you as bloodied as a fistfight; even if you win you are bruised by the experience.

Because the "statute of limitations" (the period within which you must file suit) for copyright infringement is only three years from the date the infringer commits the infringing acts, don't wait too long before you take your suspicions of infringement to a lawyer. (In the case of a continuing infringement, such as printing a large number of copies of a pirated book over a period of time, the statute runs from the date of the defendant's last infringing act.) After three years your infringement suit may be barred. That is, the court will throw it out because you did not file it within the prescribed three-year period. You snooze, you lose.

BEGINNING A LAWSUIT

If you decide to sue someone for copyright infringement, the first thing you must do is find an experienced copyright litigator to represent you. In Great Britain, lawyers are classified as either "barristers," that is, lawyers who represent clients in court, or "solicitors," lawyers who counsel clients concerning every sort of legal matter, including lawsuits, but who do not represent clients in court. In the United States, there is no such formal division among lawyers, but most lawyers consider themselves primarily either counselors or litigators. If you have an established relationship with a lawyer you trust, it is probably a good idea to ask that lawyer to refer you to a copyright lawyer for evaluation of the merits of your claim.

Deciding whether you have a real case is not a determination you should try to make yourself, even *after* reading this book. If you think someone has infringed your copyright, see a lawyer who's well versed in copyright law. Most lawyers will not charge you for an initial consultation about a possible copyright infringement lawsuit against someone else. You'll need the objective evaluation an experienced lawyer can give you, since creative people are notoriously poor judges of whether their works have actually been infringed. Your lawyer should be willing to tell you whether there has been an infringement and, if so, whether you're likely to prevail in court. A competent evaluation of whether to bring suit in a suspected case of copyright infringement involves a careful analysis of the question of whether the suspect actions actually *do* constitute copyright infringement. For this evaluation, only a lawyer who is well versed in copyright law can reliably advise you.

Copyright lawyers tend to be few and far between in some areas of the country. If your own lawyer can't refer you to a copyright lawyer he or she knows personally, call the bar association in the largest city near you and ask for names of lawyers who specialize in copyright law. (This is distinct from intellectual property law; copyright law is a variety of intellectual property law, but that term also includes patent law and trademark law.) You may be able to find free or nearly free legal help through a volunteer lawyers for the arts group. There are such groups all over the country. Search online for "volunteer lawyers for the arts" to find a group near you. And remember that a lawyer may be able to advise you by phone and through email even if you live some distance from his or her office.

Another very good way to find a lawyer capable of handling your copyright case is to consult a trade organization that promotes the interests of people in your creative profession. Many such trade groups maintain lists of lawyers around the country who are experienced in copyright litigation. If your organization does not maintain a formal list of lawyers for referral purposes, try to talk to the executive director of the organization. He or she almost certainly will be able to give you some names of lawyers experienced in lawsuits similar to yours and may even be willing to confidentially evaluate the relative merits of the lawyers recommended.

Whomever you find to evaluate your copyright infringement problem, if you don't agree with the first lawyer you consult, get a second evaluation from another lawyer.

Responsible lawyers will not bring frivolous suits on your behalf; a lawyer has an ethical duty to determine that any lawsuit he or she files for you is founded on a reasonable interpretation of the law and that your allegations against your defendant are based in fact and are not merely unfounded claims. However, no lawyer can guarantee the outcome of any suit. The best your lawyer can do is make a prediction of your chances of prevailing based on her or his interpretation of the copyright statute and the precedents set by court decisions in similar cases.

Remember, your lawsuit is brought in *your* name, not your lawyer's; your lawyer is only a skilled agent acting on your behalf. It is *your* testimony that will be required, and *you* who stand to gain from any judgment in your favor. And it is *you* who will be footing the bill for all the work your attorney must perform to represent you adequately.

LAWYERS' FEES

Lawyers' fees run from a low of around $125 per hour to $500 per hour or more in some cities. What your lawsuit will cost, in attorneys' fees and costs such as court filing fees, costs of court reporters for depositions, and expert witness fees, depends mostly on how complicated the issues in your case are, how many people are involved, how well-financed they are, how vigorously they defend against your claims, and whether the suit must be brought in another city or can be filed where you live.

However, even a relatively uncomplicated suit can cost you several thousand dollars to bring to the point of trial. Complicated lawsuits involving multiple plaintiffs and/or defendants are a litigator's dream; even despite his or her best efforts to bring the suit to a quick resolution, the legal work involved may produce fat fees for several years.

And although most clients who have been through an expensive lawsuit would hesitate to admit it, there's nothing unfair about a lawyer charging for his or her work. If anything is unfair about a lawsuit, it is the fact that circumstances compel you to be involved in one in the first place. All your lawyer can do is using every tactic at his or her disposal to get you out of it as soon as possible.

Sometimes lawyers will agree to represent clients in lawsuits on a "contingency fee" basis. This means that the lawyer will represent the client without payment for her or his services during the course of the lawsuit for a large share, usually one-third, of any sum eventually awarded the client by the court. Before accepting any case on this basis, a lawyer will look at the amount of legal work involved, the probable amount of damages that could be awarded, and the likelihood that the plaintiff will win the suit. This is because a lawyer who accepts a case on this basis earns nothing in return for sometimes literally years of work if the court rules against her or his client. And bringing a suit even on a contingency fee basis can still be expensive for the client, since the *client* will have to pay all the expenses of the suit, which can be considerable. Even if an eventual judgment in your favor includes the reimbursement of your expenses, you'll probably have to front them yourself.

Persuading a good copyright lawyer to take your case on a contingency fee basis may depend on the size of the pot of gold at the end of the lawsuit rather than the merits of your claim. If you have difficulty getting a big-gun lawyer to take your case on a contingency fee basis, look for a younger lawyer who, although possibly less experienced, will be perhaps more eager to earn his or her spurs as a copyright litigator.

Another important question that must be answered before your lawyer will begin chasing an infringer on your behalf is that of the terms of the agreement you and your lawyer make concerning fees. It is usual that a lawyer working on a contingency fee basis will expect to be paid one-third of any recovery that his or her client makes, whether that recovery results from an agreed settlement amount or an award of damages by a court. However, it is important to inquire whether the expenses of the suit are to be subtracted from the total recovery amount *before* or *after* your lawyer's fee is calculated. This is a bargaining chip. If you are fortunate enough to have caught a deep-pocket infringer red-handed, your lawyer will look more favorably on a proposal that his or her firm advance the costs of your suit, with the understanding that the firm will be repaid when you win the suit. Expect that your lawyer will ask you to sign a written fee agreement before beginning work, even if *you* must pay all the expenses connected with the suit. This is only good business. However, get another lawyer to review the terms of the fee agreement if you do not fully understand them, especially if you believe your suit could produce a large cash settlement or award of damages.

CLIENT MISCONCEPTIONS

If more people had fewer assumptions about lawsuits and the judicial process, the public image of lawyers as a group would be better. Clients somehow believe in their hearts that their lawyers can control the outcome of lawsuits and very often become disenchanted with their own lawyers, not to mention the lawyers of their adversaries, if they lose their suits. Judges decide cases based on laws passed by legislators who were elected by you. Lawyers are like guides through what is today in the United States often a legal jungle; they are stuck with the laws and the judges they encounter and must do their best to guide you through the litigation process, but they cannot change the basic rules by which the litigation must be conducted.

Nevertheless, many clients think, on some level, that all a lawyer has to do is reach into the bottom drawer of his or her desk, fill out a form marked "Lawsuit," file it at the courthouse and—voilà!—the worthless human being who has just been labeled the "Defendant" will be hauled to a cell under the courthouse that very afternoon by two or more burly federal marshals.

Unfortunately, it doesn't happen that way. You may know that your defendant is dead wrong and a sneaky, dishonest person besides, and the defendant may know it, too, but before the *court* knows it, you have to *prove* it, while simultaneously fighting the best efforts of the defendant to avoid admitting that he did anything wrong. That's why your lawyer will plot your lawsuit like a chess game and view the trial as a battle.

THE COURSE OF A LAWSUIT

Litigation is a long process, and in real life, most of it takes place before the trial. The first thing your lawyer will do after investigating the facts surrounding your grievance against your adversary and the law governing your claim is to draft what is called your "complaint." A complaint is a carefully worded document that sets out the facts of your dispute, relates them to the law, tells how the defendant has transgressed your rights under the law, and asks for certain "relief," from and on account of the defendant's transgressions, such as an injunction (an order from the court directing the defendant to do something or to stop doing something) or an award of damages (money awarded to compensate you for your losses or punish the defendant).

Plaintiffs should know that lawyers always ask for more than they have any hope of actually receiving; those "Million Dollar Lawsuit" headlines you see may result, long after the newsprint has faded, in actual awards of only a few thousand dollars, which may be barely enough to cover the legal fees of the plaintiffs.

The lawsuit officially begins when your complaint is filed with the court. After the defendant is formally notified of the suit, he or she has a specified period of time within which to file an "answer" with the court which responds to each allegation made in the complaint, giving the defendant's side of the matter.

In many suits, before and sometimes also after the answer is filed, the defendant will file various motions objecting to one or another important procedural aspect of the lawsuit in an effort to have the case dismissed, or, at least, to delay its progress. Your lawyer must file a response challenging any such motion and must support your position with a written "brief," which is a concise statement of the law and facts relating to the issue raised in the defendant's motion and which is meant to educate the judge and persuade him or her that the defendant's motion should not be granted. These motions, each countered by well-researched and carefully written briefs, can continue for a frustratingly long time.

Meanwhile, another interesting and, for the lawyers, often lucrative part of the lawsuit is going on; this is "discovery," the minuet between the parties to the suit by which each litigant "discovers" from the other as many facts as possible related to the lawsuit. Discovery tools include interrogatories (written questions), requests for production of documents (written requests for pertinent paperwork), and depositions (oral testimony taken out of court, but under oath and recorded by a court reporter). Discovery can also take forever.

Once the complaint and answer are filed, all the motions are made, answered, and ruled on by the court, and discovery is complete, the case can be set for trial. Both your lawyer and the defendant's lawyer will pore over all the facts they've gathered, assess the strengths of their arguments, and map out their plans to present those facts and arguments in court before the judge, if the trial is to be a "bench trial," or the jury.

EXPERTS

One of the people whom you may be hiring at exorbitant rates is someone called an "expert witness." Expert witnesses in copyright infringement cases may testify to prove several issues, such as the originality of the copyrighted work, whether the defendant copied from the copyrighted work, whether the copied material constitutes protectable expression, whether audiences will perceive substantial similarity between the plaintiff's work and the defendant's work, the effect of the defendant's actions on the marketability of the plaintiff's work, and the portion of the defendant's profits from the infringement that is due the plaintiff. Such testimony can be especially important in cases involving computer programs, where similarity between the works at issue cannot be judged by ordinary people. For example, the opinion of an expert may be necessary to determine whether the defendant tried to conceal the fact that the defendant's computer program was copied from the plaintiff's program by translating the plaintiff's program into another computer language.

SETTLEMENT

Lots of lawsuits are settled just prior to trial, sometimes literally in the hallway outside the courtroom just before the proceedings are to begin. This is because no one, least of all lawyers, wants to go through a trial if a settlement is offered on any basis that is at all acceptable. Even more persuasive is the attitude of most judges, who actively encourage settlements to reduce their heavy workload, to save taxpayers' money, and to clear perpetually clogged court dockets.

A settlement agreement between the litigants also usually eliminates the possibility that the lawsuit isn't over even after the fat lady sings. Many losing litigants can find reasons to appeal the judgments entered against them by their trial courts. Sometimes they appeal up the ladder of courts more than once, on one ground or another, until all the people involved in the original lawsuit feel that they have unwittingly wandered into Charles Dickens's famous never-ending fictional lawsuit, *Jarndyce v. Jarndyce*.

JUDGMENTS

If you win your copyright infringement suit, the court may issue a permanent injunction that prohibits any further use of the work that violates your copyright. It may order the seizure and destruction of any copies of the infringing work. It may award you "actual damages" (the profits the infringer made from the infringing work and the money you lost because of the infringement) or, alternately, "statutory damages" (a range of money damages the court is allowed to award you in lieu of actual damages), the expenses of the suit that you've had to pay, and attorneys' fees. Statutory damages available under the copyright statute now permit awards up to $150,000.

Although it is not required for protection, copyright registration enhances the protection the law grants automatically. Copyright registration is a prerequisite to filing a copyright infringement suit and "timely registration" makes it possible for the plaintiff in such a lawsuit to receive an award of statutory damages up to $150,000 and to recover his or her attorney fees and court costs. Both these possibilities make it much more feasible for a plaintiff to sue; in fact, many plaintiffs' claims of copyright infringement, though valid, may be all but unenforceable because the cost of bringing an infringement suit and financing it through the duration of the litigation—especially if the plaintiff must prove "actual damages" in court—is prohibitive. Statutory damages are a range of money damages specified in the copyright statute that judges are allowed to award a plaintiff in a copyright infringement suit in lieu of "actual damages," which are the money actually lost by the plaintiff as a result of the defendant's infringing actions plus the actual amount by which the infringer profited from the use of the plaintiff's work. Awards of statutory damages are often desirable, for two reasons: because actual damages can be difficult, time consuming, expensive, or impossible to prove during infringement lawsuits and because infringers often do not profit from their infringements enough to fund an adequate award to a prevailing plaintiff.

Equally important is the protection that registration provides if you are accused of having infringed someone else's copyright. Registration of your copyright establishes a public record that your copyrighted work existed in a certain form at least as early as the date of registration. This is all the proof necessary to prove that you are not guilty of infringement if the copyright you are accused of infringing was created later than yours.

IS IT INFRINGEMENT?

Q. You want to become a professional nature photographer, so you spend your weekends in state and national parks taking shots of every beautiful spot you find. You are especially pleased with a photo of a population of white trillium in full bloom that you took on your last trip to the mountains. The photo editor of the calendar published each year by your state's tourism department likes it, too, and pays you for the right to use your photo on the cover of next year's calendar. Since this is your first sale, you are ecstatic and spend the money on a new camera. You are less ecstatic, however, when you find a new issue of *National Geographic* on the newsstand; the cover story for the magazine is about the very park where you found the trilliums in bloom and the cover of the magazine itself is practically a duplicate of your photo. You are incensed and want to sue. You call a lawyer on a referral list maintained by the local chapter of the American Society of Media Photographers and set an appointment. You want to ask him: *Is it infringement?*

A. **No.** Your lawyer is going to tell you that although the National Geographic Society has enough money to make suing it profitable, no judge is going to award you any part of that money. A defendant's "deep pockets" only come into play if the plaintiff can prove that the defendant has transgressed some right of the plaintiff; apparently, you're going to have a hard time proving that the society did anything at all to you. You point out to your lawyer that the photo on the cover of the magazine is all but identical to your photo— that the photo credit inside the magazine proves that the *Geographic*'s cover shot was taken in the very same park as your photo, that the two photos both picture trilliums in full bloom and were obviously taken within a day or two of each other, and that the same fallen log appears in the background of each photo. And you point out that your photo is no longer slated as the cover shot for the tourism calendar and is now going to be used merely as an inside photo, for April. But you admit, when your lawyer asks you, that the photo on the cover of the magazine isn't yours and that there is no possible way that your photo could have ended up on the cover of the *Geographic* without your knowledge or permission. Your lawyer says that in the absence of some action by the *Geographic* that is prohibited by law, no harm, economic or otherwise, would be sufficient to turn your gripe against the magazine into a meritorious copyright infringement claim. He says that what you are experiencing is the intersection of coincidence and free expression, that the only thing that has happened is that the *Geographic* photographer had the same good idea for a photo as you and found the same beautiful natural scene to photograph, that such "coincidental similarity" does not constitute copyright infringement, no matter how closely identical the two photographs, and that the *Geographic* photographer had as much right as you did to photograph wildflowers in a national park. He says he won't file a suit for you because there has been no infringement. And then he tells you your free consultation is over and that he needs to move on to another client, one whose problems may be more profitable.

Q. You are the creative director for a company that markets motivational products to businesses, and you have an inspiration one weekend while staying at the old summer cottage that your family has owned for decades. While poking through the bookshelves there, trying to find something to read, you come across a 1930 poetry anthology. Among the poems you find in the anthology is the famous Rudyard Kipling poem "If." ("If you can keep your head when all about you, / Are losing theirs and blaming it on you; / If you can trust yourself when all men doubt you. . . .") It sends a shiver down your spine when you read it and you realize that this is just the sort of inspirational material you need for the new series of "Leadership Lessons" posters your company is marketing. You take the poetry anthology to the office on Monday, photocopy Kipling's poem, and give it to your art director so that he can have it typeset and design a poster around it. Your boss loves the resulting poster and has a copy of it framed for his office. You like it yourself, and feel pretty smug about finding the poem until a couple of months later when you are reviewing the catalog of new products from your company's chief competitor and find a nice photo of a very attractive new poster they offer their customers—it's the same Kipling poem, rendered beautifully in calligraphy and turned into a poster in your competitor's "Life Lessons" series! You are livid and remember that you saw a sales rep for the competitor company at the printer's the day you went there to watch the first copy of your poster roll off the press. You consult your boss. He is also unhappy and tells you to call the lawyer who handles your company's legal affairs. You want to ask her: *Is it infringement?*

A. **No.** Your lawyer compliments you on your new poster. She also likes the one your competitor is marketing. But she tells you that you have no reason to sue your competitor, and that she won't even write a nasty letter to them. When you tell her that you are sure that the competing company rushed out its poster version of the Kipling poem after a sales rep for the company saw your new poster, she tells you it doesn't matter. You are flummoxed and feel that the law has let you down. She explains that even if you had the idea to turn "If" into a poster before your competitor did, it doesn't matter. Kipling published the poem in 1910, which means that "If" has been in the public domain for some years. Nothing you did or could have done could change that fact or give you any rights in the poem superior to those of anyone else. Further, she tells you that the only thing that your competitor stole from you, if indeed it *was* stolen by the sales rep, was the *idea* to turn "If" into a motivational poster and, in that case, there has been no transgression because the copyright statute specifically does not protect ideas. Your competitor—and anyone else who happened to discover what you were doing—can mimic your poster with impunity. She also tells you that even though your competitor's poster is very similar to yours, there is very little basis for a lawsuit, since you and your art director have added almost nothing in the way of original, copyrightable content to Kipling's poem. The color scheme you used is not protectable. The typeface you chose is not protectable. The poster size and the fact that it is printed on high-quality archival paper are not protectable. And the poem itself, the only part of the poster that would in ordinary circumstances be eligible for copyright protection, has already enjoyed all the copyright protection the US government (and other governments of the world) will give it and is now available for anyone to use for any purpose, without permission from Kipling's heirs or anyone else. Your lawyer asks if she can keep your poster—she wants to put it on the wall of her office. You tell her to keep both posters and leave. Dejected, you try to remember what Kipling recommended in the part of his poem that says, "If you can meet with triumph and disaster. . . ." Then, when you get back to your own office, you look at the old book of poetry again and start thinking of the possibilities for a 1914 poem by Edgar A. Guest called "[Somebody Said] It Couldn't Be Done." You also start buying up all the old poetry books you run across because you want to find more great inspirational public domain poems.

Q. You are a graduate student in women's studies and are very excited when you receive a letter from a university press telling you that they want to publish your dissertation as a book. Your dissertation is a critical biography of the life and works of a now-forgotten blues singer who spent her last years with her niece in your hometown. When she died, the singer donated several large boxes of letters, scrapbooks, and memorabilia to the library of the small college where you studied as an undergraduate. You ran across them one day when you were trying to avoid studying for a French exam and, later, began a serious study of them during one Christmas break when you were visiting your parents. You see great academic success—a prestigious job, tenure, maybe even an endowed chair—in your future. Then, only a few months after your dissertation is accepted by your department, as you are revising it for publication, you see an announcement for a one-woman play based on the life of *your* blues singer. The playwright and only performer is your college nemesis, your old roommate Kay, who only knows about your blues singer *because you told her*. You are very upset because you feel sure that Kay's silly little play will cheapen the life of your blues singer by focusing on her affairs with several prominent men of her day rather than on the songs she wrote and sang and her struggles against racism. You consult a lawyer to find out: *Is it infringement?*

A. **No.** The first thing your lawyer asks is whether Kay has had access to a copy of your dissertation. You tell him no, that no one but several of your professors and one of your fellow PhD candidates has seen your dissertation or any of the research materials you gathered. Then he tells you that Kay would have been guilty of copyright infringement if she had based her play on your dissertation because she would have been using your dissertation to prepare a "derivative work"—the play—from it without your permission. You tell him that Kay hardly ever darkened the door of your college library during the years you studied literature and she studied drama, and that you know for a fact that she would never have even known about "your" blues singer if she had not found out from you what an interesting life the singer had led. He tells you that this is immaterial, that before you can sue Kay for infringement of your dissertation you must be able to prove that she had access to your dissertation to make such an infringement possible. You tell him that you have heard from mutual friends who have seen rehearsals of Kay's one-woman play that there are many similarities between her play and your dissertation. He tells you that any similarities between her play and your book must stem from the fact that they concern the life of the same woman—that any such similarities derive from the necessity of portraying the life of your blues singer factually. Then he asks you why she couldn't have simply researched the life of your blues singer using the same papers and other materials that you examined. You admit that you have heard that Kay has, since college graduation, found her way to your college library more than once to examine those materials. You voice your fears that her play will hurt sales of your book, when it is published, because people will have grown tired of hearing about your blues singer because of publicity for Kay's play. Your lawyer says that any diminishment of public interest in your book that can be attributed to Kay's play is simply a result of life in a society that values free enterprise and free speech, in art and scholarship as well as in business. You reject his ideas that you ask Kay to furnish you with a back-cover blurb for your book or that you use a picture of her onstage in a slinky satin gown on the book cover. Then he tells you, essentially, "that's all she wrote"—that there is nothing left to discuss because there has been no infringement and you have no ground for a lawsuit. You leave. But then you remember that your uncle is the editor of your hometown newspaper. The following week you send him a flattering photograph of yourself wearing your new PhD cap and gown, along with a press release about your forthcoming book. You ask your uncle to run a story about you. You consider also asking him to arrange for Kay's play to receive a bad review, but then you don't, since scholars such as you are above such petty jealousies.

Q. You work for days composing a ballad about the founding of the small city where you live. You call it "Oh, Town on the Prairie" and sing it at the annual Founders' Day celebration. You accompany yourself on your guitar and, even if you do say so yourself, you sound pretty good. You receive many compliments on your composition and performance and hope that you will be asked to sing your song as a part of every Founders' Day celebration. But, the following year, you are surprised to hear that another member of the Founders' Day planning committee, a smug little blue blood named Harold, has recorded his own ballad about the founding of your town; his song is called "Sweet Home on the Prairie." Further, when you buy a copy of the CD he is selling in local stores, you are astonished to find that the lyrics of his song are very close to yours, as is the melody, which, like yours, is a version of the tune for the old Scottish ballad "Flow Gently, Sweet Afton." You take your guitar and the CD down to your lawyer's office that same afternoon. You want to ask your lawyer *Is it infringement?*

A. **No.** Your lawyer listens patiently as you sit on the sofa in his office and play and sing your song. He is very interested in your story about the poaching of your song and agrees with you, when he plays the CD of "Sweet Home on the Prairie," that the lyrics of that song are practically identical to those of your song. Then, he tells you that, because he is not a copyright specialist, he will have to consult with a law school buddy of his and get back to you on the question of whether there has been an infringement. He asks you to leave him a tape copy of your song for purposes of comparison. You offer instead to sing "Oh, Town on the Prairie" for him again and tell him that you've never recorded or written down the song in any form because your song is a pure product of your imagination that you composed in your head behind the counter at the hardware store where you work and that you know it so well that you have never felt the need to write it down. He declines a second performance and says he will call you the following day. You can hardly wait to hear from him, but, when you do, you are unhappy. Your lawyer tells you that, for several reasons, you have no reason for threatening to sue the guy who stole your song and that you'd better tear up the long letter about him that you had planned to send to the Founders' Day planning committee and the editor of your local paper. You are astonished to hear him say this, but when you stop hyperventilating, you listen to what he has to say. He says that there are several factors that keep you from naming Harold in a federal copyright infringement lawsuit, and he enumerates them. The first is that the melody for your ballad is a public domain melody, written by one Alexander Hume in 1786 to turn a poem by the famous Scottish poet Robert Burns into a song; because you don't and can't own the public domain music, you can't prevent anyone else from using it, for any purpose. But what, you ask your lawyer, about Harold's obvious rip-off of your lyrics. Your lawyer then tells you that because you have never reduced your lyrics to writing, those lyrics—the only portion of "Oh, Town on the Prairie" that is eligible for copyright protection—are not protected by copyright. You are astonished to hear this and tell him that his law school buddy must not be much of a copyright expert because you read in a book in the library just that morning that any work is protected by copyright from the moment it is created. Then he corrects you, telling you that you should have read a little further, that, under US law, a copyrightable work is automatically protected by copyright *when it is reduced to a tangible form*, not simply when someone like you creates it in his head. You say, "Oh." You ask whether this means that your song belongs to Harold now. Your lawyer reassures you that you still own your song, but that Harold owns his song, too, despite the fact that he stole almost all of it from you and Alexander Hume. He then advises you that if you are going to write songs, to get a boom box with a cassette recorder or even to call your voice mail and sing your song to yourself, but to record your songs *somehow*. You tell him you will do so and promise not to say anything defamatory about Harold. You also spend the afternoon gloating over the fact that although Harold is two years younger than you he has lost almost all his hair. And, too, he has never had much of a chin. You feel only a little better.

CHAPTER 11

Licensing and Selling Copyrights

The market determines how much income you can create from a copyright. And it does work just in that way—*you* are the creator of both the copyrighted work *and* any income it produces. In order to get someone to reach for a checkbook, "name" writers, painters, and songwriters have only to call up the agent or publisher who made a lot of money off their last project and say, "It's finished." (J. K. Rowling could probably get six figures for her grocery list.) But very few creators are in this enviable position; most of us must actively sell and then promote what we create in order to turn it into income.

MONEY IN YOUR MAILBOX

A big obstacle to amassing a fat bank account is time. How can you write *War and Peace* if you can only work at night, after putting in a hard day at the office and getting the kids to bed? This is another question no one really knows the answer to—obviously some creators have figured out how to devote to their work the time necessary to create masterpieces (or, at least, fat bestsellers), but even they couldn't really tell you how to juggle the competing responsibilities of life and a job with creative work.

And if you manage to produce something that you think is salable, how much is it worth? One of the hardest balances to strike is that between having a healthy regard for the value of your work and having an inflated opinion of its worth. People take you seriously when you cost a lot; it's illogical (Gandhi was a modest, self-effacing man, but we all know that he and his work were very valuable) but true. It's hard to achieve the "snob appeal" of becoming an overpriced artist or author when no one will give you even enough to pay for the canvases or printer cartridges you used to create the work that won't sell.

As a practical matter, no one really has a surefire formula for creating income from copyrights, despite the hundreds of books published every year about *How to Become a Hit Songwriter* and *How to Write a Best Seller*. This is because the tastes of the consuming public—the people who spend twenty-five dollars for the newest James Patterson novel or twenty dollars for a Beyoncé CD or hundreds for a print of a Thomas Kinkade painting are fickle. Today's *New York Times'* bestseller may clog the tables at garage sales in a year or so. That means trying to become a big enough part of popular culture to produce even a living wage is a gamble.

But a lot of smart people take that gamble. Mick Jagger decided years ago that he was the best person to make decisions about the business of the Rolling Stones (his time at the London School of Economics didn't hurt). And there seems to be a steady stream of lawyers (John Grisham is the best example) willing to give up practicing their profession in order to write mystery novels. Some of the gamblers win; others never get to give up their day jobs.

If you want to earn real money from what you create, you've got to have a working knowledge of how the products of your imagination can be turned into car payments. The best way to do this is to become an expert in the business of your area of commerce—book publishing, the art world, the music industry, etc. If you are as obsessive about learning who bought what for how much and why as you are about working at your craft, you'll be able to do the best job possible with whatever you create. Although making a living from your copyrights is never a sure thing, no matter how talented you are (van Gogh sold almost no paintings during his lifetime), educating yourself to the methods and customs of the arena of art you have chosen is an important step in getting serious about earning from your art, whatever variety of art you produce.

In addition, try to begin to view your copyrights as pies. A clever baker would offer pies cut into slices as well as whole pies. That's what people whose copyrights earn income for them do—they figure out how to divide their infinitely divisible copyrights into pieces and sell or license them as wholes and in pieces, over and over again. Selling any tangible property more than once would be illegal and could land you in jail, but selling or licensing a copyright, in whole or in part, more than once is not only legal, it's smart—so long as everybody involved understands what's happening.

Think of it this way: a copyright extends through time (it will endure until seventy years after your death, under ordinary circumstances) and through space (geographic space, but also cyberspace and the "area" covered by certain uses—e.g., "areas" of trade such as movies or books). In addition, copyrights are divisible—that is, the rights that copyright embodies may be divided and sold one at a time or in pairs or according to any division you can imagine. This means that you can sell your whole copyright to a book publisher for the full term of copyright and for the territory of the world. Or, you may sell only the right to publish your book during only the next five years and only in English, to be distributed only in English-speaking countries.

Or you might turn a speech you wrote for a corporate client into an essay that is sold to both an American magazine and a British one and still use it later as the basis for a book on the same topic or a chapter in an anthology. Besides creating something others want, this is the secret to producing income from your work—that what you have created is not a pie so much as it is six or eight tasty desserts that can be sold to as many people. This is where a good understanding of licenses (both nonexclusive and exclusive licenses) is important—if you can sell a piece of your copyright for a while in a defined "area," you can sell it again later for more money and no one will object.

But don't forget assignments of copyright. The outright sale of your copyright may be advantageous—if they want to buy the copyright in your painting or song and they offer enough money for you to sell it to them, you'll go back to work and create another copyright, right after you return from the bank. The question in the case of an assignment of copyright, as with exclusive licenses of copyright for all or most of the full term of copyright and for most or all of the applicable territory, is whether the price offered is sufficient. Only you can answer this, and the answer you give will change as you become more expert at your craft and your reputation grows. The same is true of works for hire—if the money is right, it can overcome any other objections you have.

CHOICE OF METHOD

Once you understand the differences between copyright licenses and assignments and work-for-hire agreements, you can gauge which is appropriate and fair in a given situation. It's simply a matter of considering the rights conveyed by each in light of the practical aspects of the situation.

In the case of a specially commissioned work, an assignment is like a sales contract by which a freelancer transfers all copyright rights in a creative work to a commissioning party; in the assignment, the freelancer can negotiate a "sales figure" that adequately compensates him or her for his or her services in creating the work and for the sale of the copyright for the period of time agreed upon. If the assignment transfers rights in an existing work, that is, a work not specially commissioned, the freelancer's compensation may be less.

With an exclusive license, the freelancer also negotiates both the duration of the license (which is like a lease period) and a fair price for giving up the rights of copyright for that time period, but further bases his or her price on the scope of the exclusive license; that is, he or she considers the rights retained as well as those bargained away. Copyright owners who grant non-exclusive licenses consider the same factors, but the prices they can command will probably be much smaller than for an exclusive license, since the copyright owner who grants a nonexclusive license doesn't give up the right to again grant the same permission to use the work—to one or a hundred other people.

It is to the advantage of an assignee or licensee to include language in an assignment or license agreement that allows the editing or other modification of the work to accommodate its intended use. It is to the author's advantage that the assignment or license agreement includes language that provides for a reuse fee whenever the work is used.

A work-for-hire agreement, which really should be used only in situations that fit the copyright statute's requirements for works for hire, is the most exhaustive way of vesting rights in a commissioning party. This is because in a work-for-hire agreement a freelancer forfeits not only any ownership of the copyright in the work but also any right to further payment for any use of the work. He or she has no say as to how the work is used and cannot even demand credit if the work is displayed or published. Fair-minded business people will demand work-for-hire agreements only when they are really necessary and will be prepared to pay the freelancer enough to compensate him or her appropriately under all the circumstances of the situation.

This book's appendixes include four form agreements for transferring interests in copyright: a nonexclusive license (appendix C), an exclusive license (appendix D), an assignment (appendix E), and a work-for-hire agreement (appendix F). The language of the agreements is essentially the same except for the paragraphs that specify what rights are conveyed. If you read these agreements you should understand better how copyrights operate in the marketplace. You may also want to copy one or more of them for your own use. Ask a lawyer for help if you aren't sure that you understand what the agreement you want to use does.

WRITTEN AGREEMENTS

A contract is a set of legal rights and responsibilities created by the mutual agreement of two or more people or business entities—the "rules," so to speak, by which a particular business relationship is to be run. A contract is the agreement itself, not the paper document that memorializes the agreement. In fact, many contracts don't even have to be in writing to be valid, although, as we shall see, written contracts are almost always a good idea.

Except in old movies, written contracts do not depend for their effectiveness on complicated legal language. The goal of a good contract lawyer is to "draft," or write, a document that sets out in completely unambiguous language the agreement reached between the parties. This generally means that the more clearly a contract is written, the more effective it is as a contract; but eliminating ambiguity may also require more detailed language than most people are accustomed to using and may result in a much longer written agreement than the contract lawyer's client thinks is necessary. However, in a skillfully drafted agreement *every* provision is necessary. Even in the case of an apparently simple agreement, a good contract lawyer will write an agreement that not only specifies what happens when the agreement is working but also what happens when it stops working.

THE STRUCTURE OF A CONTRACT

There is no particular "architecture" required to make a written document a contract. What determines whether a document is a binding agreement is the content of the language, not the form in which the language is arranged in the document. Yet there are certain standard sections into which formal written agreements are customarily divided.

The introductory section of a formal written agreement gives the names, and sometimes the addresses, of the parties to the agreement, indicates their legal status (an individual doing business under a trade name, a partnership, or a corporation), gives the short terms by which the contracting parties will be referred to in the agreement ("Megan Clark Bowers, hereinafter referred to as the 'Writer'. . ."), and specifies the date the agreement is made or is agreed to become effective.

In the body of the written agreement, most contracts enumerate the various points of agreement between the parties in a series of headlined paragraphs, each of which sets out one facet of the agreement and all of which probably use the word *shall* to indicate the mandatory nature of the action expected from each party.

Besides all the major points of the agreement, a formal contract will also contain what are sometimes entitled "miscellaneous provisions" and what lawyers often call "boilerplate." These provisions look unnecessary to most nonlawyers, since, among other things, they set out methods for handling various contingencies that may never occur, but they can be crucially important. For example, one standard miscellaneous provision provides that any lawsuit based on the agreement will be filed in the courts of a specified state or city and that any dispute will be decided according to the laws of a specified state. This sort of provision can determine whether you sue to enforce your agreement in your home state or, at increased expense, in a distant city.

THE BENEFITS OF WRITTEN AGREEMENTS

No lawyer can include any provision in any written agreement that will compel ethical conduct from a dishonest person. The best any lawyer can do is to include provisions in the written agreement that prescribe penalties for failure to abide by the terms of the contract, and even this will not ensure that a dishonest person does not act dishonestly. Your best protection against truly dishonest people is to avoid entering agreements with them, since a true renegade has little fear of lawsuits. In any event, having to go to court to obtain what, by rights, you were due under the terms of the agreement you made is an expensive, time-consuming, and frustrating experience.

Many business people, especially those who work in the creative fields, assume that written contracts between people who know and trust each other are unnecessary and that having lawyers prepare a written agreement in such a case is an avoidable expense. Neither of these assumptions is true. Even if you enter a business agreement with another ethical person, a written agreement is necessary, for precision and for documentation.

Even honest and knowledgeable people sometimes fail to communicate to each other all the terms of their agreement. Putting an agreement in writing lets both parties "see" their agreement and provides an opportunity for them to negotiate points of the agreement they have previously omitted from their discussions. Further, a written agreement serves to document the terms of the arrangement throughout the life of the business arrangement. Human memory is fallible; even honest people can forget the precise terms of their agreements if they are not written down. And a written agreement can be crucial to proving the existence of the agreement if one of the people who originally made the agreement leaves his or her job for another company or, in the case of an individual, dies.

Generally, then, the more complex the terms of the agreement and the longer its duration, the more it should be documented in writing. Further, while it is desirable and good business practice to reduce almost any agreement to writing, some sorts of agreements are not valid or enforceable unless they are in writing. For example, the United States copyright statute requires assignments and exclusive licenses of copyrights to be in writing and provides that no creation of an independent contractor can be a work made for hire unless there is a written agreement to that effect. And contracts that may not be performed within a year are required, almost everywhere, to be in writing.

All these are good reasons for consulting a lawyer when you enter an agreement of any importance. A good contract lawyer who is familiar with your business and your concerns can not only help you define and document your agreement, but can advise you concerning the law that governs your business relationship and suggest contract provisions that can help you reach your goals and avoid disputes.

NEGOTIATING CONTRACTS

Consulting a lawyer can be just as important, or even more important, when the written contract was drafted by lawyers for the other party. In any business agreement it is important to remember that there are actually two sorts of possible written contracts documenting the relationship—their version and your version.

This is especially true when the contracting parties are not equal in power, such as when a freelancer is presented with an agreement drafted by a publishing company. Having a lawyer on your side in a situation like this can help you feel less like David confronting Goliath. Your lawyer can explain complex contract provisions to you and, by negotiating on your behalf, turn the offered agreement into one that allows you more control, gets you paid more quickly, and is generally more favorable than the unnegotiated contract you were offered originally.

However, your lawyer must know something about your business before he or she can do an effective job for you. If you take a work-for-hire agreement to your friend the real estate lawyer and he says, "Great! I've always wondered what one of these things looked like!" it's time to consult another lawyer.

Nobody ever fights over an unsuccessful project. The more successful your book or song or film, the more important it is to have the agreements concerning it reduced to unambiguous writing. This is true in most areas of business, but it is especially true with regard to any sort of intellectual property. Copyrights are intangible, but they are valuable, and their ownership and the business arrangements surrounding them should be in writing, on paper, in contracts.

CHAPTER 12

Protecting Your Ideas

Because copyright law does not protect ideas, methods, or systems, the best protection for valuable ideas (or methods or systems) is secrecy. Such ideas, methods, and systems are called "trade secrets."

The Uniform Law Commission is a body that proposes and promulgates model laws in numerous areas for adaptation by state legislatures. One of these model laws is the Uniform Trade Secrets Act, which is the basis for existing trade secrets statutes[1] in all but a few of the states.[2] The Uniform Trade Secrets, which is a very reliable guide to trade secrets laws generally, defines trade secrets as:

Information, including a formula, pattern, compilation, program, device, method, technique, or process, that: (i) derives independent

1 If you want to read the trade secrets act for your state, search online for "trade secrets act Michigan" or "trade secrets act Nevada," and so forth.

2 There is now a new *federal* trade secrets act in addition to the trade secrets statutes of the states. The federal trade secrets law, the Defend Trade Secrets Act of 2016 (DTSA), was enacted in May of 2016. (You can read the text of this new law at www.congress.gov/bill/114th-congress/senate-bill/1890/text.) This new federal statute does not replace the trade secrets statutes already in place in the states, but it does offer a choice between state law and federal law to plaintiffs who want to sue for the misappropriation of trade secrets and offers some new protections and remedies for owners of trade secrets. Unless you are involved in a dispute over a trade secret, you don't need to worry too much about which statute applies in your situation—that will be a decision for your lawyer if you are sued or need to sue. It is enough that you educate yourself as to the general, basic elements of the law of trade secrets, and this chapter is sufficient to help you do that. For advice concerning a specific situation, consult your lawyer.

economic value, actual or potential, from not being generally known to, and not being readily ascertainable by proper means by, other persons who can obtain economic value from its disclosure or use, and (ii) is the subject of efforts that are reasonable under the circumstances to maintain its secrecy.

There are, then, three requirements for trade secret protection:

- the secret must be maintained in secrecy;
- the secret must be novel (that is, not generally known in the pertinent trade or industry); and
- the secret must give its owner a competitive advantage over those who do not know or use it.

In addition, the owner of the trade secret must show the existence of a contractual or confidential relationship between the owner of the secret and the person or company that could use or disclose it; this contract or relationship must prohibit the use or disclosure of the trade secret.

CREATING A CONTRACT

Although copyright offers no protection for trade secrets, originators of such valuable ideas may create a legally enforceable contractual obligation by the careful use of a nondisclosure letter. (It's confusing, but these letters are also sometimes called "disclosure letters," as in, "I will *disclose* my trade secret to you but only on condition that you promise not to exploit it without me or tell anyone else about it.") Nondisclosure letters are merely agreements, in the form of a letter, to preserve trade secrets. They may be used whenever the originator of an idea reveals the idea to someone who is in a position to exploit it. Examples of situations in which a nondisclosure letter would be useful to the originator of an idea, method, or system are:

- the submission of the prototype for a poster or calendar to a publisher;
- the submission of a business plan for developing an application for smart phones to a potential backer for the venture;

- the submission of a proposal for an improved system for managing the use of expensive medical equipment to a health-care facility;
- the submission by an advertising agency of a proposed advertising campaign to a prospective client; and
- the submission of the prototype for a stuffed toy to a toy manufacturer.

Nondisclosure letters don't have to be long or contain particularly stern legal language in order to be effective. The form nondisclosure letter reproduced later in this chapter will adequately protect you in most situations. Besides any legal effect of a nondisclosure letter, such a document also impresses upon the people to whom you submit your idea that you are claiming ownership of the idea and that you expect them to respect your rights in it. No written document can do much to impede the underhanded schemes of truly unethical people, and the enforceability of the agreements contained in nondisclosure letters varies from state to state, so it is wise not to rely entirely on your nondisclosure letter to protect your idea. Although secrecy is still the best defense against the possibility that someone will exploit your idea without your participation, unless you own your own cannery, your method for preserving the vitamin content of canned vegetables will never earn you a penny unless you tell Hunt's or Del Monte about it. The most practical approach to protecting your trade secret is secrecy in combination with the judicious use of a nondisclosure letter.

Along these lines, there are several simple measures you can take to improve your chances of foiling anyone who may be inclined to appropriate your idea without your permission.

1. Reduce it to writing. Never simply describe your idea verbally to anyone to whom you submit it. Reduce your idea to a proposal, complete with a full written description of how your idea would work and could be exploited and drawings or photos of any prototype. However, if it is possible to communicate your idea adequately without describing every facet of it, omit whatever you can from your proposal. This approach is the equivalent of removing the firing pin from a gun or neglecting to include the secret ingredient when you give your famous

eggnog recipe to your neighbor. At the least, don't include in your proposal actual working diagrams drawn to scale—use a representational drawing that is unsuited for use in manufacture or delete important specifications from a working diagram before reducing it in size. The more complete the information included in your proposal, the more likely that someone could get the idea to eliminate you from the manufacturing loop.

2. Corral your proposal. Put every element of the proposal that explains your idea into a presentation folder and number the copies of your proposal. This allows you to bring the right number of proposals to meetings with potential exploiters of your idea. It may not hurt to let the people to whom you give copies of your proposal observe you writing the numbers of their copies of your proposal opposite their names on a list of those who receive your proposal for review. Keep track of proposals that remain in the hands of others while they consider your idea and *get them back* so they don't float around in the file cabinets of some company looking for ideas or wind up in the hands of the unscrupulous brother-in-law or employee of someone who would never dream of using your idea without your permission.

3. Use copyright notice. Even though copyright notice is optional for works first published on or after March 1, 1989, and has never been required for unpublished works such as your proposal, using it on any copies of your proposal that leave your hands will indicate that you reserve your rights in that proposal. Copyright will not protect your basic idea, even if that idea is embodied in a written proposal, but it will protect your written and visual *expressions* of your idea. Copyright protection for your expressions of your idea offers no protection at all from the possibility that someone will read your proposal, comprehend your idea, and decide to execute it; use of a nondisclosure letter is designed to do this by documenting the promise of any person who signs it to refrain from exploiting your idea without permission. However, if someone who sees your proposal notes that you have included your copyright notice on it and believes that executing or exploiting your idea would somehow violate copyright law, that's not

your problem. Copyright law is a matter of public record; if someone's misapprehensions about the law keep him or her from engaging in unethical behavior, so much the better. Use the following form of copyright notice for an unpublished work: Unpublished work © 2018 Robert W. Wilson. Use this legend on the title page of your proposal and on each separate element of it, such as a drawing or photograph.

4. Scare them. *In addition to* using copyright notice, you should include extra "no trespassing" language wherever your copyright notice appears. This extra language will have no actual legal effect but may have a certain *in terrorem* effect; that is, it may scare people. Your scary language should be formal but shouldn't overstate the punishment an idea pirate will encounter. It should also include your name and address so that proposals that fall into the hands of anyone besides those you give them to can be returned. A good form for *in terrorem* language is:

> All rights reserved. The design for a child's plush toy in the form of a black-and-white polka-dot brontosaurus and the associated information embodied and disclosed in this document are strictly confidential proprietary information. Any disclosure of any feature of that design or any portion of that information may subject the person or entity making any such disclosure to legal action. To avoid liability, return this document promptly to Robert W. Wilson, 728 Williams Street, Murfreesboro, TN 37902.

5. Warn them and be ready to walk. Let everyone to whom you present your proposal know that you will be asking them to sign a copy of your nondisclosure letter *before* you present your idea to them. You may even consider sending the necessary copies of the nondisclosure letter in advance of your meeting in order that the people whom you expect to sign it may read and consider it. In any event, collect signed nondisclosure letters from everyone present when you meet with them to make your presentation. Make no exceptions; be prepared to call off the meeting if anyone refuses to sign.

6. Don't sign their paper. Never sign *their* nondisclosure letter— not without the advice of a lawyer, anyway. Companies that

often evaluate ideas that originate outside the organization sometimes offer form nondisclosure letters to people who have ideas to peddle. Such letters are carefully drafted to give the companies the maximum latitude in using the ideas presented to them. It is unlikely that one of these nondisclosure letters will give you the protection you want; in fact, you may seriously diminish your bargaining power if you sign one. Many reputable companies will tell you up front that they will not look at your idea until you sign a nondisclosure letter. Ask for a copy of their form letter and take it to a lawyer for an explanation and possible negotiation of terms more favorable to you before signing it.

FORM NONDISCLOSURE LETTER

Use your version of this letter in submitting ideas, methods, or systems to those who could exploit them for profit.

[1] Robert W. Wilson
728 Williams Street
Murfreesboro, Tennessee 37902

[2] November 20, 2018

Jarvis Bigshot, Vice President [3]
The Cuddly Toy Company [4]
1784 Industrial Drive
Madison, Wisconsin 20087

Dear Mr. Bigshot, [5]
I am today submitting to you for your consideration my idea and design[6] for a child's plush toy in the form of a black-and-white polka-dot brontosaurus named "Bronte" containing a microchip device that plays the melody for the song "Dem Bones" when the stomach area of the toy is depressed.[7]

I submit my prototype design and the documents that express, explain, and illustrate it to you at your request and with the purpose of allowing you to consider entering a formal, written agreement with me whereby

I would grant The Cuddly Toy Company[8] the right to develop, manufacture, and market products based on my design.

My disclosure to you of the information embodied in my prototype and in the documents submitted with it is made in confidence and in consideration of your promise that neither you individually nor your company will disclose or reveal any part or portion of the ideas or design embodied in that prototype or those documents and that you, both individually and in your capacity as an officer, employee, or agent of The Cuddly Toy Company,[9] will exercise your best efforts to diligently guard against any disclosure to any other person or entity of any of the information or ideas embodied in the submitted materials or of the existence of my design or its description or the concept upon which it is based.

You further promise that no use or exploitation of any sort whatsoever of my design or of any portion of the information embodied in the documents I submit to you, whether protected under patent or copyright laws or not, will be made by you or [10]The Cuddly Toy Company until and unless a written document setting out fully the terms of any agreement that may be reached between me and [11]The Cuddly Toy Company is executed by me and an authorized representative of your company. You agree that any use by you or [12]The Cuddly Toy Company of any of the information, ideas, concepts, inventions, or other features embodied in the materials I submit to you today would cause me irreparable harm and entitle me to money damages and an injunction preventing your further such actions.

You further agree to return to me all the materials I submit to you today upon my request or on or before a date [13]ten business days after our meeting.

If you agree to the foregoing terms, please countersign this letter in the space provided below and return it to me.

Sincerely,
[14]Robert Wilson

Agreed and accepted:
[15] The Cuddly Toy Company
By: _____, an authorized signatory

Signature
[17] _____

Print Name Here

Form Nondisclosure Letter: Notes

1. Insert your name and address here, or use stationary preprinted with your name and address.

2. Use the date of your meeting with the person or company to whom you are submitting your idea.

3. Insert the name and title of each person with whom you arrange to meet. Take pains to use the correct name and title. Your aim is to document the names of the people who see your proposal and, if you are submitting your idea to a company, to reflect in the nondisclosure letter that those people are acting in their official capacity as agents for the company that employs them (i.e., that the actions of the individuals to whom you disclose your idea are attributable to their employer).

4. In addition to preparing a copy of your nondisclosure letter for each person who you know will attend the meeting at which you present your idea, prepare several copies of the letter with only the name and address of the organization in the inside address location on the letter. This will allow you to pass out these generic copies of your letter to unexpected attendees who show up at your personal meeting.

5. Insert the name of the person to whom the letter is addressed.

6. For a method use *method* instead of *idea and design*, and for a system use *system*. Adjust other language in this form letter according to your use of it, bearing in mind that specific, unambiguous language is essential if an agreement is to be easily interpreted by the parties or, potentially, by the judge in a later lawsuit.

7. In this space insert a description of the idea, method, or system you hope to protect by using a nondisclosure letter. The goal here is to describe your idea with enough specificity that anyone who later examines the nondisclosure letter can determine just what it was that the person who countersigns it agreed not to disclose.

8. Insert the name of the company to which you are submitting your idea, method, or system.

9. Insert the name of the company to which you are submitting your idea, method, or system.

10. Insert the name of the company to which you are submitting your idea, method, or system.

11. Insert the name of the company to which you are submitting your idea, method, or system.

12. Insert the name of the company to which you are submitting your idea, method, or system.

13. Use common sense in determining how long to leave copies of your proposal with the company that sees it. No business executive is going to make a decision on the spot to develop and market your design; on the other hand, giving a company a set period of time within which to decide whether it wants to exploit your idea is smart. Ask the person with whom you arrange your presentation meeting how long it will take for his or her staff to evaluate your proposal and use that time period, if it is reasonable, as the consideration period you specify in your nondisclosure letter.

14. Type your name here, leaving space for your signature above your typed name.

15. Insert the name of the company to which you are submitting your idea, method, or system.

16. Leave this space blank for the signature of the person who countersigns the letter.

17. Leave this space blank for the printed name of the person who countersigns the letter.

MAINTAINING PROTECTION

Even with careful and consistent use of a nondisclosure letter, trade secret protection will be lost if:

- the owner of the trade secret fails to keep it secret;
- a third party independently discovers the secret; or
- a third party who is not under a contractual obligation to preserve the trade secret discovers the trade secret by careful analysis of the product that embodies the secret.

One of the most common defenses raised by defendants in trade secret misappropriation suits is that the trade secret is no longer a secret. However, the requirement that the owner of a trade secret keep it secret is not absolute. The owner must merely take "reasonable measures" to preserve his or her secret. Some of the measures that courts have considered in determining the sufficiency of the efforts of trade secret owners to maintain secrecy are:

- the requirement by the trade secret owner that employees of the owner sign a nondisclosure agreement;
- the requirement by the trade secret owner that employees of the owner sign a noncompetition agreement;
- the degree of physical security of the trade secret owner's facilities, such as office space, equipment, and computer systems, including whether the owner maintains records and other documents that explain the trade secret in a secure location and whether a log book is kept to record the location of each copy of such confidential information;
- the trade secret owner's policy to reveal the trade secret only on a "need-to-know" basis;
- the efforts of the trade secret owner to educate employees of the owner as to what is secret and the proper uses of such secret information;
- the use by the trade secret owner of proprietary legends on products that embody the trade secret;
- the efforts of the trade secret owner to diminish the likelihood of disclosure of the trade secret by debriefing departing employees of the owner and reminding those employees of their continuing obligation to preserve the trade secret; and
- the requirement by the trade secret owner that departing employees of the owner sign a termination agreement that acknowledges the employee's understanding of his or her continuing obligation to preserve the trade secret.

Because trade secret owners (at least those who turn up in reported court decisions) are more often companies than individuals, these factors may seem to have little applicability to an individual who has a valuable secret to protect. However, even a trade secret owner who operates his or her business out of a spare bedroom and has no regular employees may encounter situations in which an awareness of the importance of efforts to preserve secret information is necessary. For instance, a trade secret owner may hire a typist to help reduce to an organized, written form the documents that explain the secret; the typist should be asked to sign a nondisclosure letter, should be required to do the keyboarding on the premises of the owner rather than taking confidential materials to another workplace, and should be warned not to talk about any of the information embodied in the material to be typed.

It also must be noted that although affixing a copyright notice to materials that contain a trade secret does not result in loss of trade secret protection, copyright registration may do so if care is not used in the preparation of the deposit material that must accompany any registration application. Because the information contained in a copyright registration, including the content of the work being registered, is public record, trade secret owners must take measures to avoid disclosing confidential information. For example it is possible to deposit only a portion of the work when registering certain machine-readable works, such as computer programs, omitting from the deposited portion any trade secret information. It is also possible to request from the Copyright Office special relief from registration deposit requirements so that an "identifying portion" of the work can be deposited rather than the entire work. Call the Copyright Office at (202) 707–5959 or (877) 476–0778 to discuss whether there is a way to register the copyright in material that embodies your trade secret without making your secret public. (See chapter 5 for more on copyright registration and the deposits required for registration.)

CHAPTER 13

Recapture of Copyrights

In 1976, the United States got a new copyright law, the first entirely new US copyright law since 1909. Two provisions of the new copyright law, which became effective January 1, 1978, are of potentially great benefit to creative people, since they allow, under certain circumstances, the *termination* of previous transfers of copyright. (A "transfer" of copyright is an assignment or sale of copyright to someone else.) These provisions allow a creator of a work to make a sale of the copyright in the work and later *cancel*, or terminate, that sale and regain, or "recapture," ownership of the copyright. The termination-of-transfers provisions of the new law are somewhat complicated, but if you are an author you owe it to yourself and to your heirs to learn a little about the new provisions and how they work.

There are two groups of copyrights that are affected by the new termination-of-transfers provisions. Section 203 of the copyright law provides that an assignment of copyright made on or after January 1, 1978, by the author of a work may be terminated thirty-five to forty years after the assignment. Section 304(c) of the copyright statute provides that assignments of copyright made by an author or certain members of the author's family before January 1, 1978, may be terminated after fifty-six years from the date copyright protection was first secured. The right to terminate an assignment is statutory; this means you can't waive this right or bargain it away.

When you (or certain of your heirs) exercise the right to terminate an assignment, on the date that the termination is effective you (or they) regain ownership of all the rights of copyright (with some limitations in specific situations) that were originally sold or otherwise conveyed to someone else. You (or your family) then own those rights for the remainder of the term of copyright (until seventy years after your death or the death of your last surviving coauthor for works created on or after January 1, 1978, and for thirty-nine more years for works that have been protected by copyright for fifty-six years), or the copyright may be sold or licensed again. It's important to remember, however, that only US copyright rights may be regained; the US copyright law is only effective within the United States and its termination-of-transfers provisions affect only US copyrights. Further, the termination-of-transfers provisions do not apply to copyrights that were created as works for hire.

The copyright law sets out specific procedures that must be followed by anyone who seeks to terminate a transfer of copyright and the Copyright Office has adopted certain regulations for the documents filed. Written notices of intent to terminate must be given, *by and to* the proper people, during specified periods in advance of termination. These notices will be ineffective to accomplish termination if they are given too soon or too late, or by or to the wrong people.

The termination of copyright transfers is a complicated area of the law that confuses even lawyers. This means that the termination of a copyright assignment is *not* a do-it-yourself job. If a copyright is valuable enough, decades after its creation, to make its ownership desirable, it's valuable enough to justify paying a copyright lawyer to help regain that ownership. However, before a lawyer can help you or your family regain ownership of a copyright, you or your heirs must first remember that such a procedure is possible and, second, you must be able to supply that lawyer with sufficient information about the original assignment of the copyright to enable him or her to carry out the termination. This means you should keep accurate records of every assignment of the copyright in any work you create. Keeping records concerning the assignments of your copyrights does not have to be time consuming. The best way to keep the records you need is to set aside an evening once every year (the day before your birthday?) to compile records that could result in increased old-age income for you or enhanced income for your spouse, children, and grandchildren after your death.

A form for recording important information about the copyrights in the works you create and assign to someone else appears at the end of this chapter. Make a supply of clear photocopies of the form, called "Notice to My Heirs and Executors." Fill out one of these forms for each assignment of copyright you make and attach to the filled-out form a copy of the work that was the subject of the assignment, a copy of the assignment document, and the copyright registration certificate, if you have one.

Put the records concerning all transfers of copyright made during any given year in a folder marked "Copyright Transfers—2018" (etc.). Keep these records with your other important personal papers; tell your spouse, your adult children, the executor of your will, and your lawyer that you're keeping such records and why. Your job is to gather and preserve all the information you can about your work and the transfer of the copyright in it. Your lawyer will do the rest.

The termination-of-transfers provisions of the new copyright act were included in the statute because Congress wanted to give authors and their families the chance to regain ownership of copyrights that grow to be valuable after they are originally sold. In the case of terminations made after fifty-six years of copyright protection, Congress wanted to give authors the benefit of the nineteen-year extension period it tacked onto the end of the copyright terms in existence when the new law was passed. The passage of the Sonny Bono Copyright Term Extension Act in 1998 increased this extension further, to thirty-nine years.

The copyright law is our government's way of rewarding and encouraging creativity in our society; the termination-of-transfers provisions of the new copyright law can help you make sure that your successful works benefit you and your heirs. It may be worthwhile for you or your lawyer to compile a multiyear calendar of possible terminations so that no one forgets when recapture of the copyrights becomes feasible.

FORM NOTICE TO MY HEIRS AND EXECUTORS

Follow the directions provided in this chapter for using the following form to record information about assignments of copyrights so that those assignments of copyright may be later terminated, as provided in the US copyright statute.

Notice to My Heirs and Executors

If the procedures specified in sections 203 and 304(c) of the US Copyright Act of 1976 are followed and certain requirements are met, the ownership of the copyright in the Work described below (referred to herein as "the Work") may be regained, by me or by my spouse, children, or grandchildren, even though I have previously assigned all or some part of the copyright in the Work to another person or company (referred to herein as "the Assignee"), as described below.

If the date of assignment listed below is before January 1, 1978, it is possible that the assignment may be terminated fifty-six years after copyright protection was secured.

If the date of assignment listed below is after January 1, 1978, it is possible that the assignment may be terminated between thirty-five and forty years after it was made.

The copyright in the Work may be very valuable. If the termination of the assignment of this copyright is not carried out correctly, the right to regain ownership of the copyright may be lost. This notice and any attachments[1] should be taken to a copyright lawyer not more than ten years and not less than three years (a) before the fifty-sixth anniversary of an assignment made prior to January 1, 1978, or (b) before the thirty-fifth anniversary of an assignment made after January 1, 1978.

A. Description of Work:[2, 3]

_____

_____

_____

_____

_____

_____

B. Author(s) of Work: (indicate name of each Author, including the most current address and phone number available for the Author; further, indicate ownership share of the copyright for each author):[4]

_____

_____

_____

_____

_____

_____

C. Date of Transfer of Copyright by Me:[5] _____

D. Percentage of Entire Copyright Transferred by Me:[6] _____

E. Copyright Assigned to: (indicate name of the Assignee, including the most current address and phone number available for the Assignee)[7]

_____

_____

_____

_____

_____

_____

FORM NOTICE TO MY HEIRS AND EXECUTORS: NOTES

1. If it is possible to attach a copy of the Work that was the subject of the assignment, do so. This may be a photocopy of a work on paper, a photograph for a three-dimensional work, a CD for a computer program, or a DVD for an audiovisual work. Insert the copy of the Work in a large manila envelope that is durably attached to this form; enclose a copy of the document in which the copyright assignment was made, if it is available, and the original copyright registration certificate, if the copyright in the Work has been registered.

2. Start with an appropriate short description of the Work that was the subject of the assignment—e.g., "a photograph of three-year-old twin girls, each holding a black Labrador puppy," "a poem titled *Midsummer's Eve*," "a musical composition titled 'Wind Dance,'" "a short story titled 'High Hopes,'" "a nonfiction book manuscript titled *Butterflies of the Eastern States*," and so on. Follow with a description of the Work detailed enough to allow anyone who may have a role in terminating the previous assignment to determine just which particular work, out of all similar works, was the subject of the assignment.

3. If it is practicable, attach a copy of the Work, similar to the sort of copies required for registration of copyright, to each original of the Assignment of Copyright document. If it is not practicable to do so, omit this language and use a much more detailed description of the Work or use photographs (for three-dimensional works such as sculptures) or other identifying material, such as the script for a film, and change the language describing the attached materials.

4. Insert the names and addresses of all the authors here. For example, if you and a coauthor created the Work together, use language similar to the following: "Megan Bowers, fifty percent (50%) author of the Work and Natalie Wilson, fifty percent (50%) author of the Work." If you created the Work alone, make that fact clear by using language similar to the following: "Aaron Bowers, sole author of the entire Work."

5. Insert the date of the assignment of copyright in the Work— i.e., the date of the publishing agreement or other document that transferred ownership of the copyright in the Work to someone else.

6. In the usual circumstance, you will assign your entire interest in the copyright in the Work and will use language here similar to the following: "one hundred percent (100%)." If you created the Work with a coauthor and assigned only your portion of the copyright, use language similar to the following: "fifty percent (50%) of the entire copyright in the Work." Make sure you use language that jibes with the information you gave in Paragraph B. That is, if you originally owned one-half of the copyright in the Work and assigned to a publishing company only half of your one-half ownership share, you would use "twenty-five percent (25%) of the entire copyright in the Work," since half of a one-half share of a whole is one-quarter, or twenty-five percent.

7. Insert the name, address, and phone number of the Assignee named in the document that assigned ownership of the copyright in the Work to someone else. Include any additional identifying information that may come in handy when you or your heirs later try to locate the Assignee, such as "subsidiary company of Mega Music, a Delaware corporation," or "married to Elizabeth McMillen, president of McMillen Computers," or, even, "niece of Thaddeus Bryant." Remember, both people and companies move around. You will never regret recording too *much* information.

CHAPTER 14

Copyright and the Internet

Any analysis of copyright would be incomplete without a discussion of perhaps the newest and largest area populated by copyrights, the Internet, and the increasingly intelligent robots that run it. Lots of people seem to think that copyright can't survive in cyberspace. They think that the copyright laws that exist in most of the nations of the world don't work in this new dimension and that inserting any work into the traffic on the information superhighway is tantamount to giving it away. Fortunately, these assumptions are untrue. However, it also seems obvious that copyright and copyright owners must adjust to the realities of cyberspace and the technologies that create and power it.

EXISTING LAW STILL APPLIES

In this country, the copyright statute states that "copyright protection subsists . . . in original works of authorship fixed in any tangible medium of expression, now known or later developed, from which they can be perceived, reproduced, or otherwise communicated, either directly or with the aid of a machine or device." This language allows copyright to stretch when it is necessary to extend protection to new forms of expression without language that names each new technology. Copyright has not been killed by the new methods of communications that are now possible via the Internet. In fact, it has expanded; the copyright umbrella has been enlarged by virtue of the new forms of expression to which it now applies.

Secondly, copyright is not abandoned when a work is made accessible to millions via the Internet. Cyberspace belongs to all of us, in the same way that highways and the broadcast spectrum do. Use of transportation thoroughfares does not deprive you of your private property—your car still belongs to you, no matter how many public roads you use. This is not to say that there is no danger of having your property stolen by "highwaymen" on the information superhighway, but then, the risk of car theft exists on our roadways, too.

REBELLION OF THE NETIZENS

In recent years copyright has been increasingly under attack. During the 1990s, personal computers became affordable and common and people in all walks of US life became Internet users. By the turn of the millennium, the Internet was no longer a novelty, no longer a specialized tool for academics and scientists. Although people of every age are enthusiastic citizens of cyberspace, the most enthusiastic are the young. To them, the access to every area of commerce and culture that the Internet offers is not an innovation but is, rather, simply a reality of life. Unlike those of us who can remember a time when a long-distance phone call was an event, the young have fewer adjustments to make to the possibilities that the new technology offers. They also have no fixed attitudes toward copyright that must be altered in light of the new uses of copyrighted works that are now possible. To them, instant communication and instant information are the norm; they have become accustomed to the instant gratification that the Internet offers. They feel that the Internet and everything the Internet can put on their computer screens are *theirs*, in a way older people never felt about the copyrights embodied in the phonograph records they bought and brought home or the magazines delivered by the postman or the books they borrowed from the library. Add to this proprietary attitude of some of the rhetoric of early hackers ("Information wants to be *free!*") and it is no surprise that, despite years of lobbying by software manufacturers, content providers, and entertainment-industry trade associations, many Internet users remain unconvinced that the copyright statute, which predates the widespread use of the Internet, applies to them and their activities. One prevalent attitude has been the feeling that, regardless of the provisions of the copyright statute and how copyright lawyers parse it, making copies of a copyrighted work for private use is all right. This is perhaps the heart of most present-day disputes between copyright owners and copyright users. The indignation that lots of those users feel when told that they are breaking the law by sharing copies of recordings of their favorite songs with their friends has created a lack of respect for copyright that scares copyright owners, who have traditionally sought to control *every* copy of their works and who are extremely suspicious of the technology that allows copying and the social climate that permits it.

But there are other reasons for the disconnect between enforcement of copyright rights and the activities of Internet users. One of these is that the concepts of ownership inherent in copyright law may need to be revised to better accommodate the interests of copyright users and to restore respect for copyright law. Perhaps the solution is not controlling copies of copyrighted works but limiting access to those works by controlling relationships with those who want to use the works. This can be achieved by arrangements analogous to subscriptions; only those who pay for access and thereby make themselves known to the owner of a copyright are permitted full access to it. Many newspapers and magazines are trying to activate pay policies for their online readers. Today many websites offer channels for obtaining permissions to make copies of materials posted there. Some content creators post notices that dispense with the need for website users to contact anyone for permission to copy material; such notices give advance permission to website visitors allowing them to make "up to ten" or "up to one hundred" copies of material posted there; sometimes conditions are imposed on those who would make such copies, such as that any copies made be used for personal purposes only. Other creators of copyrightable works announce that they do not claim copyright in their creations and that the works may be copied without restriction by anyone; some of these creators don't believe in copyright, others act simply in an effort to benefit society by allowing free access to computer programs or other materials they have created.

Another problem is jurisdiction—how can we and other countries figure out questions of traditional, geographic, legal jurisdiction for a "place"—cyberspace—that simultaneously exists everywhere and nowhere; whose laws apply to what cyberspace activities? Is there a need for a new set of international laws that apply to cyberspace? If so, who can enforce those laws—who is the "government" in the intangible but gigantic territory of cyberspace? It seems evident that what has been named in the US the National Information Infrastructure will have to be designed to both allow the regulation of cyberspace activities and avoid overburdening Internet activities by overregulation. That's going to be a hard problem to solve. For instance, originally no one collected sales tax on Internet sales. Now many Internet merchants pay taxes on sales to people who live in states where they maintain physical facilities. A national sales tax has been proposed, but nobody knows yet just how this would work and the largest online sellers consistently lobby against it.

THE DIGITAL MILLENNIUM COPYRIGHT ACT

In 1998 Congress passed copyright legislation designed to address some of the problems that have plagued copyright owners since the advent of widespread access to and use of the Internet. The law, an addition and amendment to the existing US copyright statute called the Digital Millennium Copyright Act (DMCA), became effective in late October that year. The DMCA addresses a wide variety of concerns and makes it possible, through new means, such as encryption technology, and older ones, such as lawsuits, for copyright owners to better protect themselves. Some of the more important provisions of the law are summarized below. (For a PDF copy of the entire DMCA, posted by the Copyright Office as a part of the current copyright statute, go to www .copyright.gov/legislation/pl105-304.pdf. For a Copyright Office summary of the DMCA, go to www.copyright.gov/legislation/dmca.pdf.)

- The DMCA protects what is called "copyright management information." Copyright management information is identifying information that accompanies a copy or performance of a work, such as the copyright notice placed on a work; other information that identifies the work, the author, and/or the copyright owner of the work; the terms and conditions for uses of the work; and information identifying any writer, performer, or other contributor to the work. With the DMCA, it is now illegal to intentionally remove, alter, or falsify any copyright management information or knowingly distribute or perform works with false copyright management information. Civil and criminal penalties are provided for those who transgress these prohibitions, which apply to copyrighted works in the print and other media, not just those in digital form.
- The DMCA prohibits the circumvention of technologies used by copyright owners to protect their works, generally referred to as "encryption devices." For example, encryption software can be used to render the electronic version

of a text unreadable on any but the specific ebook reader for which it was purchased. The DMCA also prohibits the sale or importation of any sort of device designed to be used to defeat any encryption technology.

- The DMCA generally limits the liability of online service providers (OSPs) for simply innocently transmitting content over the Internet, even if that content infringes the copyright rights of a third party. The DMCA includes several provisions to allow OSPs to escape punishment for such innocent transmissions; these are known as "safe harbors" from copyright infringement liability for OSPs. The safe harbor provision most associated with the DMCAs is the "notice and takedown" provision, which allows OSPs to escape any liability for displaying a copyrighted work placed on its system at the direction of a user of that system.[1] When an OSP receives information that material on a website for which it provides service is infringing, the OSP is expected to take down or block access to the accused material. The copyright owner can subpoena the OSP to learn the identity of the alleged infringer if an infringement suit is filed.

- In order to qualify for the DMCA's safe harbor protections, certain kinds of service providers—for example, those that allow users to post or store material on their systems, and search engines, directories, and other information location tools—must file with the Copyright Office a designation of an agent to receive notifications of claimed infringement. To designate an agent, a service provider must do two things: (1) make certain contact information for the agent available to the public on its website; and (2) provide the same information to the Copyright Office, which maintains a centralized online directory of designated agent contact information for public use. The service provider must also ensure that this information is up to date. In December 2016, the office introduced an online registration system

---

1 Other provisions that provide safe harbors to OSPs have more to do with how content is transmitted, located, or stored.

and electronically generated directory to replace the office's old paper-based system and directory. Accordingly, the office no longer accepts paper designations. To designate an agent, a service provider must register with and use the office's online system. (You can find the DMCA Designated Agent Directory on the Copyright Office website at www .copyright.gov/dmca-directory/.)

- The DMCA limits the liability of colleges and universities for copyright infringement by faculty and graduate students, under certain circumstances, when they serve as OSPs for their students, staff, and faculty.

- The DMCA protects the rights of copyright users by providing that that "nothing in this section shall affect rights, remedies, limitations, or defenses to copyright infringement, including fair use," thereby preserving existing case law on copyright infringement.

Various studies by the Copyright Office relating to the protection of copyright in the new media age are called for in the DMCA. This fact, coupled with the complexity of many of the law's provisions, means that the full effect of the DMCA won't be known for some time. Court decisions will interpret sections of the act and Congress or the Copyright Office may act to implement recommendations by the Copyright Office after the mandated studies are completed. At present, anyone who treats material available on the Internet with the same respect accorded to works available in more traditional formats will stay on the right side of the law. Think of it this way: it has been possible since Gutenberg to print multiple copies of books without the permission of their authors. If you wouldn't dream of doing this, or of pirating and selling CDs or copies of a movie, neither should you consider duplicating and disseminating most of what you find on the Internet. Reasonable people don't do whatever is possible just because the means are there. Think of the matches in your kitchen. The possibilities are endless for that box of matches, but many of the uses to which they can be put are unwise, self-defeating, or illegal. Newer technologies such as computers and the Internet should be used with similar prudence.

Frontiers are exciting, but they are also scary. Those who thrive in unstructured environments revel in the freedom that a new, unregulated business arena provides. But those who have property to protect—copyright owners—are more comfortable when law is introduced into the previously lawless new frontier. We thought all the frontiers had been conquered, but we were wrong. Perhaps the biggest frontier ever, one that encompasses the whole globe, has been born in recent years. As it grows, there will be more regulation. The freedom of some will be curtailed, but the property of others will be protected. So far, the laws applied to and created for the Internet seem to take into account the rights of all netizens. Court decisions interpreting those laws will further balance the interests of software and content providers with those who use new technology and the Internet. There may also be some amendments to the DMCA that make a little more room for some prevalent and not-too-harmful practices; advocates for various groups have been trying to persuade Congress to pass such amendments almost since the DMCA was passed. Every new term of Congress sees some bills of this sort introduced, as well as others that seek to regulate the Internet and the activities of Internet users in other important areas, such as privacy and pornography and fair trade. There are little tradition and little law and little precedent with regard to the new technologies, but such is always the case when there is a radical advance in technology. The cyberspace frontier won't become a settled place instantly, and everyone who works or plays there will have to make some changes before it does, but the very bright people who populate it are too interested in its possibilities to let it remain a nearly lawless frontier for long. Revolutions don't happen overnight; they take years. We survived the Industrial Revolution, and most people's lives are better because of it. The same will be true of our exploration and colonization of cyberspace.

INTERNET COPYRIGHT PROBLEMS

If you own and run a website or a blog or even just post the occasional video on YouTube or enthusiastically post to Facebook, you need to be aware of the most common sorts of copyright infringement on the Internet.

Copying

Any form of copying of anyone else's copyrighted material is infringement and can lead to a lawsuit or, at least, a takedown demand. This means, obviously, that if you didn't create it, you should not post any image or text or recording, audio or video, on your own website or any other, such as Facebook or YouTube. It's not somehow transformed into a public-domain work just because the owner of the work posted it on a website. Neither did the owner of the work somehow consent to the copying of the work merely by putting it online. And remember this: because of the unique capabilities of the Internet, you may be guilty of violating *several* of the exclusive rights of copyright by copying and using another person's work without permission on the Internet. Copying the work violates the exclusive right of the copyright owner to make copies, of course. Posting the work on your website violates the exclusive right of the copyright owner to display, perform, and distribute the work you copy. And, depending on how you use the work, you may also violate the right of that person to be the only one who is allowed to prepare a derivative work from the copied work. That's almost a clean sweep of the exclusive rights of copyright. The Internet is a powerful tool; don't use it to get yourself in hot water. Get permission to use anything you post, just as you would if you used that material in some nonelectronic form. Otherwise, your urge to communicate someone else's copyrighted work could result in your being named the defendant in a lawsuit.

Linking

Linking is a very popular practice. A link provides a sort of cross-reference from one website to related sites. It can greatly increase the efficiency of the time an Internet user spends searching for information or products; in a very real way, linking embodies the best aspirations of the Internet by offering everything on the web to an Internet user with the minimum amount of searching. Some website owners have complained that linking, without their prior consent, is a violation of their rights. Courts have ruled that merely linking another website to your site is not infringement because no copying takes place and have compared the practice to using a library's card catalog to direct a user to the work of another.

The practice of "deep linking," which allows visitors to a website to bypass the website's homepage and any advertisements or notices there and go directly to an internal page of the site, was originally viewed as problematic. The thinking was that deep linking violated copyright law by altering the presentation of the material intended by the owner of the linked website, perhaps by avoiding advertising on the homepage of the linked site. However, courts have not viewed the practice as copyright infringement and deep linking is now common and accepted.

"Inline linking" (also called "embedding") is another common practice. This is the sort of linking that would result if you used HTML code to enable you to display a video on your blog from another website in such a way that a reader of your blog would not know that the video actually is from another website. Inline linking has often been found not to be copyright infringement. One court held that since the linked images were not stored on the defendant's server but merely linked, there was no copyright infringement even though it appeared that the images were present on the defendant's website. (Inline linking can result in trademark infringement, however, if the linking implies some sort of association between the person or company who employs the link and the person or company who owns the linked content.) Be cautious with inline linking; it is not possible to formulate a rule that takes into account all possible scenarios, and not all courts are convinced that it is not copyright infringement. As with all copyright infringement evaluations, the *particular* circumstances of the situation that is said to constitute infringement are determinative. Don't rely on your own judgment in deciding whether your actions are infringing; get skilled legal advice about your specific proposed actions or stay away from inline linking.

"Framing" is another practice that upsets copyright owners, although it is not as common as linking. The sort of framing that is problematic is the framing, through a link, that "captures" pages from one person's website within a browser window on a second site and, sometimes, imposes on the framed web pages tools, text, logos, or ads that are not controllable by the owner of the pages that are thus "framed." There is no copying of the framed site, but framing arguably alters the appearance of the content of the framed site and, because the uniform resource locator (URL) displayed is the address of the framing site, creates the impression that some voluntary relationship exists between the framed site and the framing site. The real problem here seems to be the creation of an unauthorized association, perhaps an unwelcome one, between the framing site and the framed site, as when a smaller, more obscure website seeks to shine up its image by associating itself, without permission, with a website that belongs to a more famous and well-regarded company. Website owners whose sites have been "framed" have fought the practice through suits for copyright and trademark infringement, unfair competition, and false advertising, among other theories. There are as yet no definitive rules governing framing. It is more dangerous if copyrighted material is altered or if a false association is suggested between the two sites or products marketed on them.

The only conclusion that is reasonable from any consideration of Internet copying, linking, and framing is that any action, without permission, that involves any but the most usual and certain fair use of any copyrighted material should be examined for its potential as the basis for a lawsuit. If you are a large corporation, you have lawyers who can advise you about just what you can get away with and deep pockets to pay them in the event you are sued. If you are an ordinary person, it's more reasonable to seek permission to copy, link, or frame anything that belongs to someone else and to remember that your enthusiasm for what the Internet allows you to do from your own computer will be significantly dampened if you are sued. Permission to link to another website or to frame it may not be hard to obtain. An email to the owner of the linked site specifying exactly what you want to do that is returned to you with the owner's stated permission to do so should suffice. If you can't get permission, consider using a disclaimer on your site that states clearly that the linked site belongs to someone else and that your site has nothing to do with the linked site, its owner, or its products.

It's possible to get away with more "traditional" means of copyright infringement for a while—the guy whose painting you turned into a poster may never know of your infringement. On the Internet, copyright infringement is not only easier to commit, it is harder to hide.

New Millennium Outlaws

Trolls

Until the Internet transformed all our lives, most people thought trolls lived under bridges. They may still live under bridges, but many troublesome trolls have moved to the Internet.

A troll is a person or company that enforces its rights of copyright in an aggressive way for purposes of the litigation award or settlement fee that the enforcement can produce; they seek to profit from litigation rather than from licensing or otherwise exploiting their copyrights. At worst, copyright trolls are little more than blackmailers and bullies. After receiving a menacing letter claiming infringement, a defendant may pay to settle with the copyright troll, usually for an amount that is smaller than the damages the troll claims but is still substantial. A copyright troll can often profit with very little investment of time or money by extracting a cash settlement without having to actually take a defendant to court. A number of these troll corporations are run by predatory lawyers whose business is threatening infringement suits rather than representing legitimate clients. Individuals have been sued for illegally downloading movies, newspaper stories, photos, and pornographic material, among other sorts of media.

This is how it works. A copyright troll files a lawsuit alleging that your Internet address has unlawfully downloaded its copyrighted material, which the troll may have placed on file-sharing sites as a sort of bait for infringers. The troll uses the discovery process to request your name and address from your OSP, which notifies you that you are one of the people who has been accused of illegally downloading the troll's movie or music or other content. Then the troll will send you a letter demanding a settlement fee. If you do not settle the troll may pursue litigation against you; if the troll wins, a court may order you to pay a significant damages award.

The best thing to do in such a situation is to see a lawyer as soon as you receive a letter from your OSP telling you that a troll is after you. Let your lawyer advise you and act for you. Be very wary of contacting the troll or its "negotiators." Your lawyer may not be able to get you out of the troll's clutches without a settlement, but he or she can at least diminish the harm the troll can do.

And remember that the basis of any troll's claim is that you have downloaded the troll's copyrighted content without permission. If you are very careful never to copy anyone's work without payment or permission, you may be able to avoid becoming the victim of a troll. Downloading pornography is especially dangerous; the trolls who sue people for downloading dirty movies are counting on the fact that many of their targets would rather pay a settlement fee than be publicly charged with stealing porn. It is not uncommon that defendants are targeted unjustly; copyright trolls are not meticulous litigators and are more likely to sue indiscriminately than most plaintiffs. After all, the more people sued, the more who will pay to settle.

Copyright trolls have caused big problems for the legal systems of many countries since the Internet conquered the world and became a necessity rather than a luxury for most of us. But some courts are fighting back, awarding attorney fees and costs to defendants, imposing sanctions on trolls for lying and contempt of court, and banning suits against unrelated multiple defendants, which allow trolls to inexpensively sue many defendants. Some of the most egregious trolls have been defeated, disbarred, and even jailed and no longer operate. But as long as some people will send a check to a troll to avoid the hassle and embarrassment of a lawsuit, trolls won't disappear entirely. Be careful where you go and what you do on the Internet.

Pirates

Another of the problems that the Internet and technology present to copyright owners is an old problem: pirates. In every age, in every part of the world, there have been people who figured that the easiest way to acquire something they wanted was to steal it. The Internet offers anonymity with the opportunity to hide behind a computer screen, and no crime that a hacker or pirate can commit through the Internet requires a gun or otherwise involves physical danger. Devices that copy DVDs and CDs are easy to buy—and legal unless used for illegal purposes. And software to defeat encryption technology is sold openly on the Internet, mostly from other countries; the DMCA punishes this, but only when an offender can be caught. This means that a dishonest, cowardly person who would never dream of holding up a liquor store with a pistol can nevertheless steal copyrights worth much more than the contents of a liquor store cash register—and maybe the owners of the copyrights will never even know that they have been robbed. Thankfully, this lawless attitude isn't characteristic of all Internet users, but it does blur the distinction between what is *yours* and what is *mine* in the same way that pornography and violence in movies and on TV erode our standards of what is acceptable.

If you want to see what sort of pirates the FBI investigates, take a look at its Intellectual Property Theft/Piracy News (www.fbi.gov/investigate/white-collar-crime/piracy-ip-theft/intellectual-property-theftpiracy-news). These cases report the theft of everything from trade secrets and new varieties of seeds to movies, music, and software and the manufacture and sale of counterfeit products. Cases such as these deal with *criminal* copyright infringement,[2] which is more serious and carries more serious penalties than the sort of infringement most people are likely to commit, but they are instructive.

---

2 The copyright statute provides that an infringement is criminal if it was committed
 (A) for purposes of commercial advantage or private financial gain;
 (B) by the reproduction or distribution, including by electronic means, during any 180-day period, of 1 or more copies or phonorecords of 1 or more copyrighted works, which have a total retail value of more than $1,000; or
 (C) by the distribution of a work being prepared for commercial distribution, by making it available on a computer network accessible to members of the public, if [the accused infringer] knew or should have known that the work was intended for commercial distribution.

But most of us don't have to deal with criminal copyright infringement and don't have the resources of the FBI. Enforcing your own copyrights can present problems. One of the most prevalent is infringement by people who don't attempt to profit from the infringement. What do you do if your photograph is copied and posted on the Internet without your permission by someone who merely uses it on his or her Facebook page? And what if the use of that photo spreads so that, suddenly, your photo is everywhere on the Internet, without your permission? Sure you can ask to have the photo taken down under procedures specified in the DMCA, but if your photo "escapes" and is widely posted, do you have to make a part-time job of notifying people that it's your photo and asking them to stop using it? And what if the infringer is a sympathetic defendant? Are you really going to sue a precocious teenage blogger for copyright infringement for using your video without permission? What about a misinformed nonprofit organization that used your work on its website to raise money for flood victims? And how are you going to find and stop that college student who buys a copy of your recording but then distributes ten or twelve copies to his friends, without your permission and without compensation to you? These more "amateur" infringers, who are not part of a criminal cartel and don't have the capability to widely distribute the works they use, may need to be pursued with less vigor and punished less severely.

What are the remedies for the problems of unauthorized copying and dissemination of copyrighted works? Lots of content providers, software manufacturers, lawyers, and lawmakers are trying to figure out what solutions to such problems are fair and which will work. But they, as well as the people who say that copyright is an outmoded concept and believe that it stifles popular culture and hampers free speech, must either adjust their attitudes or remain for the foreseeable future locked in unproductive turf fights throughout cyberspace and inside millions of desktop, laptop, and notebook computers and smartphones across the country and around the world. The Internet practices and uses of technology that are problems in the eyes of copyright owners and merely innovative techniques to those who invent and employ them will probably continue to be "solved" by various means. Some present and future problems will be solved by enforcement of existing law; some will disappear as problems because they will become accepted practices; and some will be all but eliminated because copyright owners will begin to use new technology created to protect them from other technology.

ASSESSING ELECTRONIC PUBLICATION

Before cyberspace becomes as settled as the formerly chaotic and danger-ous Wild West, anyone who ventures into cyberspace—especially anyone with valuables—should take precautions. Despite the DMCA, any copyright owner should carefully consider the wisdom of making any work accessible via the Internet. As a practical matter, there is no guarantee that any work the habitués of the Internet can find and copy in cyberspace won't be used and distributed in ways to which the owner of copyright in the work objects. Copyright notice and warnings forbidding unauthorized downloading and dissemination of a work are fine, but they stop only those scrupulous enough to refrain from infringing other people's copyrights. Lots of other Internet users, who are often young, brash, and enchanted with the (mistaken) ideas that there is little law on the cyberspace frontier to restrict their actions and that no one will notice what they do, are not so conscientious. And encryp-tion codes and devices are a great idea, but somebody will know how to get around most such barriers to infringement. After all, hackers can break into the computer systems of the government and big corporations; defeating the average encryption code or device can't be impossible.

There are several characteristics of a copyrighted work that may be deter-minative in any decision whether to launch the work into cyberspace. One is the popularity of the work and the desirability of disseminating it or owning a copy of it. You may post your fake-Hemingway short story on your website with perfect safety if it's so bad that no one wants to read it, much less copy it or claim authorship of it or send it electronically to all his or her friends. However, if your science fiction story is good and is interesting to science fiction fans, you may have a problem. Think about how likely it is that what you put into cyberspace will be stolen or further disseminated. Unless you are willing, in effect, to surrender your copyright rights in your work, think twice about putting it into an "instant-infringement" form.

Consider, too, the nature of your work—especially if it's a fact-based work. Works that are primarily compilations of information and contain very little expression, such as directories, are granted much narrower copyright protec-tion than creative works. This is the reason that large annual reference works that list, for instance, names and addresses of corporation executives or of all the franchise restaurant companies in the United States, are often available only in libraries or from their publishers at substantial cost. The publishers of such directories know that (a) the information in their directories is in demand; (b) their directories, because they are compilations of facts, are only narrowly protected by copyright law; and (c) they would be hard pressed to stop infringers from lifting whole sections of the information they have gathered and published if their publications were accessible to the general public online, even for a fee. Don't make it easy for an infringer to steal your work, especially if you are doubtful about just how protectable it is.

Electronic rights are a new area of law that is growing and changing. If you are offered any contract for the use of your work on the Internet, take it to a lawyer who is experienced in copyright law and get him or her to explain what you will be allowing by signing the agreement. The more important or potentially valuable your work, the more important it is that you look before you leap into an agreement that may give someone more rights in that work than you really want to give or allows it to be published in a form that would make unauthorized copying easy. The same is true of publication of a work in a form that makes it easy to copy. Publishing a collection of photographs in a book may allow the photos to be scanned into a computer and stolen, but the chance of theft is greatly increased if those photos are published on a CD. Careful attention to the possibilities for copying that the form of publication creates may be as important as any encryption method or legal remedy—it's a lot easier to build a fence high enough to keep your horse from escaping than to capture him after he's out of your control. And remember that any electronic publisher of your work may not be obligated by your publishing agreement to go after infringers; in any event, it will make a determination as to whether any such lawsuit would be profitable and successful, and that depends on who stole your work and whether they have any money and whether they can be found to sue. And remember that, in most cases, what remedies are theoretically available to you under the law are going to be much harder to obtain than you probably realize—what you really want is never to have to consider suing. This is possible only if you protect your work well enough from infringers that you are never faced with the decision whether to sue. Consider the worst scenario that could possibly result. What if a really unprincipled person, using the most sophisticated existing technology, decided to copy your work or claim it or sell it without your permission? Then factor in the likelihood that someone will want to steal your work. Be expansive in your analysis—think like a thief. Some people do things to make a buck that would never occur to most of us, especially if they think they won't get caught. In the end, especially if your work is very desirable, the most you may be able to do is diminish the thefts that occur rather than prevent them entirely. Movie studios and CD producers and software companies are familiar with this dilemma and live with it, even as they try to stop the pirates—it may be part of the price of publishing or posting a popular creation in a form that allows it to be stolen.

In short, be careful of what you post for all the World Wide Web to see; use your own copyright notice prominently and repeatedly to protect what you post.

If you find that your photograph or song or video has been used online without your permission, you may want to send a takedown notice, as is envisioned under the DMCA. Reputable people and companies will comply with such notices; others may have to be sued.

Sending a takedown notice is not a casual undertaking; the right person must send notice of infringement to the right person(s) through the right channels, and the notice must contain certain information specified in the law. This is what the copyright statute says:

> (A) To be effective . . . , a notification of claimed infringement must be a written communication provided to the designated agent of a service provider that includes substantially the following:
>
> (i) A physical or electronic signature of a person authorized to act on behalf of the owner of an exclusive right that is allegedly infringed.
>
> (ii) Identification of the copyrighted work claimed to have been infringed, or, if multiple copyrighted works at a single online site are covered by a single notification, a representative list of such works at that site.
>
> (iii) Identification of the material that is claimed to be infringing or to be the subject of infringing activity and that is to be removed or access to which is to be disabled, and information reasonably sufficient to permit the service provider to locate the material.
>
> (iv) Information reasonably sufficient to permit the service provider to contact the complaining party, such as an address, telephone number, and, if available, an electronic mail address at which the complaining party may be contacted.

(v) A statement that the complaining party has a good faith belief that use of the material in the manner complained of is not authorized by the copyright owner, its agent, or the law.

(vi) A statement that the information in the notification is accurate, and under penalty of perjury, that the complaining party is authorized to act on behalf of the owner of an exclusive right that is allegedly infringed.

A notification from a copyright owner that fails to comply substantially with these provisions of subparagraph will be considered insufficient to compel the infringer to take down the infringed material and will be ineffective.

The Copyright Office is studying how to make the notice process more foolproof, but has not yet issued a form notice that copyright owners can use. If your copyrighted work is valuable enough to protect, it may be worth it to seek the help of a lawyer to send an appropriate—and effective—takedown notice.

WORK IN PROGRESS

No final statement can be made on any of the topics connected with copyrights in cyberspace because cyberspace copyright is a cake that isn't baked yet. There are not yet enough reported court decisions to say exactly what the law is in every situation and, in any event, it seems likely that the statutes governing copyright in cyberspace as well as the problems themselves will change—maybe more than once—in a sort of virtual evolution of this species of communications law. Until the cyberspace frontier has been settled, be cautious about what you park in its commercial district. And stay tuned. The saga will continue.

Appendices

Copyright Office Resources

The Copyright Office is the ultimate authority on any question about US copyright that does not involve a dispute over ownership or infringement. And that information is available free to anyone who requests it. It's like having a free copyright research department available twenty-four hours a day.

QUESTIONS

If you have a question about copyright or copyright registration, you may be able to find the answer on the informative and easy-to-use Copyright Office website at www.copyright.gov; click on the "Frequently Asked Questions" (FAQs) subhead on the home page. If you cannot find the answer you need by consulting the FAQs, you can use the search feature at the top of the Copyright Office homepage or ask a question directly by email by clicking on the "Contact Us" heading at the bottom of the home page. You can also call the Copyright Office with your questions. The Public Information Office telephone number is (202) 707–3000 or (877) 476–0778 (toll free). To order Copyright Office publications, the number is (202) 707–9100. Hours of service are 8:30 a.m. to 5:00 p.m. eastern time, Monday through Friday, except federal holidays.

COPYRIGHT OFFICE INFORMATION CIRCULARS AND FACT SHEETS

The Copyright Office publishes a variety of excellent short pamphlets and circulars written in simple language on an assortment of copyright-related topics. A list of these publications, along with their corresponding publication numbers, follows. These publications are available on the Copyright Office website at https://www.copyright.gov/circs/. Reading a few Copyright Office publications pertinent to your copyright, starting with Copyright Basics and including the publication that discusses copyright in your particular sort of work, is an excellent way to get answers to many of the questions you may have. You can order *paper* copies of any publications you want by calling the Forms and Publications Hotline at (202) 707–9100 twenty-four hours a day. And although the Copyright Office is phasing out the use of paper registration forms, you can also order copyright registration forms from the hotline.

Note: The U.S. Copyright Office began in September of 2017 to release refreshed and updated circulars to provide up-to-date and authoritative copyright information for a broad general audience. This effort began with the release of thirty-one circulars, re-designed for optimal online reading. This is the first design update in more than a decade. The remaining Copyright Office circulars were slated to be released on a rolling basis through the end of 2017. All circulars, including updated versions of circulars that have been revised, are available at the link above (https://www.copyright.gov/circs/).

Circulars and Factsheets

Foundations of Copyright

- Copyright Basics (1)
- Fundamentos de los Derechos de Autor (1)
- Make Sure Your Application Will Be Acceptable (1c)
- Copyright Notice (3)
- Copyright Office Fees (4)
- How to Open and Maintain a Copyright Office Deposit Account (5)
- Renewal of Copyright (15)
- Duration of Copyright (15a)
- Extension of Copyright Terms (15t)

Office Practices and Procedures

- Best Edition of Published Copyrighted Works for the Collections of the Library of Congress (7b)
- Mandatory Deposit of Copies or Phonorecords for the Library of Congress (7d)
- How to Respond to a Mandatory Deposit Notice If You Elect to Register Your Work (M 295)
- Supplementary Copyright Registration (8)
- Special Handling (10)
- Have a Question about the Single Application? (SL 4S)
- Recordations of Transfers and Other Documents (12)
- Calculating Fees for Recording Documents in the Copyright Office (SL 4D)
- Cálculo de cargos por Archivo de Documentos y Avisos de Terminación de Contratos (SL 4DE)
- Cargos por Servicios Prestados en la Oficina del Derecho de Autor (SL 4E)
- Obtaining Access to and Copies of Copyright Records and Deposits (6)
- How to Investigate the Copyright Status of a Work (22)
- The Copyright Card Catalog and the Online Files of the Copyright Office (23)
- The Effects of Not Sending a Timely Reply to Copyright Office Correspondence (7c)
- Reconsideration of a Refusal to Register a Copyright, Mask Work, or Vessel Hull Claim (SL 4A)
- Limitations on the Information Furnished by the Copyright Office (1b)
- Privacy: Copyright Public Records (SL 37)
- Changing Your Address with the Copyright Office (SL 30A)

Copyright Concepts

- Work Made For Hire Under the 1976 Copyright Act (9)
- Copyright Registration for Derivative Works (14)

- Reproduction of Copyrighted Works by Educators and Librarians (21)
- Ideas, Methods, or Systems (31)
- Blank Forms and Other Works Not Protected by Copyright (32)
- Computing and Measuring Devices (33)
- Copyright Protection Not Available for Names, Titles, or Short Phrases (34)
- International Copyright Relations of the United States (38a)
- Copyright Restoration under the URAA (38b)
- Federal Statutory Protection for Mask Works (100)
- Pseudonyms (FL 101)
- Contribution to Collective Work (FL 104)
- How to Obtain Permission (M 10)

Visual Arts Works

- Copyright Registration for Pictorial, Graphic, and Sculptural Works (40)
- Deposit Requirements for Registration of Claims to Copyright in Visual Arts Material (40a)
- Copyright Claims in Architectural Works (41)
- Cartoons and Comic Strips (44)
- Electronic Registration of Groups of Published Photographs (SL 39)
- Useful Articles (FL 103)
- Copyright Registration of Photographs (FL 107)
- Copyright Registration of Games (FL 108)
- Group Registration Published Photos (FL 124)

Performing Arts Works

- Copyright Registration for Motion Pictures Including Video Recordings (45)
- Copyright Registration for Musical Compositions (50)
- Copyright Registration for Multimedia Works (55)
- Copyright Registration for Sound Recordings (56)
- Musical Compositions and Sound Recordings (56a)
- Dramatic Works: Choreography, Pantomimes, and Scripts (FL 119)

Literary Works

- Copyright Registration for Computer Programs (61)
- Copyright Registration for Single Serial Issues (62)
- Group Registration of Newspapers and Newsletters on Form G/DN (62a)
- Copyright Registration for Group of Serial Issues (62b)
- Copyright Registration for Secure Tests (64)
- Copyright Registration for Automated Databases (65)
- Copyright Registration for Online Works (66)
- Copyright Registration of Poetry (FL 106)
- Copyright Registration of Books, Manuscripts, and Speeches (FL 109)

Licensing

- Compulsory License for Making and Distributing Phonorecords (73)
- How to Make Statutory License Royalty EFT Payments via Wire (74a)
- How to Make Statutory License Royalty EFT Payments via ACH Credit (74b)
- How to Make Statutory License Royalty EFT Payments Using Pay.gov (74c)
- The Licensing Division of the Copyright Office (75)
- Copyright Office Licensing Division Service Fees (SL 4L)

THE ELECTRONIC COPYRIGHT OFFICE (ECO)

The Copyright Office is phasing out most paper registrations and now refers to electronic copyright registration as the "primary" method of registering a claim to copyright. As with most matters regarding the Copyright Office, the best information available is from the Copyright Office itself. Go to www .copyright.gov/eco/help/ for the eCO Help Desk, a list of questions about eCO and how it works. It's really a convenient system and is designed to be easy for most applicants to use.

Fair Use Checklist

Courts consider a long list of factors in determining whether a use is "fair." The factors that courts must weigh in determining whether a use of a copyrighted work is a fair use are set out in section 107 of the US copyright statute. They are also embodied in the Fair Use Checklist reproduced below. Notice that the checklist leaves the decision whether a use is fair or infringing up to you. However, it can help you evaluate your use on a point-by-point basis using the only binding standard that exists—the four factors of the copyright statute (and their subcategories). There is no definite boundary between fair use and infringement because no general rule defining infringement is possible—the copyright infringement evaluation is made by weighing *particular* circumstances. Make a few photocopies of the Fair Use Checklist and use it like a worksheet the next time you have a question about how much of someone else's work you can use without permission—or whether you can use it at all without tracking down the copyright owner and asking for a license, which is the only way to make sure no one sues you if your use does not qualify as a fair use of the copyrighted work.

Fair Use Checklist[1]

Preliminaries

Name:[2] _____

Date:[3] _____

Project

Name or title of project:[4]

_____

_____

_____

Description of project:[5]

_____

_____

_____

_____

_____

Work to Be Used[6]

Description of work to be used, including name or title:

_____

_____

_____

_____

_____

Author or owner of copyright in work to be used:

_____

_____

_____

_____

Address and phone number of author or owner of copyright in work to be used:

_____

_____

_____

_____

_____

Copyright information for work to be used: [7]

_____

_____

_____

_____

_____

Copyright Status of Work to Be Used

Is the work you want to use a public-domain work? _____ yes _____ no
(If you answer "yes" and are *sure* that the work is no longer protected by copyright, no permission to use the work is necessary. If you answer "no," answer the questions below to help you determine whether your use of the work is a fair use.)

Evaluation

Factors in Fair Use

Purpose of the proposed use:[8]

_____

_____

_____

_____

_____

Character of the use:[9]

_____ nonprofit educational use[10]   _____ **commercial use**[14]

_____ research use   _____ **advertising use**

_____ scholarship use   _____ **profit from use**[15]

_____ criticism use

_____ comment use

_____ news reporting use

_____ parody use[11]

_____ restricted use[12]

_____ transformative or productive use[13]

_____ credit will be given to author   _____ **credit will not be given to author**[16]

Nature of the copyrighted work:[17]

_____ factual work   _____ **creative work**[18]

_____ published work   _____ **unpublished work**[19]

Amount of the portion of the work used in relation to the copyrighted work as a whole:[20]

_____ 5% or less   _____ **15%**[21]

_____ 10%   _____ **more than 15%**

Substantiality[22] of the portion of the work used in relation to the copyrighted work as a whole:

_____ portion used is not substantial   _____ **portion used is substantial**

Effect of the use upon the potential market for or value of the copyrighted work:[23]

_____ does not impair market for   _____ **significantly impairs**
       the work   **market for the work**[24]

_____ will not replace a sale of the   _____ **could replace a sale of**
       work   **the work**

_____ will not diminish the market   _____ **will diminish the market**
       for the work   **for the work**

_____ does not increase exposure   _____ **significantly increases**
       of the work   **exposure of the work**[25]

_____ use of the work limited in   _____ **repeated use of the work**
       time   **over longer period**[26]

Other pertinent factors:

_____ you own a copy of the work[27]   _____ **you borrowed a copy of**
_____ permission to use the work is   **the work**
       not available   _____ **permission to use the**
                                               work is readily available[28]

Conclusion

Completed analysis:[29]

If you check more than two items in the right-hand column of answers under Factors in Fair Use, your proposed use is probably not a fair use.

Two right-hand-column answers indicate that you should further examine your planned use and, possibly, revise your plans for using the copyrighted work. One right-hand-column answer indicates that your planned use is probably a fair use, unless that one answer results from checking "commercial use" under "Character of the Use." "Commercial use" is the spoiler in any fair use evaluation. *If your planned use involves earning money from your project in any way, get legal advice before you proceed with your project; **there is no substitute for the opinion of a lawyer** well versed in copyright law, and any important project deserves a careful fair use evaluation as a preliminary to work.*

_____ Based on the answers to the questions above, I have determined that my use of the copyrighted work is a fair use of that work.

_____ Based on the answers to the questions above, I have determined that my use of the copyrighted work is not a fair use of that work. I will either obtain permission from the copyright owner before using the copyrighted work in my project, will decrease my use of the work so that my use will constitute fair use, or will abandon my plans to use the copyrighted work in my project.

Notes[30]

_____

_____

_____

_____

_____

_____

_____

_____

_____

_____

FAIR USE CHECKLIST: NOTES

1. Use this checklist to help you decide whether you need permission to use a work in your own project and to keep a record of information about that work. If you don't have complete information to enter in every blank, just enter what you know; you can do the research to fill in the blanks later, if necessary. The goal in using this form is to assemble and organize the information you have in an effort to consider the work you want to use in light of the use you want to make. Retain the completed checklist so that you can later recreate your fair use evaluation if you need to explain how you reached the decision you made. Remember that you may have to make the fair use evaluation again if the circumstances surrounding your project change—for instance, if a classroom use of a copyrighted work expands outside the classroom.

2. Write your name here.

3. This date may be important in the case of a copyright that is still valid but will expire before your project is completed. After a while, it can also let you know that you have spent too much time trying to get permission to use a work and should give up.

4. Write the name of your project here. Use a working title or a title that is a description, e.g., "American Love Songs of the Fifties," or "Fifties Love Songs Compilation CD."

5. Describe your project in as much detail as possible, including the medium in which you are working (a documentary film, an anthology of short stories, a musical composition, etc.).

6. Recording the information about the work you want to use when you gather it can save a lot of time later; further, in addition to helping you make the fair use analysis, it can also expedite the process of getting permission to use the work, if you decide that permission is necessary.

7. If there is a copyright notice on the work you want to use, copy it here; include any other information you have about the work, such as "This play was first produced on Broadway in 1965" or "This story was published in Good Housekeeping magazine in 1970." Some of this information may be important in determining the copyright status of the work or the owner of copyright in it, if you do not already have that information.

8. For example, "segment of song (music and lyrics) used in soundtrack of documentary film"; "section of photograph used in collage of images of young children"; "two lines of poem used as epigraph for magazine article." Remember, too, the uses enumerated as fair uses in the House Report that accompanied the draft copyright statute during its progress through Congress before its passage; these are fair uses, barring any unusual circumstance connected with them: "Quotation of excerpts in a review or criticism for purposes of illustration or comment; quotation of short passages in a scholarly or technical work, for illustration or clarification of the author's observations; use in a parody of some of the content of the work parodied; summary of an address or article, with brief quotations, in a news report; reproduction by a library of a portion of a work to replace part of a damaged copy; reproduction by a teacher or student of a small part of a work to illustrate a lesson; reproduction of a work in legislative or judicial proceedings or reports; incidental and fortuitous reproduction, in a newsreel or broadcast, of a work located in the scene of an event being reported."

9. Nonprofit educational, research, criticism, and news reporting uses are almost always fair; commercial uses, such as uses in advertising, are seldom fair uses.

10. Remember that although the entity making use of the copyrighted work is a legitimate nonprofit organization, the use itself may be a fundraising use, which makes it a commercial use.

11. Parody use of a copyrighted work is risky unless done carefully. The conventional wisdom that a permissible parody takes from the underlying copyrighted work only the amount of material that is necessary to call to mind the original, copyrighted work and

make the point of the parody. This generally means that attempts at parody that rely far too much on mere replication of the original, copyrighted works or significant portions of them are not fair uses. One court characterized the circumstances surrounding a permissible, fair use of a copyrighted work in a parody thusly: "the audience [is] aware that underlying the parody there is an original and separate expression, attributable to a different artist."

12. A restricted use of a work, such as copies of one poem circulated only to students in a classroom by a teacher, argues for fair use of the work.

13. The "transformative or productive use" question gauges whether the purported "fair" use changes the copyrighted work for a new utility or adds value to it. One court said that the question whether the alleged fair use is "transformative" is an inquiry into whether the second use "adds something new with a further purpose of different character, altering the first with new expression, meaning or message." Unlike the four factors discussed in footnote 8 above, this question is not part of the copyright statute but has, rather, been created by some court decisions on fair use. The purported "fair" uses that have been held by these courts to be "transformative or productive" are usually unusual uses of the copyrighted work and often involve some element of parody. Legitimate, fair use parodies are transformative because they add to the underlying work by their wit and the acute observation and commentary inherent in the added expression; that is, they take only what is necessary to call to mind the parodied work and create a new work whose purpose is distinct from the parodied copyrighted work. It is worth noting that true "transformative" works—like true, permissible parodies—are rare and hard to achieve. Because the evaluation that a use is "transformative or productive" is highly subjective and, despite being applied in a number of reported cases, somewhat ambiguous, because truly transformative uses are rare, and because most ordinary people are not equipped to make the decision that a use is "transformative or productive" with any accuracy, it is best not to rely on your own judgment that your use will qualify as a fair use on this

ground. Remember, fair use is a defense to infringement; relying on your own evaluation that a use qualifies as a fair use because it is a "transformative or productive" use of a copyrighted work is simply asking for the opportunity to try to make that point in court, in the course of a lawsuit for copyright infringement. It is far better to be certain enough of a use before you complete your project that the risk of such a dispute is all but eliminated than to wait to see if the owner of copyright in the work that you used in that project will claim infringement. Nevertheless, the "transformative or productive" question is given here for the sake of accuracy and completeness. Two examples of uses ruled by courts to be "transformative" are a photograph used in an ad of the head of actor Leslie Nielsen superimposed on a photograph of the body of a nude pregnant model, in a parody of the famous and controversial Annie Leibovitz photograph of actress Demi Moore on the cover of the magazine Vanity Fair; and a book titled The Seinfield Aptitude Test, which quizzed readers regarding characters, dialogue, and plot details of almost every episode of the television comedy series Seinfeld. The defendant in the first case won; those in the second case lost—the court ruled that even though they had made a "transformative" use, the other three factors of the fair use test were against them. The court also paid attention to the fact that the authors and publishers of the book The Seinfield Aptitude Test had used a high percentage of scripts from the show in the book.

14. Whether a proposed use is a commercial use can be a problematic question. For instance, quoting a small section of a long poem in a short story is probably fair use, even if the short story is published by a magazine for a fee. Printing a long section of the same poem on coffee mugs or T-shirts and selling those is not a fair use and would require the permission of the poet to avoid copyright infringement.

15. Some uses that are arguably noncommercial in the ordinary sense of that term nevertheless produce profits. For instance, sales of tickets to a performance of a copyrighted play with no remuneration to the playwright would be a for-profit use of the play, and

not a fair use, even if the group presenting the production was an informal group such as a little-theatre association that used all the play proceeds to pay for staging the production. The use of the play would be a fundraising use only, but fundraising uses are commercial uses even for nonprofit organizations.

16. Credit should be given to the author of the material from another work that is used if possible in the context of your project; however, it is also important to realize that giving credit to the author of the material used does not turn an infringing use into a noninfringing use.

17. The permissible uses that may be made of informational works are considerably broader than permissible uses of creative works. However, courts have yet to permit the fair use defense to infringement in a case involving an unpublished work, where the private nature of the work is ordinarily protected.

18. A creative work is a work that owes its existence more to the imagination of the author than to the author's gathering of facts or information; this includes, among other creative works, stories, poems, novels, films, musical compositions, plays, and paintings. Creative works such as fiction are given more protection than factual works.

19. Unpublished works, like creative works, are given more protection from unauthorized uses than published works, since the decision whether or not to publish is a right of the copyright owner and a use without permission of an unpublished work by definition eliminates that choice of the copyright owner, at least to the extent the user publishes the unpublished copyrighted work.

20. This is the quantitative part of the evaluation. Make your best guess here as to the percentage of the work you want to use. Remember that "the copyrighted work as a whole" means the whole of the individual work you want to use—for example, if you want to use part of a song off a CD, "the copyrighted work as a whole" means the whole song, not the whole CD; and if you want to use part of a story, determine your estimated percentage used in relation to the story itself, not in relation to the book-length collection of stories that includes the story you want to use.

21. Using more than 10 percent of a copyrighted work without permission is dangerous, but whether the use is a fair use depends also on the other factors. Any use of 10 percent or more of the copyrighted work is almost certainly going to be held to be too great a use by a court—in the case involving the book The Seinfield Aptitude Test, the court said that 3.6 percent verbatim quoting of the original scripts was too great.

22. This is the qualitative part of the evaluation. "Substantial" means the portion of the work used is central or significant to the entire work. That is, did you quote the twelve-page climactic scene of a mystery novel, thereby disclosing the identity of the killer, or did you quote only a three-paragraph section that describes the city where the detective works? Even if your use is relative small from a quantitative standpoint, if it takes the "heart" from the copyrighted work, it may not be a fair use.

23. This evaluation is often determinative in a court's decision whether the use constitutes infringement. It is undoubtedly the most important of the four factors to be weighed in determining fair use. If the market for the copyrighted work is significantly diminished because of the purported fair use, then it is not a fair use. Fewer readers will want to buy a book if its most sensational and newsworthy sections have been previously excerpted in a magazine. A related factor that is considered is the effect of the purported fair use on any of the rights in the copyright of the work said to be infringed. If, without permission, one person writes and sells a screenplay based on another person's copyrighted novel, the right to prepare and sell a screen adaptation of the novel may have been lost to the author of that novel. And the questions raised under this factor is not limited to whether use of the copyrighted work will result in loss of revenue for the copyright owner. Rather, they seek to gauge the effect of the use on the entire potential market for the copyrighted work.

24. For instance, the right of the copyright owner to sell the movie rights to his novel is impaired because you based your independent film on his book without permission.

25. For instance, you posted the copyrighted work on the Internet, thereby making it accessible to millions of web users.

26. A repeated use of the copyrighted work has the effect of eroding, over time, the rights of the copyright owner, even if one use of the work does not. For instance, even if you make only ten copies of a poem for use in teaching a college literature class, if you keep those copies and use them term after term, you will expose scores of students to the poem over time; some of those students may have bought a book that contains the poem and the fact that you eliminated the need to do so hurts the poet's and his or her publisher's sales.

27. Check this if you or, in the case of a project prepared for your employer, your employer owns a legally acquired copy of the copyrighted work. Check it if you or your professor or college or university own a copy. In many circumstances, your actions, even if they constitute infringement, are attributable to your employer or college or university.

28. The ability to get permission to use the copyrighted work for a reasonable price (if any) and with reasonable effort argues against a fair use, but is not, by itself, determinative.

29. Check one of the following statements after completing this checklist.

30. Write here any actions you take with regard to use of the copyrighted work, such as phone calls to the copyright owner or a trimming down of the portion of the copyrighted work used or a change in the circumstances surrounding the use that will change the outcome of your fair use analysis. Date each notation and write down phone numbers and addresses. Remember, this checklist, when completed, is your record that you made reasonable efforts to avoid committing copyright infringement and that you took reasonable action to solve any problems. Attach additional sheets with a history of your actions, if necessary.

Form Permission Request Letter

Although copyright law does not require nonexclusive licenses of copyright to be in writing (and most permissions to use copyrighted works fall into this category), a written permission is an excellent idea, if for no other reason than that the person requesting the permission and the one granting it will have, in writing, documentation of the scope of the permission. This form permission request letter allows the would-be user of a work to request and receive permission to use the work in one document. Use a version of this form letter to request permission to use any work that is not a public domain work.

[1]Timothy Wilson St. Charles
726 Edgemont Avenue
Montclair, New Jersey 94202
January 30, 2018

Ms. Lulu Bluestocking[2]
630 Park Avenue
New York, NY 10021

Dear [3]Ms. Bluestocking,
I am researching the life of your late friend Dallas McMillen in preparation for writing a critical biography of Mr. McMillen.[4] Bifocal Books, a noted publisher of scholarly nonfiction, has contracted to publish my book.[5]

In this connection, I am writing to request your permission to quote from your letters to Mr. McMillen between the years 1949 and 1951.[6] Your donation of these letters to the Harry Ransom Humanities Research Center at the University of Texas in Austin has made it possible for me to gain a more complete picture of Mr. McMillen's life and writings during those years.[7]

I have attached to this letter a list of the excerpts from your letters that I would like to quote in my manuscript.[8] You will note that in any instance where you mentioned a person who is still living, I have referred to that person in the excerpt I have made as "Miss A" or "Mr. B" in order to preserve her or his privacy, as well as yours.[9] Similarly, you will note that I have not included in the excerpts I am requesting permission to publish any material that is not of legitimate interest to literary scholars; specifically, in three of the excerpts that appear on the third page of the attachment I have omitted several passages of a purely personal nature that could possibly embarrass your son or Mr. McMillen's grandchildren.[10]

I also enclose photocopies of several photographs, also from the collections of the Harry Ransom Center. I believe that the first four of these photographs were taken by you at your country house in Connecticut during the six years that Mr. McMillen spent his summers with you there. I want to include these photos in my book. I need your permission to reproduce them.[11] I also need your consent to the publication of the two photos of you with Mr. McMillen, one in your parlor at Stonehaven and one on the front porch there, photocopies of which are also enclosed.[12] These photographs were taken by your and Mr. McMillen's mutual friend Frances Barton, who, as owner of the copyrights in those photographs, has given me permission to publish them in my book.[13]

I enclose a letter from my publisher confirming my book contract and attesting to my reliability and competence as a biographer. Perhaps you have seen my previous book, a biography titled *Bon Mots: The Life and Works of Carolyn T. Wilson.*[14]

If you will consent to my request to reprint from your letters to Mr. McMillen the excerpts listed on the attachment to this letter and the publication of the photos described above and enclosed in the form of photocopies, please countersign this letter in the space below reserved for your signature and return one copy of the letter and excerpts list to me in the enclosed, self-addressed, stamped envelope.[15] I am sending two copies of this letter and its attachment so that you may retain a copy for your files.[16] Thank you for considering my request.

Sincerely,
[17]Will St. Charles

Agreed and accepted:
Lulu Bluestocking

[18] _____   _____
Copyright Owner   Date of Signature

Form Permission Request Letter: Notes

1. Insert your name and address here, or use stationery preprinted with your name and address.
2. Insert the name of the owner of the copyright in the work or works you want permission to use. This person may be the author of those works, as in this example, or may instead be the publisher or heir or executor of the estate of the author.
3. Insert the name of the person to whom the letter is addressed.
4. Briefly describe your project.
5. If you have a book contract or some other commitment that will result in the distribution and dissemination of your finished project, describe it here. If you have no such commitment, state your plans regarding your project, as "I intend to use excerpts from your letters in my dissertation; I am a PhD candidate at the University of Wisconsin at Madison."
6. Describe as specifically as possible your source material. Further, if you can limit the scope of your request to include only material that you may actually use, permission to use the material may be more easily obtained.
7. It's not a bad idea to state where and how you gained access to the materials you want to use, especially in the case of unpublished materials, as in this example, access to which may be restricted as a condition of the donor's gift of those materials to a library or other institution. However,

if you have stumbled across useful material in a less conventional manner, such as discovering in a used-book store a cache of manuscripts with the author's notations concerning revisions, state the fact forthrightly. Deception of any sort is likely to make the person to whom you address your request suspicious of you and your motives.

8. Again, be as specific as possible about the material you want to use. The narrower the request, the more likely it is to be granted.

9. If it is possible to obscure the identity of living people who are mentioned in previously unpublished materials such as the fictitious letters which are the subject of this permission letter, it may be desirable to do so. The owners of such materials may be reluctant to have their comments about identifiable living people published during their lifetime.

10. Similarly, the owners of copyright in unpublished materials may wish to avoid causing pain or embarrassment to their own or others' families by allowing the disclosure of their personal affairs; gaining permission to quote from unpublished materials may depend on your willingness and ability to shield the author of those materials and other concerned people.

11. The owner of the copyright in a photograph, under ordinary circumstances, is the photographer. Permission from the copyright owner is required to publish even snapshots of friends and relatives such as these. If a photograph depicts someone who is a public figure, such as the man who is the subject of the biography proposed in this form permission letter, it is not necessary to obtain permission from that person (or his or her heirs) for the use of that person's image in any noncommercial context.

12. However, in the situation portrayed in this form permission letter, the woman to whom the letter is addressed and who appears in two of the photos is a private individual who can and may object to the publication of photographs of herself. (For a more detailed discussion of the law of privacy and publicity, see the book by Lee Wilson *The Advertising Law Guide* from Allworth Press.)

13. Again, it is necessary to obtain from the photographer permission to publish his or her photographs.

14. A letter such as this is not a job interview, but it doesn't hurt to briefly present your credentials to the person from whom you are requesting the permission; a track record and association with credible institutions can only bolster the chance that the requested permission will be granted.

15. Since this portion of the letter recites your proposed course of action and asks for the consent to that course of action from the person to whom the letter is addressed, it is very important to make sure that the language you use states exactly what you want permission to do. Any vague language may cast doubt on what was agreed to.

16. It is best to make it as easy as possible for the person from whom the permission is requested to say yes to your request. This means that you should not expect the person to whom you address your letter to have to photocopy it or type an envelope to return it to you.

17. Your signature on the letter will serve to demonstrate your agreement to abide by whatever conditions on the use of the materials you want to use that you have proposed to abide by.

18. Leave this space blank for the signature of the person who countersigns the letter. The signature of that person at the bottom of the letter transforms your proposal (to use and publish certain materials, on stated conditions) into an agreement between you.

Form Nonexclusive License of Copyright

Although exclusive licenses of copyright must be in writing, it is not necessary that nonexclusive licenses of copyright be written. However, a written nonexclusive license is an excellent idea, if for no other reason than that the parties to the agreement will have, in a written license, documentation of the duration and scope of the license as well as of other important terms of their agreement. This form agreement allows the author of a work to license it to another person or company on a nonexclusive basis—that is, other users of the copyright may be granted the same rights by the owner of the copyright.

Nonexclusive License of Copyright

This agreement is made between Aaron Bowers[1] (hereinafter referred to as "the Author"[2]) and Ace Publishing Company[3] (hereinafter referred to as "the Licensee"), with reference to the following facts:

That the Author, an independent contractor,[4] is the creator of and owner of the copyright in a certain unpublished[5] drawing[6] (hereinafter referred to as "the Work"), which may be more fully described as follows:

a three-by-five-inch pen-and-ink portrait of the poet Seamus Heaney,[7] a photocopy[8] of which is attached hereto and made a part of this agreement by this reference.

The Author and the Licensee agree as follows:

1. That the Author hereby grants to the Licensee the nonexclusive right to reproduce, publish, prepare derivative works
of and from, combine with other materials, display publicly,
and otherwise use, control the use of, and exploit the Work[9]
for a period of thirty-six (36)[10] months from the date written
below.

2. That, during the term of this License of Copyright, the
Licensee shall have the nonexclusive right to exercise the
rights granted herein throughout the United States and
Canada.[11]

3. That the Licensee shall have the right to crop, edit, alter, or
otherwise modify the Work to the extent that the Licensee,
in the sole discretion of the Licensee, deems necessary to
suit it to such uses as the Licensee may choose to make of
the Work.[12]

4. That the Licensee will pay to the Author the sum of Five
Hundred Dollars ($500), which amount it is agreed will
constitute the Author's only compensation for the grant of
rights made herein.[13]

5. That the Author warrants that he or she is the owner of
copyright in the Work and possesses full right and authority
to convey the rights herein conveyed. The Author further
warrants that the Work does not infringe the copyright in
any other work, and does not invade any privacy, publicity,
trademark, or other rights of any other person.[14] The Author
further agrees to indemnify and hold the Licensee harmless
in any litigation in which a third party challenges any of the
warranties made by the Author in this paragraph if any such
litigation results in a judgment adverse to the Author in a
court of competent jurisdiction;[15] and

6. That this agreement shall be governed by the laws of the
State of Massachusetts[16] applicable to contracts made and
to be performed therein and shall be construed according to
the Copyright Law of the United States, title 17, section 101,
et seq., United States Code; and

7. That this agreement shall ensure to the benefit of and bind the parties and their respective heirs, representatives, successors, and assigns.[17]

In witness whereof, the Author and the Licensee have executed this document in two (2) counterpart originals[18] as of[19] the fifth day of September, 2018.[20]

AUTHOR   LICENSEE

[21] _____   [22] _____
Author signature   Licensee signature

Address: Address:
[23] _____   [24] _____

_____   By: [25] _____
[26] _____   [27] _____
Author Social Security Number   Title

Nonexclusive License of Copyright: **Notes**

1. Insert the name of the author of the work. If two or more people created the work as coauthors, insert all their names here and add enough spaces for their signatures and so on at the end of the agreement.
2. If you want to be more specific, use "Photographer," "Writer," "Songwriter," "Composer," "Illustrator," or similar terms; use the same designation throughout the document everywhere the word "Author" appears here. If two or more people created the work as coauthors, use the following language: "(hereinafter jointly referred to as 'the Author')."
3. Insert the name of the person or company to whom the copyright in the work is being licensed.
4. This form license agreement is inappropriate for use by anyone who is *not* an independent contractor. The works created by employees as part of their jobs are works for hire; no written agreement is necessary to document the work-for-hire situation in such a circumstance because the

relationship of the employee and employer determines, as a matter of law, the ownership of the copyright in any work created on the job by the employee. However, even someone who works at a full-time job is an independent contractor with regard to any activity outside his or her job responsibilities. This language makes clear that the Author is not an employee of the Licensee.

5. If the Work has been published, use language similar to the following to specify the year of first publication of the Work: "a certain drawing first published in 2018." One of the three elements of copyright notice is the year date of first publication of the work. See chapter 1, on copyright protection for more information about copyright notice.

6. Use an appropriate short designation for the type of work that is the subject of the assignment—e.g., "a photograph of three-year-old twin girls, each holding a black Labrador puppy," "a poem titled 'Midsummer's Eve,'" "a musical composition titled 'Wind Dance,'" "a short story titled 'High Hopes,'" "a nonfiction book manuscript titled *Butterflies of the Eastern States*," and so on.

7. Insert a detailed description of the Work sufficient to allow the parties to the license and everyone else to determine just which particular work, out of all similar works, is the subject of the license.

8. If it is practicable, attach a copy of the Work, similar to the sort of copies required for registration of copyright, to each original of the Nonexclusive License of Copyright document. If it is not practicable to do so, omit this language and use a much more detailed description of the Work or use photographs (for three-dimensional works such as sculptures) or other identifying material, such as the script for a film, and change the language describing the attached materials.

9. These are the exclusive rights of copyright given to copyright owners by the US copyright statute and the copyright statutes of other countries. However, since this is a nonexclusive license, the Author may also grant the right to other parties to exercise these rights; further, the Author retains the right to exercise these rights simultaneously with any licensee.

10. When they draft agreements, lawyers traditionally use both words and figures to specify important numbers and sums of money one party must pay the other. This is done to diminish the possibility that a typographical error will lead to a misunderstanding of some important provision of the agreement, such as its duration, or the underpayment of one party or

overpayment by the other. This is a good practice to adopt in modifying this form agreement for your own use. The period of the license may be as short or as long (up to a maximum of the remainder of the term of copyright protection for the Work) as the parties wish. Use "for the full term of copyright protection" to license the copyright for the remainder of the term of copyright protection; otherwise, specify the number of months or years the license will endure.

11. Specify the territory to which the license applies. If the Author's intent is to grant a nonexclusive license for the entire world, use this language: "That the Licensee shall have the nonexclusive right to exercise the rights granted herein throughout the world. . . ."

12. Unless permission to alter the work is given by the Author of the work, anyone who significantly modifies it may be legally liable to the Author for distorting his or her work. This paragraph may be omitted if the Author objects to any modification of the Work. Or, any such modification may be made dependent upon the prior written approval of the Author: "That the Licensee shall not have the right to crop, edit, alter, or otherwise modify the work without the prior written consent of the Author to any such modification."

13. If payment is to be made in installments, use language similar to the following: "That the Licensee will pay to the Author the sum of Ten Thousand Dollars ($10,000), which amount it is agreed will constitute the Author's only compensation for the grant of rights made herein and which shall be paid according to the following schedule: Five Thousand Dollars ($5,000) shall be paid upon the execution of this agreement; Twenty-five Hundred Dollars ($2,500) shall be paid on a date not later than thirty days after the date of execution of this agreement; and Twenty-five Hundred Dollars ($2,500) shall be paid on a date not later than sixty days after the date of execution of this agreement." The phrase "only compensation" refers to the fact that this agreement does not provide for the periodic payment of royalties to the Author, as do many agreements in which authors license copyrights to others, such as book publishers or music publishers. This simple form Nonexclusive License of Copyright is inadequate to document a license of copyright made in return for the promise of the payment of royalties.

14. This sort of provision is common in licenses of copyright to protect the person or company acquiring the license of copyright from lawsuits for

infringement based on actions of the Author. This seems reasonable if you consider that licensees usually have no knowledge of the circumstances surrounding the creation of the work of others and need to make sure that they are buying only rights in copyrights, *not* lawsuits.

15. This is called a "hold harmless" clause and is very common in book publishing, music publishing, and other agreements in which one party acquires rights in the copyright in a work created by an independent contractor. This is a fairly mild example of a "hold harmless" clause. Authors should expect to see a similar provision in any document that licenses a copyright for any substantial period of time; no licensee should agree to acquire a license of copyright unless the author of the work will make, in writing, promises similar to these in the document that grants the license of copyright.

16. Insert the name of the state where you live here. It is an advantage to a litigant to be able to file or defend a suit in his or her home state. However, it may be that each party to the agreement will want any suit concerning it to be filed in his or her home state. This is a point of negotiation but, as a practical matter, the more powerful of the two parties to the agreement will prevail.

17. This allows the Author to assign any sums due under the agreement to a third party or the estate of an Author who dies to collect any such sums on his or her behalf. It also permits the Licensee to in turn assign its nonexclusive license to another person or company. However, under some circumstances, especially those where the license is granted in return for the periodic payment of royalties, the Author will not want the Licensee to assign its nonexclusive license to any other party; the usual reason for this objection is that the Author may not know and trust this secondary licensee and may have no confidence in the ability of any such secondary licensee to exploit the copyright in the Work. In such an event, add this language to limit the right of the Licensee to assign the license of copyright to another entity: "However, the Licensee shall not attempt to convey any of the rights granted herein to the Licensee by the Author to any third party without the prior written consent of the Author."

18. Specify how many original copies of the agreement (i.e., copies of the agreement, even if they are photocopies that bear the original signatures of the parties).

19. In agreements, "as of" means "We are signing this agreement today, but we mean for it to take effect *as of* two weeks ago," or "next month." A date specified that is before or after the agreement is actually signed is referred to as the "effective date" of the agreement.

20. If you want the agreement to become effective on the date it is signed, use that date here. If you want it to be effective as of a previous date, use that date. If you want to postpone the time when the agreement becomes operative until a later date, use that future date.

21. Leave this space blank for the signature of the Author.

22. Leave this space blank for the signature of the Licensee.

23. Insert the Author's address here.

24. Insert the Licensee's address here.

25. Insert here the name of a person who is acting on behalf of his or her company when that company is the Licensee. If the Licensee is an individual, this line may be omitted.

26. It may be necessary for the Licensee to file a report of the Licensee's payments to the Author with the Internal Revenue Service; if so, the Author's Social Security number will be necessary for any such filings.

27. Insert here the title of a person who is acting on behalf of his or her company when that company is the Licensee. If the Licensee is an individual, this line may be omitted.

Form Exclusive License of Copyright

To be legally effective, exclusive licenses of copyright must be in writing and must be signed by at least the owner of the copyright licensed. This form agreement allows the author of a work to license it exclusively to another person or company.

Exclusive License of Copyright

This agreement is made between Natalie Wilson[1] (hereinafter referred to as "the Author"[2]) and Ace Publishing Company[3] (hereinafter referred to as "the Licensee"), with reference to the following facts:

A. That the Author, an independent contractor,[4] is the creator of and owner of the copyright in a certain unpublished[5] essay[6] (hereinafter referred to as "the Work"), which may be more fully described as follows:

a three-thousand-word original essay titled "The Changing Face of the American Voter: From World War II to the First Gulf War,"[7] a photocopy[8] of which is attached hereto and made a part of this agreement by this reference.

B. That the Work was completed during 2018.[9]

C. That the Author's date of birth is July 7, 1976.[10]

The Author and the Licensee agree as follows:

1. That the Author hereby grants to the Licensee the sole and exclusive right to reproduce, publish, prepare derivative works of and from, combine with other materials, display publicly, and otherwise use, control the use of, and exploit the Work[11] for a period of thirty-six (36)[12] months from the date written below.

2. That, during the term of this License of Copyright, the Licensee shall have the right to exercise the rights granted herein throughout the United States and Canada.[13]

3. That the Licensee shall have the right to crop, edit, alter, or otherwise modify the Work to the extent that the Licensee, in the sole discretion of the Licensee, deems necessary to suit it to such uses as the Licensee may choose to make of the Work.[14]

4. That the Licensee will pay to the Author the sum of Five Hundred Dollars ($500), which amount it is agreed will constitute the Author's only compensation for the grant of rights made herein.[15]

5. That the Author warrants that he or she is the owner of copyright in the Work and possesses full right and authority to convey the rights herein conveyed. The Author further warrants that the Work does not infringe the copyright in any other work, and does not invade any privacy, publicity, trademark, or other rights of any other person.[16] The Author further agrees to indemnify and hold the Licensee harmless in any litigation in which a third party challenges any of the warranties made by the Author in this paragraph if any such litigation results in a judgment adverse to the Author in a court of competent jurisdiction;[17] and

6. That this agreement shall be governed by the laws of the State of Massachusetts[18] applicable to contracts made and to be performed therein and shall be construed according to the Copyright Law of the United States, title 17, section 101, *et seq.*, United States Code; and

7. That this agreement shall ensure to the benefit of and bind the parties and their respective heirs, representatives, successors, and assigns.[19]

In witness whereof, the Author and the Licensee have executed this document in two (2) counterpart originals[20] as of[21] the fifth day of September, 2018.[22]

AUTHOR

LICENSEE

[23] _____

[24] _____

Author signature

Licensee signature

Address:

Address:

[25] _____

[26] _____

_____

_____

[28] _____

By: [27] _____

Author Social Security Number

[29] _____

Title

Exclusive License of Copyright: Notes

1. Insert the name of the author of the work. If two or more people created the work as coauthors, insert all their names here and add enough spaces for their signatures, etc., at the end of the agreement.
2. If you want to be more specific, use "Photographer," "Illustrator," "Songwriter," "Composer," or similar terms; use the same designation throughout the document everywhere the word "Author" appears here. If two or more people created the work as coauthors, use the following language: "(hereinafter jointly referred to as "the Author)."
3. Insert the name of the person or company to whom the copyright in the work is being licensed.
4. This form license agreement is inappropriate for use by anyone who is *not* an independent contractor. The works created by employees as a

part of their jobs are works for hire; no written agreement is necessary to document the work-for-hire situation in such a circumstance because the relationship of the employee and employer determines, as a matter of law, the ownership of the copyright in any work created on the job by the employee. However, even someone who works at a full-time job is an independent contractor with regard to any activity outside his or her job responsibilities. This language makes clear that the Author is not an employee of the Licensee.

5.   If the Work has been published, use language similar to the following to specify the year of first publication of the Work: "a certain drawing first published in 2018." One of the three elements of copyright notice is the year date of first publication of the work. See chapter 1, on copyright protection, for more information about copyright notice.

6.   Use an appropriate short designation for the type of work that is the subject of the assignment—e.g., "a photograph of three-year-old twin girls, each holding a black Labrador puppy," "a poem titled 'Midsummer's Eve,'" "a musical composition titled 'Wind Dance,'" "a short story titled 'High Hopes,'" "a nonfiction book manuscript titled *Butterflies of the Eastern States*," and so on.

7.   Insert a detailed description of the Work sufficient to allow the parties to the license and everyone else to determine just which particular work, out of all similar works, is the subject of the license.

8.   If it is practicable, attach a copy of the Work, similar to the sort of copies required for registration of copyright, to each original of the Exclusive License of Copyright document. If it is not practicable to do so, omit this language and use a much more detailed description of the Work or use photographs (for three-dimensional works such as sculptures) or other identifying material, such as the script for a film, and change the language describing the attached materials.

9.   Specify the year during which the Work was finished by the Author. (The Copyright Office permits exclusive licensees to register with the Copyright Office their interests in the copyrights they license; the year date the Work was completed is required on any application for copyright registration.)

10.   Insert the correct date. (The author's date of birth is also required in any application for copyright registration.)

11.   These are the exclusive rights of copyright given to copyright owners by the US copyright statute and the copyright statutes of other countries.

12. When they draft agreements, lawyers traditionally use both words and figures to specify important numbers and sums of money one party must pay the other. This is done to diminish the possibility that a typographical error will lead to a misunderstanding of some important provision of the agreement, such as its duration, or the underpayment of one party or overpayment by the other. This is a good practice to adopt in modifying this form agreement for your own use. The period of the license may be as short or as long (up to a maximum of the remainder of the term of copyright protection for the Work) as the parties wish. Use "for the full term of copyright protection" to license the copyright for the remainder of the term of copyright protection; otherwise, specify the number of months or years the license will endure.

13. Since a copyright owner may grant simultaneous exclusive licenses to a copyright in different geographic areas, specify the territory to which the license applies. If the Author's intent is to grant an exclusive license for the entire world, use this language: "That the Licensee shall have the right to exercise the rights granted herein throughout the world. . . ."

14. Unless permission to alter the work is given by the Author of the work, anyone who significantly modifies it may be legally liable to the Author for distorting his or her work. This paragraph may be omitted if the Author objects to any modification of the Work. Or, any such modification may be made dependent upon the prior written approval of the Author: "That the Licensee shall not have the right to crop, edit, alter, or otherwise modify the work without the prior written consent of the Author to any such modification."

15. If payment is to be made in installments, use language similar to the following: "That the Licensee will pay to the Author the sum of Ten Thousand Dollars ($10,000), which amount it is agreed will constitute the Author's only compensation for the grant of rights made herein and which shall be paid according to the following schedule: Five Thousand Dollars ($5,000) shall be paid upon the execution of this agreement; Twenty-five Hundred Dollars ($2,500) shall be paid on a date not later than thirty days after the date of execution of this agreement; and Twenty-five Hundred Dollars ($2,500) shall be paid on a date not later than sixty days after the date of execution of this agreement." The phrase "only compensation" refers to the fact that this agreement does not provide for the periodic payment of royalties to the Author, as do many agreements in which

authors license copyrights to others, such as book publishers or music publishers. This simple form Exclusive License of Copyright is inadequate to document a license of copyright made in return for the promise of the payment of royalties; while the *license* provisions of this agreement are adequate for such an arrangement, agreements that provide for the payment of royalties universally make many other provisions, such as a provision specifying the right of the author to occasionally examine the books of the Licensee.

16. This sort of provision is common in licenses of copyright to protect the person or company acquiring the license of copyright from lawsuits for infringement based on actions of the Author. This seems reasonable if you consider that licensees usually have no knowledge of the circumstances surrounding the creation of the work of others and need to make sure that they are buying only rights in copyrights, *not* lawsuits.

17. This is called a "hold harmless" clause and is very common in book publishing, music publishing, and other agreements in which one party acquires rights in the copyright in a work created by an independent contractor. This is a fairly mild example of a "hold harmless" clause. Authors should expect to see a similar provision in any document that exclusively licenses a copyright for any substantial period of time; no licensee should agree to acquire an exclusive license of copyright unless the author of the work will make, in writing, promises similar to these in the document that grants the license of copyright.

18. Insert the name of the state where you live here. It is an advantage to a litigant to be able to file or defend a suit in his or her home state. However, it may be that each party to the agreement will want any suit concerning it to be filed in his or her home state. This is a point of negotiation, but, as a practical matter, the more powerful of the two parties to the agreement will prevail.

19. This allows the Author to assign any sums due under the agreement to a third party or the estate of an Author who dies to collect any such sums on his or her behalf. It also permits the Licensee to in turn assign its exclusive license to another person or company. However, under some circumstances, especially those where the license is granted in return for the periodic payment of royalties, the Author will not want the Licensee to assign its exclusive license to any other party; the usual reason for this objection is that the Author may not know and trust this secondary

licensee and may have no confidence in the ability of any such second-ary licensee to exploit the copyright in the Work. In such an event, add this language to limit the right of the Licensee to assign the license of copyright to another entity: "However, the Licensee shall not attempt to convey any of the rights granted herein to the Licensee by the Author to any third party without the prior written consent of the Author."

20. Specify how many original copies of the agreement (i.e., copies of the agreement, even if they are photocopies, that bear the original signatures of the parties).

21. In agreements, "as of" means "We are signing this agreement today, but we mean for it to take effect *as of* two weeks ago," or "next month." A date specified that is before or after the agreement is actually signed is referred to as the "effective date" of the agreement.

22. If you want the agreement to become effective on the date it is signed, use that date here. If you want it to be effective as of a previous date, use that date. If you want to postpone the time when the agreement becomes operative until a later date, use that future date.

23. Leave this space blank for the signature of the Author.

24. Leave this space blank for the signature of the Licensee.

25. Insert the Author's address here.

26. Insert the Licensee's address here.

27. Insert here the name of a person who is acting on behalf of his or her company when that company is the Licensee. If the Licensee is an individual, this line may be omitted.

28. It may be necessary for the Licensee to file a report of the Licensee's payments to the Author with the Internal Revenue Service; if so, the Author's Social Security number will be necessary for any such filings.

29. Insert here the title of a person who is acting on behalf of his or her company when that company is the Licensee. If the Licensee is an individual, this line may be omitted.

Form Assignment of Copyright

To be legally effective, assignments of copyright must be in writing and must be signed by at least the owner of the copyright transferred. This form agreement is for use in transferring ownership of a copyright from the author of the work to another person or company.

Assignment of Copyright

This agreement is made between Megan Bowers[1] (hereinafter referred to as "the Author"[2]) and Ace Publishing Company[3] (hereinafter referred to as "the Assignee"), with reference to the following facts:

A. That the Author, an independent contractor,[4] is the creator of and owner of the copyright in a certain unpublished[5] essay[6] (hereinafter referred to as "the Work"), which may be more fully described as follows:

a three-thousand-word original essay titled "The Changing Face of the American Voter: From World War II to the First Gulf War,"[7] a photocopy[8] of which is attached hereto and made a part of this agreement by this reference.

B. That the Work was completed during 2018.[9]

C. That the Author's date of birth is July 7, 1976.[10]

The Author and the Assignee agree as follows:

1. That the Author hereby assigns, transfers, and conveys to the Assignee all[11] right, title, and interest in and to the Work described above[12] together with the copyright therein and the right to secure copyright registration therefor, in accordance with sections 101, 204, and 205 of title 17 of the United States Code, the Copyright Law of the United States. The above assignment, transfer, and conveyance includes, without limitation, any and all features, sections, and components of the Work, any and all works derived therefrom, the United States and worldwide copyrights therein, and any renewals or extensions thereof, and any and all other rights that the Author now has or to which he or she may become entitled under existing or subsequently enacted federal, state, or foreign laws, including, but not limited to, the following rights: to reproduce, publish, and display the Work publicly, to prepare derivative works of and from the Work, to combine the Work with other materials, and to otherwise exploit and control the use of the Work.[13] The above assignment further includes any and all causes of action for infringement of the Work, past, present, and future, and any and all proceeds from such causes accrued and unpaid and hereafter accruing; and

2. That the Assignee shall have the right to crop, edit, alter, or otherwise modify the Work to the extent that the Assignee, in the sole discretion of the Assignee, deems necessary to suit it to such uses as the Assignee may choose to make of the Work.[14]

3. That the Assignee will pay to the Author the sum of Five Hundred Dollars ($500),[15] which amount it is agreed will constitute the Author's only compensation for the grant of rights made herein.[16]

4. That the Author warrants that he or she is the owner of copyright in the Work and possesses full right and authority to convey the rights herein conveyed. The Author further

warrants that the Work does not infringe the copyright in any other work, and does not invade any privacy, publicity, trademark, or other rights of any other person.[17] The Author further agrees to indemnify and hold the Assignee harmless in any litigation in which a third party challenges any of the warranties made by the Author in this paragraph if any such litigation results in a judgment adverse to the Author in a court of competent jurisdiction;[18] and

5. That this agreement shall be governed by the laws of the State of Massachusetts[19] applicable to contracts made and to be performed therein and shall be construed according to the Copyright Law of the United States, title 17, section 101, *et seq.*, United States Code; and

6. That this agreement shall enure to the benefit of and bind the parties and their respective heirs, representatives, successors, and assigns.[20]

In witness whereof, the Author and the Assignee have executed this document in two (2) counterpart originals[21] as of[22] the fifth day of September, 2018.[23]

AUTHOR

[24] _____

Author signature

Address:

[26] _____

_____

[29] _____

Author Social Security Number

ASSIGNEE

[25] _____

Assignee signature

Address:

[27] _____

_____

By: [28] _____

[30] _____

Title

Assignment of Copyright: Notes

1. Insert the name of the author of the work. If two or more people created the work as coauthors, insert all their names here and add enough spaces for their signatures, etc., at the end of the agreement.

2. If you want to be more specific, use "Photographer," "Illustrator," "Songwriter," "Composer," or similar terms; use the same designation throughout the document everywhere the word "Author" appears here. If two or more people created the work as coauthors, use the following language: "(hereinafter jointly referred to as "the Author)."

3. Insert the name of the person or company to whom the copyright in the work is being assigned, or transferred.

4. This form assignment agreement is inappropriate for use by anyone who is *not* an independent contractor. The works created by employees as a part of their jobs are works for hire; no written agreement is necessary to document the work-for-hire situation in such a circumstance because the relationship of the employee and employer determines, as a matter of law, the ownership of the copyright in any work created on the job by the employee. However, even someone who works at a full-time job is an independent contractor with regard to any activity outside his or her job responsibilities. This language makes clear that the Author is not an employee of the Assignee. This is an important point because an author who does not create a work as part of his or her job responsibilities may terminate an assignment of the sort made in this agreement at the halfway point of copyright protection. See chapter 13, on recapture of copyrights, for more information about terminations of copyright assignments.

5. If the Work has been published, use language similar to the following to specify the year of first publication of the Work: "a certain drawing, first published in 2018." One of the three elements of copyright notice is the year date of first publication of the work. See chapter 1, on copyright protection, for more information about copyright notice.

6. Use an appropriate short designation for the type of work that is the subject of the assignment—e.g., "a photograph of three-year-old twin girls, each holding a black Labrador puppy," "a poem titled 'Midsummer's Eve,'" "a musical composition titled 'Wind Dance,'" "a short story titled 'High Hopes,'" "a nonfiction book manuscript titled *Butterflies of the Eastern States*," and so on.

7. Insert a detailed description of the Work sufficient to allow the parties to the assignment and everyone else to determine just which particular work, out of all similar works, is the subject of the assignment.

8. If it is practicable, attach a copy of the Work, similar to the sort of copies required for registration of copyright, to each original of the Assignment of Copyright document. If it is not practicable to do so, omit this language and use a much more detailed description of the Work or use photographs (for three-dimensional works such as sculptures) or other identifying material, such as the script for a film, and change the language describing the attached materials.

9. Specify the year during which the Work was finished by the Author. (This year date is required on any application for copyright registration.)

10. Insert the correct date. (The author's date of birth is also required in any application for copyright registration.)

11. It is, of course, possible to convey by assignment less than the entire copyright in a work. If this is desired, use language similar to the following: "That the Author hereby assigns, transfers, and conveys to the Assignee Fifty Percent (50%) of the entire right, title, and interest in and to the Work described above. . . .")

12. This assignment language does not convey ownership in any physical object or objects that embody the Work, since copyright ownership is separate from ownership of copies of the Work. If the parties intend to convey both the copyright in the work and ownership of a physical object or objects (such as a sculpture or an original painting), a separate sales agreement should be drafted to provide for the sale of any such physical object or objects. However, as a practical matter, implied in any transfer of copyright in a work that requires possession of a particular physical object, such as a flash drive to allow the work to be copied is the promise that the author of the work will at least make available for copying any such necessary physical object.

13. These are the exclusive rights of copyright given to copyright owners by the US copyright statute and the copyright statutes of other countries.

14. Unless permission to alter the work is given by the Author of the work, anyone who significantly modifies it may be legally liable to the Author for distorting his or her work.

15. When they draft agreements, lawyers traditionally use both words and figures to specify sums of money one party must pay the other. This is

done to diminish the possibility that a typographical error will lead to the underpayment of one party or overpayment by the other. It is a good rule to follow in modifying this form agreement for your own use.

16. If payment is to be made in installments, use language similar to the following: "That the Assignee will pay to the Author the sum of Ten Thousand Dollars ($10,000), which amount it is agreed will constitute the Author's only compensation for the grant of rights made herein and which shall be paid according to the following schedule: Five Thousand Dollars ($5,000) shall be paid upon the execution of this agreement; Twenty-five Hundred Dollars ($2,500) shall be paid on a date not later than thirty days after the date of execution of this agreement; and Twenty-five Hundred Dollars ($2,500) shall be paid on a date not later than sixty days after the date of execution of this agreement." The phrase "only compensation" refers to the fact that this agreement does not provide for the periodic payment of royalties to the Author, as do many agreements in which authors transfer copyrights to others, such as book publishers or music publishers. This simple form Assignment of Copyright is inadequate to document a transfer of copyright made in return for the promise of the payment of royalties; while the *transfer* provisions of this assignment are adequate for such an arrangement, agreements that provide for the payment of royalties universally make many other provisions, such as a provision specifying the right of the author to occasionally examine the books of the assignee.

17. This sort of provision is common in assignments of copyright to protect the person or company acquiring the copyright from lawsuits for infringement based on actions of the Author. This seems reasonable if you consider that assignees usually have no knowledge of the circumstances surrounding the creation of the work of others and need to make sure that they are buying only copyrights, *not* lawsuits.

18. This is called a "hold harmless" clause and is very common in book publishing, music publishing, and other agreements in which one party acquires the copyright in a work created by an independent contractor. This is a fairly mild example of a "hold harmless" clause. Authors should expect to see a similar provision in any document that transfers ownership of a copyright; no assignee should agree to buy a copyright unless the author of the work will make, in writing, promises similar to these in the document that transfers ownership of the copyright.

19. Insert the name of the state where you live here. It is an advantage to a litigant to be able to file or defend a suit in his or her home state. However, it may be that each party to the agreement will want any suit concerning it to be filed in his or her home state. This is a point of negotiation, but, as a practical matter, the more powerful of the two parties to the agreement will prevail.

20. This allows the Author to assign any sums due under the agreement to a third party or the estate of an Author who dies to collect any such sums on his or her behalf. It also permits the Assignee to in turn assign ownership of the copyright in the Work to another person or company. However, under some circumstances, especially those where the assignment is made in return for the periodic payment of royalties, the Author will not want the Assignee to assign the copyright in the Work to any other party; the usual reason for this objection is that the Author may not know and trust this secondary assignee and may have no confidence in the ability of any such secondary assignee to exploit the copyright in the Work. In such an event, add this language to limit the right of the Assignee to assign the copyright to another entity: "However, the Assignee shall not attempt to convey any of the rights granted herein to the Assignee by the Author to any third party without the prior written consent of the Author."

21. Specify how many original copies of the agreement (i.e., copies of the agreement, even if they are photocopies that bear the original signatures of the parties).

22. In agreements, "as of" means "We are signing this agreement today, but we mean for it to take effect *as of* two weeks ago," or "next month." A date specified that is before or after the agreement is actually signed is referred to as the "effective date" of the agreement.

23. If you want the agreement to become effective on the date it is signed, use that date here. If you want it to be effective as of a previous date, use that date. If you want to postpone the time when the agreement becomes operative until a later date, use that future date.

24. Leave this space blank for the signature of the Author.

25. Leave this space blank for the signature of the Assignee.

26. Insert the Author's address here.

27. Insert the Assignee's address here.

28. Insert here the name of a person who is acting on behalf of his or her company when that company is the Assignee. If the Assignee is an individual, this line may be omitted.

29. It may be necessary for the Assignee to file a report of the Assignee's payments to the Author with the Internal Revenue Service; if so, the Author's Social Security number will be necessary for any such filings.

30. Insert here the title of a person who is acting on behalf of his or her company when that company is the Assignee. If the Assignee is an individual, this line may be omitted.

Form Work-for-Hire Agreement

To be legally effective, work-for-hire agreements must be in writing and must be signed by both the creator of the specially commissioned work and the person or company that commissioned the work. For information about the situations in which work-for-hire agreements are appropriate, see chapter 2, on copyright ownership, for more information about works made for hire.

Work-for-Hire Agreement

This agreement is made between Rob Wilson[1] (hereinafter referred to as "the Writer"[2]) and Ace Publishing Company[3] (hereinafter referred to as "the Commissioning Party"), with reference to the following facts:

A. That the Writer, an independent contractor,[4] has prepared, at the instruction and under the direction of the Commissioning Party, a certain unpublished[5] essay[6] (hereinafter referred to as "the Work"), which may be more fully described as follows:

a three-thousand-word original essay titled "The Changing Face of the American Voter: From World War II to the First Gulf War,"[7] a photocopy[8] of which is attached hereto and made a part of this agreement by this reference.

B. That the Work was completed during 2018.[9]

C. That the Writer's date of birth is July 7, 1976.[10]

The Writer and the Commissioning Party agree as follows:

1. That the Work, including every embodiment thereof, was specifically prepared for the Commissioning Party and constitutes a work for hire, as defined in title 17, section 101, *et seq.*, United States Code, the Copyright Law of the United States. The Writer acknowledges and agrees that the Commissioning Party is and will be considered the author of the Work for purposes of copyright and is the owner of all rights of copyright in and to the Work and that the Commissioning Party will have the exclusive right to exercise all rights of copyright specified in title 17, section 101, *et seq.*, United States Code, the Copyright Law of the United States, for the full term of copyright and will be entitled to register the copyright in and to the Work in the Commissioning Party's name.

2. That the Commissioning Party will pay to the Writer the sum of Five Hundred Dollars ($500),[11] which amount[12] it is agreed will constitute the Writer's entire fee and only compensation[13] for the Writer's services in creating and preparing the Work and for the agreement made herein (excluding reimbursement for such reasonable expenses as may have been incurred by the Writer in connection with the creation of the Work) within thirty (30) days after delivery to the Commissioning Party of the complete text of the Work. Notwithstanding the foregoing, the Writer may represent himself or herself as the author of the Work, may use the Work as a specimen of the Writer's writings in the context of presenting his or her abilities as a writer, and may include the Work in the Writer's professional portfolio or use it as an entry in writing competitions.[14]

3. That this agreement shall be governed by the laws of the State of Massachusetts[15] applicable to contracts made and to be performed therein and shall be construed according to the Copyright Law of the United States, title 17, section 101, *et seq.*, United States Code; and

4. That this agreement shall enure to the benefit of and bind the parties and their respective heirs, representatives, successors, and assigns.[16]

In witness whereof, the Writer and the Commissioning Party have executed this document in two (2) counterpart originals[17] as of[18] the fifth day of September, 2018.[19]

WRITER   COMMISSIONING PARTY

[20] _____   [21] _____

Writer signature   Commissioning Party signature

Address: Address:
[22] _____   [23] _____

_____   _____

[25] _____   By: [24] _____
Writer Social Security Number   [26] _____

                                          Title

Work-for-Hire Agreement: Notes

1. Insert the name of the Writer of the work. If two or more people created the work as coauthors, insert all their names here and add enough spaces for their signatures, etc., at the end of the agreement.

2. In every other situation where the creator of a work conveys the copyright in the work to another party, that creator is forever considered the author of the work, even after the copyright is owned by someone else. With a work for hire, the entity that commissions the work is considered, for copyright purposes, the "author" of the work from the inception of the work. Therefore, in this work-for-hire agreement, it is preferable to use a term other than "Author" to designate the creator of the Work. The best approach is to refer to the creator by a name that describes his or her profession, such as "Photographer," "Illustrator," "Songwriter," "Composer,"

and so on. Use the same designation throughout the document to refer to the creator of the work. If two or more people created the work as coauthors, use the following language: "(hereinafter jointly referred to as 'the Songwriters')."

3. Insert the name of the person or company that commissioned the Work.

4. This form work-for-hire agreement is inappropriate for use by anyone who is *not* an independent contractor. The works created by employees as a part of their jobs are works for hire; no written agreement is necessary to document the work-for-hire situation in such a circumstance because the relationship of the employee and employer determines, as a matter of law, the ownership of the copyright in any work created on the job by the employee. However, even someone who works at a full-time job is an independent contractor with regard to any activity outside his or her job responsibilities.

5. If the Work has been published, use language similar to the following to specify the year of first publication of the Work: "a certain essay, first published in 2018." One of the three elements of copyright notice is the year of first publication of the work. See chapter 1, on copyright protection, for more information about copyright notice.

6. Use an appropriate short designation for the type of work that is the subject of the work-for-hire agreement—e.g., "a photograph of three-year-old twin girls, each holding a black Labrador puppy," "a poem titled 'Midsummer's Eve,'" "a musical composition titled 'Wind Dance,'" "a short story titled 'High Hopes,'" "a nonfiction book manuscript titled *Butterflies of the Eastern States*," and so on.

7. Insert a detailed description of the Work sufficient to allow the parties to the agreement and everyone else to determine just which particular work, out of all similar works, is the subject of the agreement.

8. If it is practicable, attach a copy of the Work, similar to the sort of copies required for registration of copyright, to each original of the work-for-hire agreement document. If it is not practicable to do so, omit this language and use a much more detailed description of the Work or use photographs (for three-dimensional works such as sculptures) or other identifying material, such as the script for a film, and change the language describing the attached materials.

9. Specify the year during which the Work was finished by the Writer. (This year date is required on any application for copyright registration.)

10. Insert the correct date. (The Author's date of birth is also required in any application for copyright registration.)

11. When they draft agreements, lawyers traditionally use both words and figures to specify sums of money one party must pay the other. This is done to diminish the possibility that a typographical error will lead to the underpayment of one party or overpayment by the other. It is a good rule to follow in modifying this form agreement for your own use.

12. If payment is to be made in installments, use language similar to the following: "That the Commissioning Party will pay to the Writer the sum of Ten Thousand Dollars ($10,000), which amount it is agreed will constitute the Writer's entire fee and only compensation for the Writer's services in creating and preparing the Work and for the agreement made herein (excluding reimbursement for such reasonable expenses as may have been incurred by the Writer in connection with the creation of the Work) and which shall be paid according to the following schedule: Five Thousand Dollars ($5,000) shall be paid upon the execution of this agreement; Twenty-five Hundred Dollars ($2,500) shall be paid on a date not later than thirty days after the date of execution of this agreement; and Twenty-five Hundred Dollars ($2,500) shall be paid on a date not later than sixty days after the date of execution of this agreement."

13. The phrase "entire fee and only compensation" refers to the fact that this agreement does not provide for the periodic payment of royalties to the Writer, as do some other agreements in which authors transfer copyrights to others, such as book publishers or music publishers. This work-for-hire agreement is inappropriate for use in any such situation.

14. Although the Commissioning Party will own the copyright in the Work, it is considerate to allow the Writer of the Work to use the Work as an example of his or her professional ability, if that does not contravene the goals of the Commissioning Party (as in a case where the Writer is a ghostwriter of a speech or an "autobiography" for the Commissioning Party). This courtesy to the Writer does not diminish or endanger the rights of the Commissioning Party, since the Writer cannot exercise any rights of copyright.

15. Insert the name of the state where you live here. It is an advantage to a litigant to be able to file or defend a suit in his or her home state. However, it may be that each party to the agreement will want any suit concerning it to be filed in his or her home state. This is a point of negotiation, but, as

a practical matter, the more powerful of the two parties to the agreement will prevail.

16. This allows the Writer to assign any sums due under the agreement to a third party or the estate of a Writer who dies to collect any such sums on his or her behalf.

17. Specify how many original copies of the agreement (i.e., copies of the agreement, even if they are photocopies, that bear the original signatures of the parties).

18. In agreements, "as of" means "We are signing this agreement today, but we mean for it to take effect *as of* two weeks ago," or "next month." A date specified that is before or after the agreement is actually signed is referred to as the "effective date" of the agreement.

19. If you want the agreement to become effective on the date it is signed, use that date here. If you want it to be effective as of a previous date, use that date. If you want to postpone the time when the agreement becomes operative until a later date, use that future date.

20. Leave this space blank for the signature of the Writer.

21. Leave this space blank for the signature of the Commissioning Party.

22. Insert the Writer's address here.

23. Insert the Commissioning Party's address here.

24. Insert here the name of a person who is acting on behalf of his or her company when that company is the Commissioning Party. If the Commissioning Party is an individual, this line may be omitted.

25. It may be necessary for the Commissioning Party to file a report of its payments to the Writer with the Internal Revenue Service; if so, the Writer's Social Security number will be necessary for any such filings.

26. Insert here the title of a person who is acting on behalf of his or her company when that company is the Commissioning Party. If the Commissioning Party is an individual, this line may be omitted.

Glossary

access—the first element of the three-part test for copyright infringement. That is, in a case for infringement of a novel, did the defendant have access to the manuscript or a published version of the plaintiff's book so that copying was possible? Usually access must be proved before the other two parts of the copyright test (copying of protected expression and substantial similarity) are considered.

actual damages—the profits a copyright infringer made from the infringing work and the money the plaintiff lost because of the infringement. A court deciding a copyright infringement case may award either actual damages or statutory damages.

anonymous work—a work on the copies or phonorecords of which no natural person is identified as author.

assignment of copyright—like a sale of a copyright, usually made in return for a lump-sum payment or the promise of the payment of a share of the income produced by the work. For example, in the case of a music publishing agreement, a transfer of ownership of the song copyright from the songwriter to the music publisher is made in return for the promises the publisher makes in the music publishing agreement regarding advance and periodic payments of royalties to the author. In addition to assignment of an entire copyright, an author may also assign only part of a copyright. The copyright statute requires that the transfer of ownership of any copyright be made in a written document signed by the person assigning the ownership of the copyright to someone else; no verbal assignment of copyright is possible. Anyone who acquires any right of copyright by assignment can, in turn, sell that right to someone else unless the written assignment document provides otherwise. An assignment of copyright may also be referred to as a "transfer" of copyright. Assignment of copyright is one of three ways that ownership of rights in copyright is transferred to someone besides the author of the copyrighted work; the other two are license and work for hire.

audiovisual work—a work that consists of a series of related images which are intrinsically intended to be shown by the use of machines or devices such as projectors, viewers, or electronic equipment, together with accompanying sounds, if any, regardless of the nature of the material objects, such as films or tapes, in which the works are embodied.

author—in the language of the US copyright statute, the creator of any copyrightable work, whether that work is a book, photograph, painting, poem, play, musical composition, or other sort of work. The exception to this is a work for hire; if a work is created as a work for hire, the employer of the creator of the copyright owns the copyright from the inception of the work and is considered the author of the work for purposes of copyright.

Berne Convention—the Convention for the Protection of Literary and Artistic Works, signed at Berne, Switzerland, on September 9, 1886, and all acts, protocols, and revisions thereto.

A work is a "Berne Convention work" if (1) in the case of an unpublished work, one or more of the authors is a national of a nation adhering to the Berne Convention, or in the case of a published work, one or more of the authors is a national of a nation adhering to the Berne Convention on the date of first publication; (2) the work was first published in a nation adhering to the Berne Convention, or was simultaneously first published in a nation adhering to the Berne Convention and in a foreign nation that does not adhere to the Berne Convention; (3) in the case of an audiovisual work—(a) if one or more of the authors is a legal entity, that author has its headquarters in a nation adhering to the Berne Convention; or (b) if one or more of the authors is an individual, that author is domiciled, or has his or her habitual residence in, a nation adhering to the Berne Convention; (4) in the case of a pictorial, graphic, or sculptural work that is incorporated in a building or other structure, the building or structure is located in a nation adhering to the Berne Convention; or (5) in the case of an architectural work embodied in a building, such building is erected in a country adhering to the Berne Convention. An author who is domiciled in or has his or her habitual residence in, a nation adhering to the Berne Convention is considered to be a national of that nation. A work is considered to have been simultaneously published in two or more nations if its dates of publication are within thirty days of one another.

best edition—the "best edition" of a work is the edition, published in the United States at any time before the date of deposit, that the Library of Congress determines to be most suitable for its purposes. This usually means the best quality version of the work available at the time registration is applied for.

case law—law that originates in the decisions of courts as opposed to written laws passed by state legislatures or the US Congress, which are called "statutes."

cease and desist letter—a letter written by the lawyer for the plaintiff telling the defendant to immediately cease certain specified actions that infringe the plaintiff's copyright and thereafter desist from any further such actions. These letters are usually the first indication to a defendant that his or her actions may have violated the plaintiff's rights. Depending on the merits of the plaintiff's claims of infringement, a defendant will decide to comply with the plaintiff's demands and try to settle the infringement dispute out of court or to fight the plaintiff's assertions of infringement in court.

children—according to the copyright statute, a person's "children" are that person's immediate offspring, whether legitimate or not, and any children legally adopted by that person.

collective work—a work, such as a periodical issue, anthology, or encyclopedia, in which a number of contributions, constituting separate and independent works in themselves, are assembled into a collective whole.

compilation—a work formed by the collection and assembling of preexisting materials or of data that are selected, coordinated, or arranged in such a way that the resulting work as a whole constitutes an original work of authorship. The term *compilation* includes collective works.

constructive notice—the presumption that because a copyright registration is reflected in the records of the Copyright Office, which are public, everyone knows of the claim of copyright ownership the registration embodies, regardless of whether any examination of those records is actually made.

contingency fee—a lawyer's fee taken from an award of damages to the plaintiff. Copyright infringement suits are often filed by lawyers who agree to work for a contingency fee; that is, the lawyer agrees that the fee for his or her work is to be taken from and is contingent upon an award by the court in favor of the plaintiff. If the plaintiff loses, the lawyer is not paid a fee. In any event, a plaintiff is still responsible for bearing the costs of the suit, such as his or her lawyer's travel expenses, the costs of court reporters for depositions, and the fees of expert witnesses. Lawyers never agree to work on a contingency fee basis for defendants, who have no expectation of any awards.

copies—material objects, other than phonorecords, in which a work is fixed by any method now known or later developed, and from which the work can be perceived, reproduced, or otherwise communicated, either directly or with the aid of a machine or device. The term *copies* includes the material object, other than a phonorecord, in which the work is first fixed.

copying—the second part of the three-part test for copyright infringement. That is, was part of the protected expression of the plaintiff's work copied by the defendant? Usually a defendant must be found to have copied significant portions of the plaintiff's work before this part of the copyright infringement test is satisfied. The mere fact that two works share certain similarities, even if those similarities are significant, is not sufficient to prove infringement unless the defendant copied from the plaintiff's work. Coincidental creation of a similar work, without copying, is not actionable under the US copyright statute, even if the works in question are so similar as to be nearly identical.

copyright—the set of exclusive rights that are granted, initially to the creators of copyrightable works, by the various copyright statutes that exist in most countries.

copyright infringement—the unauthorized exercise of any of the exclusive rights reserved by law to copyright owners. The most usual sort of copyright infringement lawsuit claims that the defendant is guilty of unauthorized copying from the plaintiff's work. In this situation, copyright infringement is judged by a three-part circumstantial evidence test: (1) Did the accused infringer have access to the work that is said to have been infringed, in order to make copying possible? (2) Is the defendant actually guilty of copying from the plaintiff's work part of the plaintiff's protectable expression? and (3) Is the accused work substantially similar to the work the plaintiff says was copied? Coincidental creation of a work similar to an existing copyrighted work is not infringement; the gist of most copyright infringements is unauthorized copying.

copyright notice—the three elements that legally serve to give notice to the world that a copyright owner is claiming ownership of a particular work. Copyright notice consists of three parts: the word "copyright" or the © symbol (or, for sound recordings, the ℗ symbol), the year of first publication of the work, and the name of the copyright owner. No formalities are required to use copyright notice, and although it is no longer required to secure copyright protection, use of copyright notice does confer certain valuable procedural benefits (in a copyright infringement lawsuit) on the copyright owner.

copyright protection—the protection the law gives copyright owners from unauthorized use of their works during the term of copyright.

copyright registration—the registration of a claim to ownership of a copyright, made in Washington, DC, in the US Copyright Office, a division of the Library of Congress. Copyright registration enhances the rights an author gains automatically by the act of creating a copyrightable work but does not, of itself, create these rights. The Copyright Office prescribes a specific form for the registration of copyright in each particular variety of work. Form TX is used for the registration of "literary" works—that is, works, other than dramatic works—that consist primarily of Textual Matter. Form VA is used to register works of the Visual Arts. Form PA is used to register copyrights in works of the Performing Arts, including plays, songs, and movies. Form SR is used to register the copyrights in Sound Recordings. There are other forms for other sorts of works; the name of the major varieties of copyright registration forms and the sort of works to be registered with each are listed in chapter 5, on copyright registration, in this book.

copyright statute—in the United States, the written copyright law passed by Congress, as opposed to copyright law that originates in the decisions of courts, which is called "case law." The current US copyright statute became effective January 1, 1978, and changed significantly many aspects of copyright law operative under the previous statute. Because the copyright statute is a federal statute and federal law outranks state law, there is no such thing as a state copyright statute. Most other countries also have copyright statutes, the provisions of which often vary from those of the US statute.

creation—a work is created when it is fixed in a copy or phonorecord for the first time; where a work is prepared over a period of time, the portion of it that has been fixed at any particular time constitutes the work as of that time, and where the work has been prepared in different versions, each version constitutes a separate work.

defendant—the person or company whose actions are complained of in a lawsuit. In criminal trials, a defendant is presumed innocent until proven guilty. In civil lawsuits, such as a suit for copyright infringement, no such presumption is made. Nothing is presumed about the actions of either the defendant and the plaintiff (the person or company that files the suit) until it is proven to the court. This means that even an innocent defendant is in the same position as a plaintiff—i.e., the defendant must prove his or her innocence just as the plaintiff must try to prove the truth of the allegations made in the complaint.

defenses—the arguments a defendant in a lawsuit makes in self-defense. The most important and the most commonly used defense in copyright infringement suits is the defense of "fair use," which is the argument that the complained-of actions by the defendant are allowable under the law as a permitted use of the plaintiff's work.

deposit copies—copies of the "best edition" of a work that are required to be deposited with the Copyright Office as a part of an application for copyright registration. The copyright statute requires that copies of works first published in the United States with copyright notice be deposited with the Copyright Office even if no application for copyright registration is made. Copyright registration forms give information on what sort of copies and how many copies of a work should accompany the application for registration of that work. The Copyright Office also publishes a free pamphlet concerning mandatory deposit of copies.

derivative work—an alternate version of a copyrighted work, i.e., a work "derived" from or based upon one or more preexisting works, such as a translation, musical arrangement, dramatization, fictionalization, motion picture version, sound recording, art reproduction, abridgment, condensation, or any other form in which a work may be recast, transformed, or adapted. A work consisting of editorial revisions, annotations, elaborations, or other modifications, which as a whole represent an original work of authorship, is a derivative work. The right to prepare derivative works from a copyrighted work is one of the exclusive rights of copyright reserved to copyright owners in the US copyright statute.

display—to display a work means to show a copy of it, either directly or by means of a film, slide, television image, or any other device or process or, in the case of a motion picture or other audiovisual work, to show individual images nonsequentially.

exclusive rights of copyright—those rights pertaining to a copyright that may be exercised only, or exclusively, by the owner of that copyright. Under the United States copyright statute, the creator of a copyrighted creative work has the exclusive right to copy or reproduce the work, to prepare alternate or "derivative" versions of the work, to distribute and sell copies of the work, and to perform or display the work publicly. Usually these rights may not be exercised by anyone other than the author of the work or a person to whom he or she has sold or licensed one or more of these "exclusive rights."

exploitation of copyright—the use of a work to produce income. Book publishers exploit book copyrights. Song copyrights are exploited by music publishers; the copyrights in recorded performances of songs are exploited by record companies. Copyrights in plays and film scripts are exploited by theatre and movie producers.

expression—copyright subsists only in the expression embodied in a work and not in the underlying ideas upon which the work is based. The copyright statute specifically limits copyright protection to works that embody some expression and excludes from protection a list of various products of the imagination that do not embody sufficient expression to qualify for copyright protection: "in no case does copyright protection for an original work of authorship extend to any idea, procedure, process, system, method of operation, concept, principle, or discovery, regardless of the form in which it is described, explained, illustrated, or embodied in such work."

fair use—a kind of public-policy exception to the usual standard for determining copyright infringement; that is, there is an infringing use of a copyrighted work, but, because of a countervailing public interest, that use is permitted and is not called infringement. Any use that is deemed by the law to be "fair" typically creates some social, cultural, or political benefit, which outweighs any resulting harm to the copyright owner. The copyright statute identifies six purposes that will qualify a use as a possible fair use: criticism, comment, news reporting, teaching, scholarship, or research. Once any use of a copyrighted work has been proved to have been made for one of these six purposes, the use must be examined to determine whether it is indeed fair. The copyright statute lists four factors that courts must weigh in determining fair use: the purpose and character of the use, including whether such use is of a commercial nature or is for nonprofit educational purposes; the nature of the copyrighted work; the amount and substantiality of the portion used in relation to the copyrighted work as a whole; and the effect of the use upon the potential market for or value of the copyrighted work. (For more information on fair use of copyright, see the book *Fair Use, Free Use, and Use by Permission* by Lee Wilson, published by Allworth Press.)

fixation—"Fixation" is one of three statutory requirements for copyright protection; the other two are that the work must embody some "expression" of the author, rather than consisting only of an idea or ideas, and the work must be "original," that is, the work was not copied from another work. The US copyright statute provides that the moment a work that is otherwise eligible for copyright protection is "fixed" in any tangible form that allows the work to be perceived by the senses (with or without the aid of a mechanical device, such as a CD player or videocassette player), that work is automatically protected by copyright. A work is "fixed" in a tangible medium of expression when its embodiment in a copy or phonorecord, by or under the authority of the author, is sufficiently permanent or stable to permit it to be perceived, reproduced, or otherwise communicated for a period of more than transitory duration. A work consisting of sounds, images, or both, that are being transmitted, is considered by the copyright statute to be "fixed" if a fixation of the work is being made simultaneously with its transmission.

independent contractor—one who performs work for an employer but is not an employee of that employer. Another term for independent contractor is *freelance* or *freelancer*. The status of one who creates a work is important to the determination of whether that work is a work made for hire. Several factors are relevant to the evaluation of the status of the creator of a work vis-à-vis the party who commissions the work to be created: the skill required to produce the work; the source of the instrumentalities and tools that will be used to produce the work; on whose premises the work will be produced; the duration of the relationship between the party who commissions the work and the person who will create it; whether the party who commissions the work has the right to assign additional projects to the person who will create the work; the extent of the discretion that may be exercised by the person who will create the work over when and how long he or she works during the process of creating it; the method by which the person who creates the work will be paid for his or her services; the role of the party who commissions the work in hiring and paying assistants for the person who will create the work; whether the work is part of the regular business of the party who commissions it; whether the party who commissions the work is in business; whether the party who commissions the work provides employee benefits to the person who will create the work; and the tax treatment of the person who will create the work.

injunction—a court order that directs the enjoined party to do something, or more typically, to cease doing something and to refrain from doing it in the future. Plaintiffs in copyright infringement suits typically seek injunctions to stop defendants from continuing to infringe the plaintiffs' copyrights. The scope of an injunction and whether a litigant's motion for one is granted is at the discretion of the judge who hears the suit. A temporary injunction is usually granted at the same time a suit is filed and endures only ten days. A preliminary injunction is granted by a judge after hearing arguments for and against the injunction from both the plaintiff and the defendant and usually lasts until the end of the lawsuit, when it may ripen into a permanent injunction by means of a paragraph to that effect in the judge's written order rendering his or her decision.

joint work—a work prepared by two or more authors with the intention that their contributions be merged into inseparable or interdependent parts of a unitary whole.

judgment—the ruling of the judge, rendered at the conclusion of a lawsuit. Judgments in civil (as opposed to criminal) trials usually include an order that the defendant, if the defendant is found to be guilty of the actions that caused the plaintiff to sue, pay the plaintiff money damages and, sometimes, attorneys' fees. Judgments in copyright infringement cases may also include orders to destroy the defendant's infringing copies of the plaintiff's work and injunctions to prevent further infringing actions of the defendant.

license of copyright—if an assignment of copyright is like a sale of the copyright, a license of copyright is like a lease. A nonexclusive license of a copyright may be verbal, but an exclusive license is required by the copyright statute to be in writing.

literary work—a work, other than an audiovisual work, that is expressed in words, numbers, or other verbal or numerical symbols or indicia, regardless of the nature of the material object, such as a book, periodical, manuscript, phonorecord, film, tape, disk, or card, in which it is embodied.

nondisclosure letter—also called a "nondisclosure agreement" or a "disclosure letter," a nondisclosure letter is a document used by the owner of a trade secret to create a legally enforceable contractual obligation to preserve the trade secret, which is disclosed to the person or company that signs the nondisclosure letter for the sole purpose of allowing that person or company to consider exploiting the trade secret under an arrangement whereby the owner of the trade secret would be compensated for its use.

ordinary observer test—the test courts use in determining whether substantial similarity exists in copyright infringement cases. Courts try to decide whether an ordinary observer would believe that the defendant's work and the plaintiff's work are the same. If so, substantial similarity, the third part of the three-part test for copyright infringement, exists.

originality—"originality" means simply that a work was not copied from another work rather than that the work is unique or unusual. Originality is one of three statutory requirements for copyright protection; the other two are that the work must embody some "expression" of the author, rather than consisting only of an idea or ideas, and that the work must be "fixed" in some tangible medium of expression. For purposes of copyright protection, if a work is not copied from another work, it is said to be "original." Similarities between two works are immaterial so long as they do not result from copying.

parody—a work that satirizes another work. A parody becomes infringement of the parodied work when it takes more from the parodied work than is absolutely necessary to call that work to mind.

patent—the rights granted by the federal government to the originator of a physical invention or industrial or technical process (a "utility patent") or an ornamental design for an "article of manufacture" (a "design patent"). A patent for an invention is the grant of a property right to the inventor, issued by the United States Patent and Trademark Office. Generally, the term of a new patent is twenty years from the date on which the application for the patent was filed in the United States. Design patents are granted for ornamental designs used for nonfunctional aspects of manufactured items; design patents last fourteen to fifteen years from the date the design patent is granted, depending on when it was filed.

perform—to "perform" a work means to recite, render, play, dance, or act it, either directly or by means of any device or process or, in the case of a motion picture or other audiovisual work, to show its images in any sequence or to make the sounds accompanying it audible.

performing rights societies—one of three US organizations, BMI, ASCAP, and SESAC, that collects royalties for broadcast uses of musical compositions.

phonorecords—material objects in which sounds, other than those accompanying a motion pictures or other audiovisual work, are fixed by any method now known or later developed, and from which the sounds can be perceived, reproduced, or otherwise communicated, either directly or with the aid of a machine or device. The term *phonorecords* includes the material object in which the sounds are first fixed.

permission—a consent to use a work, usually by reprinting it or reproducing it in some other work, such as the reproduction of photographs in a biography of the subject of the photographs. Permissions are actually nonexclusive licenses to use a work in a specified way. The owner of copyright in the materials sought to be used may or may not be compensated for the use.

pictorial, graphic, and sculptural works—two-dimensional and three-dimensional works of fine, graphic, and applied art, photographs, prints and art reproductions, maps, globes, charts, diagrams, models, and technical drawings, including architectural plans. Such works shall include works of artistic craftsmanship insofar as their form but not their mechanical or utilitarian aspects are concerned; the design of a useful article shall be considered a pictorial, graphic, or sculptural work only if, and only to the extent that, such design incorporates pictorial, graphic, or sculptural features that can be identified separately from, and are capable of existing independently of, the utilitarian aspects of the article.

plaintiff—in a civil lawsuit, the person or company that files a lawsuit to complain of the actions of the defendant that the plaintiff believes violate the plaintiff's rights. In a copyright infringement lawsuit, the plaintiff asks the court to order the defendant to stop its infringing actions and asks for an award of money damages to compensate the plaintiff for the harm the defendant's actions caused.

protectable expression—those elements of a work that are protected by copyright. The most basic premise of copyright law is that copyright does not protect ideas, only expressions of ideas. Therefore, the idea on which a copyrighted work is based is not granted protection under copyright law. Other unprotectable elements of otherwise copyrightable works are *scènes à faire* (stock literary themes); literary characters (to the extent that they are "types" rather than original expressions of an author); titles of books, stories, poems, songs, movies, etc.; short phrases and slogans; the rhythm or structure of musical works; themes expressed by song lyrics, short musical phrases, and arrangements of musical compositions that do not constitute alternate versions of the compositions; social dance steps and simple routines; uses of color, perspective, geometric shapes, and standard arrangements dictated by aesthetic convention in works of the visual arts; jewelry designs that merely mimic the structures of nature; names of products, services, or businesses; pseudonyms or professional or stage names (names and titles may be protected under trademark law, however); mere variations on familiar symbols, emblems, or designs, such as typefaces, numerals, or punctuation symbols, and religious emblems or national symbols; information, research data, and bare historical facts; blank forms, such as account ledger page forms, diaries, address books, blank checks, restaurant checks, order forms, and the like; and measuring and computing devices such as slide rules or tape measures; calendars, height and weight charts, sporting event schedules, and other assemblages of commonly available information that contain no original material; and raw information and bare historical facts, although many compilations of such information and extended expressions based on historical facts are protectable by copyright.

pseudonymous work—a work on the copies or phonorecords of which the author is identified under a fictitious name.

publication—the distribution of copies or phonorecords of a work to the public by sale or other transfer of ownership, or by rental, lease, or lending. The offering to distribute copies or phonorecords to a group of persons for purposes of further distribution, public performance, or public display constitutes publication. A public performance or display of a work does not of itself constitute publication. To perform or display a work "publicly" means (1) to perform or display it at a place open to the public or at any place where a substantial number or persons outside of a normal circle of a family and its social acquaintances is gathered; or (2) to transmit or otherwise communicate a performance or display of the work to a place specified by clause (1) or to the public, by means of any device or process, whether the members of the public capable of receiving the performance or display receive it in the same place or in separate places and at the same time or at different times. Because publication, in the context of copyright, can determine the expiration of the term of copyright for a work created as work for hire or under a pseudonym, it can be very important to determine whether and when such a work has been published within the meaning of the copyright statute.

public domain—primarily, works for which copyright protection has expired. The US copyright statute is based on the assumption that creative people will be encouraged to be creative if they are given exclusive control for a period of time over the use of their works. After that control ends, the public benefits from the right to make unlimited use of the previously protected creations. When a work falls into the public domain the work has become available for use in any way by anyone. Besides works for which copyright protection has expired, the other major category of public domain works is works created by officers or employees of the US government as part of their government jobs, which are in the public domain because the government has chosen not to claim copyright in works created at the taxpayers' expense.

recordation—the recording in the Copyright Office of the document that evidences an assignment of copyright or an exclusive license agreement. Recordation confers several benefits, such as creating a public record of a change in ownership of rights in a work and of the current ownership of those rights.

scènes à faire—common literary or dramatic conventions such as the star-crossed lovers or the pauper who is actually the lost heir to a fortune. Such devices are a variety of idea and are therefore, in themselves, not protected by copyright, although particular expressions of these conventions are protectable.

settlement—either the termination of a dispute or lawsuit by mutual agreement of the plaintiff and the defendant or the sum of money that is often paid, as an incentive to reach such an agreement, to the plaintiff by the defendant in lieu of any award of damages a court could make. The majority of lawsuits are settled before trial. The contract that embodies the agreement reached, in addition to providing for a payment to the plaintiff in settlement of the dispute or suit, which may include promises by one party to do or in future refrain from doing something.

sound recordings—works that result from the fixation of a series of musical, spoken, or other sounds, but not including the sounds accompanying a motion picture or other audiovisual work, regardless of the nature of the material objects, such as disks, tapes, or other phonorecords, in which they are embodied.

statute of limitations—the period within which a lawsuit must be filed. The statute of limitations for copyright infringement is three years from the date the infringer commits the infringing acts. In the case of a continuing infringement, the statute runs from the date of the defendant's last infringing act. After the three-year period has passed, an infringement suit will likely be barred by the court.

statutory damages—a range of money damages the copyright statute allows courts to award a plaintiff in a copyright infringement suit instead of the money lost by the plaintiff as a result of an infringer's actions plus the actual amount by which the infringer profited from the use of the plaintiff's work. Because actual damages can be very difficult, time-consuming, expensive, or impossible to prove during infringement lawsuits, and because infringers often do not profit from their infringements, awards of statutory damages are often desirable.

substantial similarity—the third part of the three-part test for copyright infringement. That is, in a case for infringement, is the defendant's work substantially similar to the plaintiff's work? Substantial similarity is more than isolated, insignificant similarities, but the "infringed" work and the accused work need not be identical for substantial similarity to be found.

term of copyright—the period during which copyright protection endures for a copyrightable work. For any work created after December 31, 1977, copyright protection begins the moment the work is first fixed in a tangible form. How long it lasts depends to a large extent on who wrote it and under what circumstances. Under ordinary circumstances, copyright protection lasts for the remainder of the life of the author of the work plus seventy years; if two or more authors jointly create a work, copyright protection will endure until seventy years after the last of the authors dies. If a work is created as a work for hire, anonymously, or under a fictitious name, the term of copyright will be either one hundred twenty years from the date the work was created or ninety-five years from the date it is published, whichever period expires first.

termination of transfers—a right given authors (and certain of their heirs) in the current US copyright statute by which they may recover ownership of copyrights previously assigned or licensed to someone else. The termination-of-transfers provisions of the statute specify precise procedures for exercising this right of recovery, and these procedures require that good records be kept of copyrights that are assigned to others. The rules for copyrights created before 1978 and those created after December 31, 1977, are significantly different. In most cases, consulting a copyright lawyer is an important step in ensuring that the required termination-of-transfers procedures are followed and the termination is effected.

trademark—a word or symbol used to identify a product or service in the marketplace. Rights in a trademark accrue only by use of the trademark in commerce and belong to the company that applies the mark to its products rather than to the person who creates the name or logo. A company gains rights in a trademark in direct proportion to the geographic scope and duration of its use of the mark; ordinarily, the company that uses a mark first gains rights in that mark superior to any other company that later uses it for the same product or services. Unauthorized use of a mark is trademark infringement. (For more information about trademarks, see *The Trademark Guide*, by Lee Wilson, published by Allworth Press.)

trade secrets—valuable formulas, patterns, compilations, programs, devices, methods, techniques, or processes, that are not generally known or discoverable and that are maintained in secrecy by their owners. Because copyright does not protect ideas, methods, or systems, trade secrets are usually unprotectable by copyright. Such secret information is preserved by the use of nondisclosure letters that obligate those to whom trade secrets are disclosed to keep them secret.

transfer of copyright—another term for assignment of copyright ownership. A transfer of copyright ownership is an assignment, mortgage, exclusive license, or any other conveyance, alienation, or hypothecation of a copyright or of any of the exclusive rights comprised in a copyright, whether or not it is limited in time or place of effect, but not including a nonexclusive license.

unpublished work—any work that has not been to the public by sale or other transfer of ownership, or by rental, lease, or lending. The offering to distribute copies or phonorecords to a group of persons for purposes of further distribution, public performance, or public display, constitutes publication. However, a public performance or display of a work does not of itself constitute publication. The law generally allows fewer "fair" uses of unpublished works than of published works.

useful article—an article having an intrinsic utilitarian function that is not merely to portray the appearance of the article or to convey information. An article that is normally a part of a useful article is considered a "useful article."

utilitarian elements of industrial design—the elements of pictorial, graphic, and sculptural works that are specifically excluded from copyright protection in the copyright statute. Only the nonfunctional aspects of such works are protectable; generally, decorative elements of designs for useful articles are protected while the "mechanical or utilitarian aspects" of such designs are not.

widow or widower—the surviving spouse under the law of the author's domicile at the time of his or her death, whether or not the spouse has later remarried.

work—in the language of the US copyright statute, any copyrightable product of the imagination, whether it is a book, photograph, painting, poem, play, musical composition, movie, or other sort of work.

work of visual art—a work of visual art is an original pictorial, graphic, or sculptural work, including two-dimensional and three-dimensional works of fine, graphic, and applied art.

work made for hire—a work created by an independent contractor (a freelancer) if the work falls into one of nine categories of specially commissioned works named in the US copyright statute, and both the independent contractor and the person who commissions the creation of the work agree in writing that it is to be considered a work for hire, or a work that is created by an employee as part of his or her full-time job. Works made for hire belong to the employers of the people who create them, and those employers are considered the authors of those works for copyright purposes from the inception of the works. (Work for hire is one of three ways that ownership of rights in copyright are transferred to someone besides the author of the copyrighted work; the other two are assignment of copyright and license of copyright.)

Index

 **Books from Allworth Press**

ASMP Professional Business Practices in Photography (Seventh Edition)
by the American Society of Media Photographers (6 × 9, 480 pages, paperback, $35.00)

Business and Legal Forms for Authors and Self-Publishers (Fourth Edition)
by Tad Crawford with Stevie Fitzgerald and Michael Gross (8½ × 11, 176 pages,
paperback, $24.99)

Business and Legal Forms for Fine Artists (Fourth Edition)
by Tad Crawford (8½ × 11, 160 pages, paperback, $24.95)

Business and Legal Forms for Graphic Designers (Fourth Edition)
by Tad Crawford and Eva Doman Bruck (8½ × 11, 256 pages, paperback, $29.95)

Business and Legal Forms for Illustrators (Fourth Edition)
by Tad Crawford (8½ × 11, 168 pages, paperback, $24.99)

Business and Legal Forms for Photographers (Fourth Edition)
by Tad Crawford (8½ × 11, 208 pages, paperback, $24.95)

The Business of Being an Artist (Fifth Edition)
by Daniel Grant (6 × 9, 344 pages, paperback, $19.99)

The Business of Writing
by Jennifer Lyons with foreword by Oscar Hijuelos (6 × 9, 304 pages, paperback, $19.95)

Legal Guide for the Visual Artist (Fifth Edition)
by Tad Crawford (8½ × 11, 304 pages, paperback, $29.95)

Starting Your Career as a Freelance Editor
by Mary Embree (6 × 9, 240 pages, paperback, $19.95)

Starting Your Career as a Freelance Photographer (Second Edition)
by Tad Crawford and Chuck Delaney (6 × 9, 352 pages, paperback, $19.99)

Starting Your Career as a Freelance Writer (Third Edition)
by Moira Allen (6 × 9, 352 pages, paperback, $19.99)

Starting Your Career as a Graphic Designer
by Michael Fleishman (6 × 9, 384 pages, paperback, $19.95)

Starting Your Career as a Musician
by Neil Tortorella (6 × 9, 240 pages, paperback, $19.95)

Starting Your Career as an Artist (Second Edition)
by Stacy Miller and Angie Wojak (6 × 9, 304 pages, paperback, $19.99)

Starting Your Career as an Illustrator
by Michael Fleishman (6 × 9, 520 pages, paperback, $24.99)

The Trademark Guide (Third Edition)
by Lee Wilson (6 × 9, 256 pages, hardcover, $24.99)

The Writer's Legal Guide (Third Edition)
by Tad Crawford and Kay Murray (6 × 9, 320 pages, paperback, $19.95)

To see our complete catalog or to order online, please visit *www.allworth.com.*